The Prophetic Spirit

of Catechesis

The Prophetic Spirit of Catechesis

How We Share the Fire in Our Hearts

Anne Marie Mongoven, O.P.

PAULIST PRESS
New York / Mahwah, N.J.

Book design by Theresa M. Sparacio

Cover design by Cynthia Dunne

Library of Congress Cataloging-in-Publication Data

Mongoven, Anne Marie.
    The prophetic spirit of catechesis : how we share the fire in our hearts / Anne Marie Mongoven.
        p.   cm.
    Includes bibliographical references and index.
    ISBN 0-8091-3922-7 (alk. paper)
        1. Catechetics—Catholic Church. I. Title.
BX1968.M642000
268'.82

                                                                99-049017
                                                                CIP

Published by Paulist Press
997 Macarthur Boulevard
Mahwah, New Jersey 07430

www.paulistpress.com

Printed and bound in the
United States of America

Contents

Contents

To every catechist I have met during the past thirty years either in person or through our writings, each of whom has said to me in her or his own way, I am a catechist because

> *There is a fire burning in my heart,*
>   *imprisoned in my bones;*
> *The effort to restrain it wearies me,*
>   *I cannot.*

With apologies to Jeremiah 20:9

Abbreviations

AAS   *Acta Apostolicae Sedis.*

AG   Vatican II. *Decree on the Church's Missionary Activity (Ad Gentes).*

CCC   *Catechism of the Catholic Church.* Washington, D.C.: United States Catholic Conference, 1994.

CMW   Vatican II. *Pastoral Constitution on the Church in the Modern World (Gaudium et Spes).*

CSL   Vatican II. *Constitution on the Sacred Liturgy (Sacrosanctum Concilium).*

CT   Pope John Paul II. *Catechesi Tradendae (On Catechesis in Our Time).* Washington, D.C.: United States Catholic Conference, 1979.

DCC   Vatican II. *Dogmatic Constitution on the Church (Lumen Gentium).*

DS   *Enchyridion Symbolorum Definitionum et Declarationum de Rebus Fidei et Morum,* edited by H. Denzinger and A. Schönmetzer, S.J., 33rd edition, Freiburg im Breisgau, 1965.

EMW   Pope Paul VI. *On Evangelization in the Modern World.* Washington, D.C.: United States Catholic Conference, 1975.

GCD   Sacred Congregation for the Clergy. *General Catechetical Directory.* Washington, D.C.: United States Catholic Conference, 1971.

GDC   Congregation for the Clergy. *General Directory for Catechesis.* Washington, D.C.: United States Catholic Conference, 1997.

IBC   Pontifical Biblical Commission. *The Interpretation of the Bible in the Church.* Vatican City: Libreria Editrice Vaticana, 1993.

MLP   Vatican II. *Decree on the Ministry and Life of Priests (Presbyterorum Ordinis).*

RCIA   *Rite of Christian Initiation of Adults.* Translated by the International Committee on English in the Liturgy. Chicago: Liturgy Training Publications, 1988.

RL   Vatican II. *Declaration on Religious Liberty (Dignitatis Humanae).*

RM   John Paul II. Encyclical Letter. *Redemptoris Missio.*

SLF   National Conference of Catholic Bishops. *Sharing the Light of Faith: National Catechetical Directory for Catholics of the United States.* Washington, D.C.: United States Catholic Conference, 1979.

TDNT   *Theological Dictionary of the New Testament.* Edited by G. Kittel and G. Friedrich. Grand Rapids: 1964–76.

TTJD   National Conference of Catholic Bishops. *To Teach As Jesus Did: A Pastoral Message on Catholic Education.* Washington, D.C.: United States Catholic Conference, 1972.

Introduction

Thirty years ago, as an associate director of religious education for the Diocese of Madison, Wisconsin, I often drove in the evenings to distant parishes to do catechist training sessions or parent programs. The Madison diocese includes eleven counties and often a parish workshop would be a two-hour drive each way. When pastors or directors of religious education invited me, I would try to set the session for a 7:00 or 7:30 P.M. starting time. The convenience of starting at that hour enabled me to be home by 11:00 o'clock or shortly thereafter.

One day the pastor in St. Joseph Parish, Dodgeville, Wisconsin, invited me to conduct such a session. I requested my usual starting time, but he adamantly refused, saying I could not begin before 8:00 in the evening. Reluctantly I accepted his time and began the session promptly at 8:00 P.M.

At 8:40 a woman arrived, rushing in, out of breath, apologizing for her tardiness. Later at the coffee break, this woman, who had driven from Yellowstone, a mission a distance from Dodgeville, explained why she was late. Before coming to our session she had prepared the dinner, finished the supper dishes, done the evening farm chores, and prepared the younger children for bed. I stood in awe of her. This woman, in her early forties, had done her family and farm duties and had then driven a half hour to Dodgeville to attend a two-hour catechist formation session.

This woman personifies for me the catechists, both men and women, with whom I have worked during the past thirty years. Strong, faithful people committed to sharing their faith, they have

1

generously given of themselves for decades. They are the heart and backbone of their parishes. I met these people again half a continent away when I came to Santa Clara University in 1982. In California I live not in a rural area but in the heart of Silicon Valley. In this high-tech area I find the same energy, commitment, faith, and intelligence in the parish catechists and the graduate students as I found in the catechists in rural Wisconsin in 1966.

At this writing, however, I am not so much concerned with the catechists of the past or even the catechists of the present. I am looking toward the catechists of the future, the catechists of the new millennium. With nostalgia I can return, happily, to the days of the 1970s and early 1980s, when the church was full of energy and hope and Spirit. But presently my concern is for the church of the future, the church that is to come, whose shape is now seen only darkly, through a glass that is not always clear.

How can the church, the Roman Catholic Church, renew its energy and life and go forth to "preach the good news" as the apostolic church did? As it has done for centuries? The world is changing. Society has changed. Cultures are conflicting. Most of the people of Asia and of the southern hemisphere are so concerned about how to feed and clothe their children that they cannot begin to hear the preaching of the gospel. Too many children in our own country go to bed hungry at night. If they have the time or energy to think about it, what do they and their families think the gospel means to them? How is our church carrying out its mission to preach the gospel at the beginning of the twenty-first century? In what way are we proclaiming the coming of God's reign today?

At the time of this writing I live on a short block in San Jose, California, a block that has five houses. The people who live in the house on my right are from India. Those who live in the house on my left are from Korea. The home beyond the Indian family houses a family from Taiwan, and next to the Taiwanese family lives a couple with two children—the husband is Japanese and the wife is from Great Britain. This is the world of the present, and it is the world of the new millennium. What do we as church have to say to this world? What word does the Catholic Church in the United States have to say to this new multicultural society?

What good news do we have to bring to our neighbors? Why should they recognize Jesus, the Christ, as their liberator, as the image of the Mystery of God made flesh? What word do we bring to the hundreds of highly educated and thoughtful people who are not Christian but live within our parishes and are searching for meaning and purpose in life? What do we as a Catholic people have to say to the thousands and thousands of poor and hungry people, many of them immigrants, many of them children who are suffering from the effects of poverty in their daily lives?

This book is about the present and the future, particularly the future of catechetical ministry in the United States. It is a book from an author filled with hope though painfully aware of the failings of the church to which I belong and which I love. It is a book about the future which sees the future in both continuity and discontinuity with the past. And it asks how we can enliven the faith of our people through the ministry of catechesis.

What Is to Come?

This book describes one among many approaches to catechesis that has emerged from the worldwide renewal of catechesis during the twentieth century. I call this approach "symbolic catechesis" because in this approach the catechist and the community seek meaning by correlating the events of their daily lives with the primary Christian symbols of God's presence: the Sacred Scriptures and the teaching, life, and worship of the church. In symbolic catechesis the community discovers how God relates to us and how we relate to God, to one another, and to the universe in which we live.

The book is divided into two parts. The first part, "Foundations of Catechesis," considers the nature of catechesis, the history of catechetical renewal in this century, an analysis of post–Vatican II church documents on catechesis, and the theology of catechesis that is the foundation for the symbolic catechesis approach. The second part, "The Process of Symbolic Catechesis," describes the process of symbolic catechesis and demonstrates how the biblical, ecclesial, and liturgical symbols of God embrace us and lead us to understand the meaning of life. The Afterword describes catechesis as a prophetic ministry in the twenty-first century.

Chapter 1 considers reasons why people minister. It examines our relationship to the mystery of God, the mystery of Christ, and the mystery of the church. It presents faith as the source of the community's desire to minister. At the same time it notes that catechesis is a ministry of the word that calls the community to stronger faith.

Chapter 2 describes the main historical events and people who influenced the renewal of catechesis from the publication of the *Baltimore Catechism* in 1885,[1] to the conclusion of the International Catechetical Study Week in Medellín, Colombia, in 1968. It includes the story of John Lancaster Spalding, bishop of Peoria, Illinois, the churchman primarily responsible for the publication of the *Baltimore Catechism,* and the stories of four other men who had an extraordinary influence on the renewal of the church's catechetical ministry, Pope Pius X; Josef A. Jungmann, S.J.; Joseph Colomb, S.S.; and Johannes Hofinger, S.J. Chapter 2 also acknowledges briefly those responsible for initiating the catechetical renewal in the United States during the 1960s.

Chapter 3 describes seven official church documents issued since the Second Vatican Council which affirmed and projected into the future the grass-roots renewal that climaxed in 1968 at the Study Week in Medellín. These documents are (1) the *General Catechetical Directory* (1971);[2] (2) the *Rite of Christian Initiation of Adults* (1972), which is both a catechetical and a liturgical document;[3] (3) *On Evangelization in the Modern World* (1975), an apostolic exhortation of Pope Paul VI;[4] (4) *Catechesis in Our Time* (1979), the apostolic exhortation of Pope John Paul II;[5] (5) *Sharing the Light of Faith: National Catechetical Directory for Catholics of the United States* (1979);[6] (6) the *Catechism of the Catholic Church* (1994);[7] and the *General Directory for Catechesis* (1997),[8] a revision of the 1971 *General Catechetical Directory.* In this chapter I ask four questions of each document: When and why was it written? Who wrote it and for whom was it written? What is its purpose? And how does it contribute to catechetical renewal?

Chapter 4 presents a theology of catechesis derived from the renewed understanding of both *revelation* and *faith* as stated in the *Dogmatic Constitution on Divine Revelation (Dei Verbum)* of Vatican Council II. It examines in some detail chapter 1 of that constitution in order to explain the conciliar teaching on revelation and faith. The theology of catechesis described in chapter 4 is the foundation for the pastoral action which I call symbolic catechesis.

Part II, "The Process of Symbolic Catechesis," describes the pastoral dimensions of symbolic catechesis. Chapter 5 describes the process of symbolic catechesis and how it relates to ordinary life experiences or events. It shows how the essential tasks of catechesis, that is, building community, sharing the church's stories and beliefs, doing justice, and community prayer are integrated in this symbolic approach.[9] Although symbolic catechesis is designed particularly for adults it can readily be adapted for both youth and children. The *Living Waters* catechetical series for children in grades 1 through 8 used this approach, with the necessary adaptations for children, successfully.

Chapter 6 examines the "signs of the times" from a biblical and conciliar point of view. What do we mean by the signs of the times? Are they always social or are there personal "signs of the times"? What are some present signs and how does the catechist lead the catechetical community to distinguish and interpret them? The chapter will also suggest ways to bring together a catechetical community of adults to consider "signs of the times." In this chapter pastoral questions relating to the parish community will be explored. Why is it important that catechists know about the people in their parishes, and how can they discover information that will help them respond to the peoples' needs? If catechesis is a process of inculturation, as the *General Directory for Catechesis* indicates it is, then what is inculturation? And finally, how do catechists prepare, promote, plan, and process a catechesis?

Because in symbolic catechesis the community understands the meaning of its life by interpreting life through the primary symbols of faith, the next three chapters examine how normative symbols of faith, the Bible (chapter 7), the church through its doctrine

5

and witness of life (chapter 8), and the church's liturgy (chapter 9) help us find meaning in our daily lives. In each chapter I describe the primary faith symbol and ask: What is the place of this symbol in symbolic catechesis? How do these symbols of faith help us find meaning in our daily lives? How do they interpret, validate, or question our experiences, and how do our experiences and insights enable us to recognize these symbols as revelatory gifts? How can these symbols so filled with the past speak clearly in the present? And most important, how do they strengthen the faith of the community and call it to conversion?

Chapter 7 examines the place of the Bible in the life of the church and in catechesis. It considers the question of biblical interpretation and how "amateurs," that is, "lovers of the Bible," such as catechists can interpret the Bible with their communities. It looks not only at the church's official recommendations for pastoral interpretation but examines briefly both fundamentalism and feminist biblical interpretation because they are pastoral questions for the church today. Finally, it describes how the catechist and the community can turn to the Bible in trying to make sense of a particular life situation.

Chapter 8 asks many of the same questions about the church, its doctrine, and its life as chapter 7 asked about the Bible. This chapter examines the different forms of language the human community uses to respond to or refer to God and shows how these forms of language are related to one another. It examines doctrine and dogma as symbolic forms of language through which the church articulates and expresses its ultimate meaning. It distinguishes between doctrines and dogmas and considers them symbolic forms of language which are rich in meaning, which challenge us, call us to conversion and give praise to the Mystery of God. Doctrines lift us up, restore us, energize us, relate us to the Mystery. Doctrines are gifts that need constant renewal if they are to continue to be life-giving. This chapter examines the anthropocentric nature of some doctrinal language and suggests forms of language for the catechists to use in their ministry.

Chapter 9 reflects on liturgy in the life of the church and on some forms of liturgical catechesis. It considers the nature of liturgy, the symbolic language of liturgy, the relationship between catechesis and liturgy, liturgical catechesis, and finally lectionary catechesis as a form of liturgical catechesis. Since approximately 80 percent of parish catechesis is liturgical catechesis, this chapter will, I hope, be particularly helpful to parish directors and catechists.

An afterword, or epilogue, follows chapter 9. In this afterword I compare the prophet and the catechist, prophecy and catechesis, and find that catechesis is indeed a prophetic ministry. The ministries themselves have so many characteristics in common that one begins to wonder why it took us so long to recognize the relationship. And if catechesis is a prophetic ministry within the church why is it sometimes seen as ineffectual? How do catechists fulfill their prophetic role, and what will happen to us if we begin to listen and respond to the new prophets?

Throughout this book I will consider questions that seem to be of concern to women in the church. I do this for two reasons. First, since approximately 87 percent of the catechists in the United States are women,[10] these questions need to be addressed, for they are the women's questions. Second, both women and men catechists will be working with women in their parishes. My concern is to help catechists respond honestly to women's questions and bring others with whom they work to be sensitive to the seriousness of women's concerns.[11]

Though at this time the church often seems at odds with itself, divided into opposing camps, the future cannot be bleak for those who are filled with faith. The Spirit lives with us; believers still proclaim the gospel; we still do justice; and we still celebrate Eucharist. Most of all, even in the midst of both civil and ecclesiastical oppression women and men still have faith and still desire to nurture faith in other men and women. The Holy Mystery whom we call God still loves us unconditionally and through that love continually recreates us. We still remember that we are all related to one another in love and that the whole earth in one way or another breathes worship with us. What more can we hope for?

Acknowledgments

My catechizing, teaching, writing, research, and working with creative people have all brought me to the point of writing this book. I write it for all those who taught me—professors, students, parents, friends, colleagues, and family members. I write it especially for those who serve their parishes as directors of catechetical ministry, and for those whom they direct, the parish catechists. It is meant to say to many of them, "Your insights are correct. Keep on!" I hope it will confirm what many catechists are already doing and show other catechists a renewed approach to catechizing, a way that will be as attractive to adults as it has been to children.

The debt the church owes to parish catechists is enormous. A recent study shows that there are in the United States 448,000 catechists in approximately 19,000 parishes.[12] Through workshops, classes, and days of retreat they take time to strengthen their own faith life so that they may share it with others. They give of their time, their energy, their knowledge, and their love. They are prophetic as they constantly call their parish faith community to conversion and commitment. They are the Catholic Church's hidden treasure.

My life has been enriched and my faith supported by these women and men, by my students and colleagues, by publishers (whom we seldom thank and whom neither the church nor parishes could do without) and their professional catechetical consultants. This book is one way of thanking all who have enriched me by their gifts to my life.

The writing of this book has been both a joy and a burden. I have wanted to write it for decades, and the delight of being given a year's sabbatical by my Sinsinawa Dominican congregation in which to complete it brought me great joy. The burden comes from not always being able to express adequately the fullness of my thought or my experience.

No one writes a book alone. We learn from others even when we are unaware of how much we are absorbing from them. I have learned from innumerable catechetical, liturgical, and biblical scholars, from theologians, sociologists, anthropologists, historians, and artists, so many that it is impossible for me to name them. But I can name a number of people who have been of enormous help to me. I am indebted to them for their support, for their ideas, for reading drafts of text, for whatever is of value in this book.

Rita Claire Dorner, O.P., offered the kind of service only a true friend and sister can offer, critically reading and rereading draft after draft and offering suggestions for improvement until the book reached its final form. Stephen Privett, S.J., my colleague in catechetics at Santa Clara University, read the text through chapter by chapter and provided many helpful insights and suggestions. Mary Paynter, O.P., encouraged me to write this book more than twenty-five years ago and gave invaluable assistance to me. Donna Lecrivain Brock; Kate Dooley, O.P.; Dr. Maureen Gallagher; Joseph Grassi; Jean Marie Hiesberger; Berard Marthaler, O.F.M.; Michael Moynahan, S.J.; Jean Richter, O.P.; Dr. Marilyn Schaub; Francis Smith, S.J.; Fr. Gerard Sloyan; and Ann Willits, O.P.; encouraged me, read parts of the text, and made helpful suggestions. To each one of them I owe a debt of gratitude and appreciation.

For seventeen years my students in the graduate program in pastoral ministries at Santa Clara University worked with me to formulate the catechetical approach offered here. Among ourselves we discussed it, debated it, tried it out, and finally embraced it. These students challenged me and gave me extraordinary insights and questions that only those working daily in catechetical ministry can offer. I cannot name them all here, but they know who they are, and they will recognize their insights in the text.

During my years in the Religious Studies Department at Santa Clara University, the administrators of the university, Paul Locatelli, S.J., president, and Stephen Privett, S.J., provost, encouraged and supported me as did my colleagues in the Religious Studies Department, particularly James Reites, S.J., as chair, who provided time for me to do research. I shall always be grateful for their confidence in me and their support.

Finally, I give thanks to and for my Sinsinawa Dominican Sisters who over the years sent me away to study again and again and in so doing gave me the pearl of great price, energy for living, a vibrant theology, a soaring faith, and a love for all that both Sinsinawa and Dominican mean. In particular I wish to thank Jean McSweeney, O.P., Prioress General of the Sinsinawa Dominicans; Carol Coenen, O.P. and Mary Ann Nelson, O.P., Prioress Provincials of the Western Province.

Whatever inconsistencies or inadequacies you find here are mine and mine alone. I have written from my experience, my research, and my teaching, from both head and heart. Whenever I wrote I had the memory of a particular TV interview in mind. Michael Malone asked a prominent economist who had just published a book if his new book was as boring as most books on economics, implying that economics was a boring topic. The author replied that he had read some pretty boring books on God. I hope and pray that his description does not fit this book.

PART I

The Foundations
of Catechesis

The Mystery as the Source of Ministry

It is always a surprise to be loved. Even when we seek the love and love the lover, being loved astonishes and amazes us. It is a wonder of life that startles us so that ordinary daily life takes on an extraordinary luster and promise. If we are loved, the sun shines brighter. We stand taller. When we are loved we can handle almost any experience. When love embraces us we can embrace ourselves.

Loving another is life-giving. When you or I love, the love we give renews not only the life of the beloved but also our own life. Loving recreates the lover by calling forth from her that which is most creative in her. Love diminishes fear and self-doubt. It enables us to see the good that is not always readily seen in others or in ourselves. Loving gives us new sight, or fresh insight. It frees us to accept love and be whole.

Loving affects all that we are and all that we do. Being in love organizes our whole world. It is not a sporadic experience but a constant one. Even when not attending to the beloved we know we are loving beings. And we see our world through the eyes of one who is deeply aware of being both a lover and a beloved.

If loving another person is life-giving, and being loved by that person is creative of our best selves, then what must it be like to be loved unconditionally? Is it possible that such ordinary people as the men and women we travel with on the subway, sit near in the office, drive by in our cars can be loved unconditionally? Who is so foolish, or so benevolent, as to love humankind, individually and communally, in an unconditional way? Is it even possible to love unconditionally?

The Mystery of God's Love

There are occasions in life when most people experience exhilaration, an awareness of the beauty and joy of life. Happiness permeates them and makes them glad to be alive. Exhilaration may come from a visit to Yosemite National Park and seeing the clear fresh water rushing through the rocky streambeds. It may come from the realization that a loved one has been healed from a threatening sickness. Or exhilaration springs from a feeling, an awareness, that at this time "all's right with the world." At these moments many people recognize the benevolent power of another One who guides and gives order to the universe. And at these special moments most of us recognize that this someone loves us, miracle of miracles.

We cannot bear daily exhilaration. So the days come and go in ordinary ways and we make our livelihood and build our families and share our strengths and call out for help in our weaknesses. Sometimes peoples' lives are filled with pain and loneliness, and they experience the terrible absence of a benevolent power. Life seems meaningless. But even in that meaninglessness they find hope. Being able to hope in the midst of suffering, defeat, or desolation is a gift that enables people to continue to seek acceptance.

Biblical people experienced being loved, and the knowledge that they were loved in all circumstances seldom left them. Historically the first people in the Judeo-Christian tradition to discover this love were Abraham and Sarah. When the patriarch first recognized God's presence and heard the demand that he leave his native land, he recognized that the Holy One who challenged him also blessed him. For the Holy One promised Abraham and Sarah progeny, as many as the stars in the sky. Not only children but a great nation would be born of them (Gn 12:3). This blessing was an act of love.

Now, why would Abraham and Sarah believe that this was God who was acting in their lives? Were they naive? Or uneducated? Or insightful? Or were they people who were ready to trust their own

14

experience? Abraham and Sarah were religious people. They were pagans, people who worshiped many gods, gods of the household and gods of the family. It seems they were people who had experienced the benevolence of a godly power in the world, a power beyond all human or created power. They responded to this experience and became believers, people committed to this God whom they could not name. They trusted their own experience, and a community of believers was born.

For two millennia the Israelites turned to their God in thanksgiving and praise and away from God in sin and selfishness. They alternated between being a faithful and an idolatrous people. They loved the one who gave them life, and such love led them to reach out in justice and love to others who were in need or in pain. They turned away from the "rock" of their salvation and became introspectively preoccupied and selfish. Their relationship with the Holy One led them to know that they were related not only to the One who blessed them but to one another and to all of creation.

Prophets rose up among the people of Israel, men and women called to speak in God's name a word of condemnation and forgiveness. These prophets ministered to the people and called them to live faithful lives. The prophets excoriated the people for their sinfulness and rejection of the God with whom they were united in a covenant of love. They urged them to be forgiving and faithful and to let justice roll down through the nation like a river through the mountain streams.

Two millennia after Abraham's experience of the Holy One, God sent his only Son, Jesus, to reawaken and renew the faith of the people. And this renewal involved the building of God's reign on earth through living out the Beatitudes. Jesus' followers were to build the reign of God by being poor in spirit, by grieving because of injustice or loss, by being meek and merciful and pure of heart. They were to be peacemakers and to be willing to suffer persecution for justice' sake. No one should be left in need. Widows, orphans, children, strangers, immigrants, those who were sick or disabled, uneducated, or in any way deprived should all be taken

15

care of. Justice was not optional. Followers of Jesus must hunger and thirst for justice, suffer persecution for its sake. Jesus renewed the covenant, which was a covenant with those who were undeserving of God's love.

Through his humanity Jesus reminded his followers of the exalted nature of humankind. He reminded his listeners that humankind emerges from the Holy Mystery and shares in the divine life of the Mystery, not as fully as he did, but nonetheless it has been deified. Jesus noted that human beings carry within themselves the life and the blessing of the Creator, with whom they are intimately related as creature, child, son, or daughter. Our creation in the image and likeness of the Divine Mystery is an extraordinary sign of God's love and friendship. Humanity has been grasped by the Mystery, lifted up in an embrace of love. It has been loved beyond all expectations.

The early Christian community experienced God's love as unconditional, as a life-enhancing gift that flowed from God through Jesus and the Spirit to the community and back to God. They recognized it as an unending and energizing gift of unconditional and continuing love. Paul wrote to the Romans:

> God's love has been poured into our hearts through the Holy Spirit that has been given to us. For while we were still weak, at the right time Christ died for the ungodly. Indeed, rarely will anyone die for a righteous person—though perhaps for a good person someone might actually dare to die. But God proves his love for us in that while we still were sinners Christ died for us. (Rom 5:5–8)

God's steadfast love available to the apostolic community still abides with us. This gift is an outpouring of the Spirit. It is a love that both transforms and divinizes us.

The Christian Scriptures tell us that "God is love" and "love is from God" (1 Jn 4:7–8). In the Synoptic Gospels, God's love is the central, though implicit, message of Jesus. John's Gospel is, however, quite explicit: the incarnation took place because "God so loved the world" (Jn 3:16). This love was not abstract but concretized in Jesus, the ultimate symbol of God's love. Jesus is the

16

fullest expression of God's love. He is the divine self-communication to humanity and the fullest human response of faith to the divine self-communication. The incarnation is a definitive sign of the unconditional love of God for humankind.

People became disciples of Jesus and ministers of the gospel because they felt called to do so by the Spirit of Jesus. They became preachers and teachers because they could not keep the good news of God's love to themselves but felt bound to share it with others. The gospel brought sense to a world that spiraled furiously and purposelessly without it. The gospel brought harmony to all of creation. It brought peace and enthusiasm to those who embraced it.

People minister today because they recognize the presence of the Mystery in their lives, a Mystery that exhilarates and builds enthusiasm *(en theos)* for life. People minister because they hear the gospel of Jesus and recognize that living according to it will lessen the presence of misery in the world. People turn to ministry because they are called by God through Christ and in the power of the Spirit to build a world of peace and justice where the lion lies down with the lamb. People minister because in their moments of loneliness or desolation others minister to them and do not let them forget that they are loved. People minister because the gospel enables them to make sense of the world.

The Bible is a love story. It is the story of God's inimitable, infinite, eternal, and unconditional love for all of humanity. It is the story of how that Holy Being whose love the Israelites and Christians experienced, tendered care and compassion, support and protection to all creatures and all of creation. It is a story that doesn't make sense unless you have been loved and been a lover. It is a love story that calls many to ministry.

For millennia people have tried to name the God who loves them. The Israelites would not speak the name of God, YHWH. It was too sacred a name to be uttered. But they needed to speak about this Holy One, and so they began to speak of God through metaphor. They imaged God as rock, shepherd, nurse, midwife, lord. But every name was inadequate. So the Israelites piled metaphor upon metaphor to name God: the almighty, king, creator, ancient of days. More and more their discourse about the God of Abraham became anthropomorphic. Over the millennia God was named as judge, lover, helper, friend, monarch, father, mother. God is all of these and none of these, and no name names God rightly. So how can we speak about the Holy One who is always surprising us with love? How can we best name the source of our life and happiness? How can we speak of God without creating an idol? How can we name the unnamable one who loves us completely, always and everywhere?

In this book I have chosen to name God "the Mystery," or "the Holy Mystery." This is not a new or original naming. Recognizing the incomprehensibility of God, theologians and mystics have for centuries named God "the Mystery." God is the one and only Holy Mystery, beyond all comprehension, transcendent and infinite. At the same time God is immanently present, *lovingly sustaining* our very life. God is the Holy Mystery.

Naming God "the Mystery" has both negative and positive aspects. Negatively it can diminish in the reader's mind the "personalness" or "relatedness" of God to humankind. Further, the word *mystery*, when associated with something people do not know or understand but which is both knowable and understandable, may seem to diminish the grandeur of God, who is neither fully knowable nor fully understandable. Positively, naming God the Mystery keeps us in continuity with our ancestors in faith.

We are not creating a new metaphor, for this name has a history in theology.[1] Karl Rahner wrote that "God is the holy mystery, so essentially and perpetually, that this mysterious Whither of transcendence, mastering, unmastered and holding sovereign sway, can be given the name of God—as indeed the name of God is the nameless infinity."[2] Daring to name the Divine brings us into relationship with the Holy Mystery whom we name.

The Greek word for *mystery*, *mystērion*, is equivalent to the Latin *sacramentum*, a visible sign of an invisible reality. The Mystery, though an invisible reality, is everywhere and always available to us through visible signs: creation, the signs of the times, the church. All of creation reveals the Mystery.[3] The Trinity is the Holy Mystery, an all-embracing, unconditionally loving God *for us*.[4]

This is what Christians profess: the Mystery embraces us as a people with unconditional love through every moment of our existence. The Mystery of Christ is always with us, gracing us and freeing us from sin and evil. The Mystery of the Spirit sustains, comforts, energizes us and sends us out in service and love to others. The Mystery we call Trinity lovingly lifts us up above our own sinfulness. And this Mystery sends us to embrace all other human beings and all of the world with our love. The Mystery is the source of the church's mission to proclaim the reign of God throughout the world.

Catechesis is a proclamation in many and varied ways of the unconditional love of the Trinity poured out on humankind always and everywhere, from the beginning, now, and forever, as long as the Mystery lives and loves. It is the Holy Mystery which catechists proclaim. The Greek word *katēcheo* means "to echo." Catechists through their ministry echo the Mystery of God to the community. The word catechists echo is not their own word, but the word of God. They echo the Mystery. In every word and every action catechists proclaim the Mystery of Christ and summon both individuals and the community to respond to the unconditional love of God. They do this in response to the great love of the Mystery poured forth on them through Christ and the Holy Spirit.

The Ministries of the Church

The ministries of the church take many forms. We minister as we worship, as we do works of justice, and as we proclaim the word. Whatever forms of ministry the church does, *God for us* is the source and origin of all our works. Ministries are our loving response to the love of God poured out on us. In our ministries we reach out to the world in service. Our ministries are a response to the Mystery which loves us so fully.

Jesus proclaimed the unconditional love of the Mystery and its fulfillment as he preached "the reign of God." His mission was to initiate and reveal God's reign in which the blind would see, captives would be freed, and the poor would have the good news preached to them. At the beginning of his ministry he identified himself with "the anointed one" on whom "the Spirit of the Lord" rested.

The good news that Jesus preached in many words can be summed up in a few words: God loves us unconditionally. Jesus' many stories and images proclaim this love. God is the one who cares for the lilies of the field. God is like the good shepherd, like the woman searching for a lost coin. God is the healer, the compassionate one, the one who drives out demons. If God provides for all creatures, how much more will the Mystery provide for us. God's love is unconditional, and we are to love even as God loves us. Loving is a godly way of life.

As Jesus proclaimed the unconditional love of the Mystery and ushered in the reign of God, so today we as Jesus' disciples carry on his mission. We do this by the witness of our lives and by our word. We are now the anointed ones who proclaim liberty to the captives and recovery of sight to the blind. We are the ones called to preach the good news to the poor. We are the ones who witness to God's reign. We do this in our daily interchange with others, and if we come to offer service in and through the church, we do it through our particular ministry.

Through the centuries the Christian community has tried to fulfill its mission through three forms of ministry: the ministry of worship, the ministry of service, and the ministry of the word. Worship, service, and word are related ministries. The community seldom does one without doing another. They cannot really be separated, but for purposes of clarity we will examine them separately.

The ministry of worship includes the church's liturgical celebrations. These celebrations are ritual prayers of praise and thanksgiving, of penitence and petition in which the church remembers and celebrates its liberation through the life-death-resurrection-glorification of Christ. In its liturgical celebrations the faith community celebrates its life with the Lord and remembers who it is. Worship gives the church its identity. In worship the church calls upon all of creation to join with it in giving praise and thanksgiving and as it worships the church is reminded of its responsibility to reach out in mercy, justice, and love to the world, the concrete world in which it lives.

The ministries of service include the church's works of justice and mercy, not only feeding the hungry, caring for the sick, teaching the ignorant, providing shelter for the homeless, bringing peace on earth but also setting up structures of advocacy for all who are in need or dispossessed. These structures may include lobbying Congress for those who are voiceless as Network does, or building homes for the homeless as Habitat for Humanity does. The ministry of justice is at the very heart of Christianity. It is not an option or an effect of being Christian. It is *being* Christian. Ministries of service are ministries of deeds and of witness. All Christians are obligated to works of mercy, but some accept the responsibility as ministers in the name of the church.

The ministry of the word includes different forms of the church's proclamation of God's gracious love and salvation as well as God's word of denunciation of evil through evangelization, catechesis, theology and liturgy, particularly through the homily. The ministry of the word is a service primarily of the word, through bodily and verbal language. It is the linguistic expression of the faith of the community.

The Ministry of the Word

What does the church proclaim through the ministry of the word? Ministers of the word announce the surprising love of the Mystery for each one of us and all of us and summon individuals and communities to recognize God's love in their lives. Every ministry of the word, whatever its form, whether it be evangelization, catechesis, theology, or the homily is meant to be a proclamation of the good news of God's love.

The phrase "the ministry of the word" is first used in the New Testament in the Acts of the Apostles. Luke tells the story of dissension between the Hellenistic and Hebrew Christians. The Hellenists felt they were neglecting their widows in the daily ministry of distributing food and services (a ministry of service). So the Twelve called the community together and redistributed the ministries. They asked the community to choose seven to do the ministry of service while they continued to devote themselves "to prayer (a ministry of worship) and to the ministry of the word" (Acts 6:4).

From the beginning the ministry of the word was a liberating echo of the original gospel. It was the proclaiming of the story of our freedom through Christ, the One who fully revealed God's unconditional love for us, through evangelization, or preaching, or theologizing, or catechesis. The ministries of the word bolstered the community's faith. They reminded the people that the Mystery loved them, particularly those who were poor or ill or abandoned or in any need. The ministries of the word called the people to love one another and to reconciliation, peace, and unity. They denounced evil, selfishness, and all forms of unethical behavior. In the beginning the ministries of the Word were the church's speech, a proclamation in which the community's voice was freed to speak, to sing and shout in words and actions of the Mystery of God's love for us.

Ministers of the word communicated the Mystery of God's love and of our participation in that love both to those who believed and to those who were simply curious. The words were never adequate, and everyone knew that the words were unsatisfactory, but the church also knew that no words describing the Mystery would ever be appropriate. Through the centuries ministers of the word have continuously tried to find better language to sing or speak of the Mystery. Thomas Aquinas is alleged at the hour of his death to have dismissed his extraordinary theological writings as "straw." He recognized that whatever we say about God is inadequate and limited, but he also knew that we must do the best we can to name and share through language our experience of the Divine.

Though words are insufficient, they still have extraordinary power. They communicate meaning. They praise or condemn. They lift up or tear down and both give life and take life away. Words transform and heal and wound and renew. They are neither insignificant nor unimportant. "Be careful with words, they're dangerous," said Elie Wiesel.[5] The nursery rhyme "Sticks and stones will break my bones, but names will never hurt me" hides the deep injury that words sometimes convey.

But words also heal and give life. We have carved our best words on marble and stone and they still inspire us. We inscribed the welcoming words of Emma Lazarus to all immigrants on our statue of liberty, "Give me your tired, your poor, Your huddled masses yearning to breathe free," and through those words millions of immigrants have been raised up, given hope and courage. In his Emancipation Proclamation Abraham Lincoln's words set a race of people free:

> On the first day of January in the year of our Lord, one thousand eight hundred and sixty-three, all persons held as slaves within any state, or designated part of a state, the people whereof shall then be in rebellion against the United States shall be then, thenceforward, and forever free.[6]

Words can be effective. They can change the world.

The words of the gospel echo the healing words of Jesus. They give meaning to our lives and express our deepest values. They fill us with hope and inspire us to give of ourselves. They themselves heal and liberate. Those who are ministers of the word bring the word of Jesus and the word of the church to the world. The ministry of the word echoes the gospel.

This book is about catechesis as a ministry of the word. It is about the renewal of catechesis during the twentieth century and its promise for the new twenty-first century. It is about the prophetic word, the word of God which our catechists proclaim. In the United States, in parish after parish, women and men catechists, ministers of the word, speak the word of God, the word of Christ, through the Holy Spirit to the people—to adults, to youth, to children. They praise and thank and call the community to conversion, and are both accepted and rejected by the people as were the prophets who spoke before them.

Many stories have been told about the courage and love of the catechists of Central America during the recent wars. In El Salvador and in Guatemala it was the catechists who most often spoke the word of the gospel, a word that strengthened the faith of the poor and the oppressed. It was their word that gave hope to the hopeless and brought people together as communities of faith. It was their words of compassion and grace that brought their authoritarian governments to fear and kill them.

Catechists in the United States labor under different circumstances. Our lives are not endangered because of our proclamation of God's word, for we speak only too often to a culture that simply does not care about religious faith, a world that treats religious faith as irrelevant to the times. How does one penetrate the frozen wall of indifference? What do we need to do to help our brothers and sisters understand that the word of the gospel is a freeing word for them, whoever they are, whatever their way of life may be.

Catechists in the United States need to minister more frequently with adults, for it is adults who are able to hear the word of God and respond freely to it. Parishes have spent so much time, energy, and money on the catechesis of children and youth that they seem to have little left for catechesis with adults. But it is only when we reach out to adults, share with them the reality of God's love and their own divinization that we can begin to call them to religious conversion. Maybe then the authorities and the ruling culture will begin to take the church and the word it speaks seriously.

The ministry of catechesis is a prophetic ministry. Our new prophets, primarily but not only women, address the church and the world with strength and with clarity. They speak the word which seems foolish. "Our God is a loving God. Our God is a compassionate God. Our God cares most of all for those most in need." And the word they speak emerges from their Christian faith commitment, a word of power and a word of life, a word of condemnation and a word of grace.

During the twentieth century the church began to remember again that catechesis is a prophetic ministry. During this century it considered its catechetical beginnings and heritage, and it recognized that it needed to catechize its adult members as well as its new members and children. Theoretically the church knows that children are not the only ones to be catechized, but it has not always acted on its theory. The twenty-first century can be the century of adult catechesis, of catechesis on the signs of the times in the adult's world. If so, all of us will need to recognize that adults need a community within which to be catechized. For them the place for catechesis is not the classroom but a comfortable adult space, and the topic for catechesis is their world. Through such a renewal the church can help the community to recognize God's love in its life, as well as the reality of sin.

The Ministry of Catechesis

During the twentieth century the catechetical renewal brought the church into harmony with the way in which it catechized in the apostolic age and in the first six centuries of church life. During these early centuries catechesis was the ministry through which new members, generally adults or families as a whole, were initiated into the church. This initiation eventually took a particular form which included the catechumenate and mystagogical catechesis.

Both Paul and Luke use the verb "to catechize" in their New Testament writings.[7] As noted earlier, the Greek verb for "to catechize" means to resound or to echo.[8] In English it is frequently translated as "to teach or to instruct," in the sense not of giving facts but of sharing insights, knowledge, wisdom, love. Walter Burghardt notes that instruction for catechumens in the early church was contextualized in the Scriptures and the liturgy.[9] From the beginning the purpose of catechizing was neither purely academic nor purely notional. Its purpose was to strengthen the commitment and dedication of faith.[10] It was a way of introducing adult believers into the Christian community and a Christian way of life. It was a way in which the church shared the Mystery and called others to recognize the unconditional love of the Mystery in their own lives.

Today we cannot repeat exactly what the early church did when it catechized. We are not living in the first century. Nor can we ignore twenty centuries of history. But we can look back at the early history of the church and see what it tells us about the way in which the community built up the faith commitment of its members. During the twentieth century catechetical leaders throughout the world did that kind of research. They also evaluated twentieth-century catechetical ministry and, out of their research and evaluation, articulated a new vision of the nature and purpose of catechesis. This renewed vision recognizes that the goal of catechesis is not information, as it was thought to be in the first half of the twentieth century, but conversion, the conversion of both individuals and the community.

The Goal of Catechesis: The Conversion of the Community

Catechesis is an ecclesial ministry that calls both individuals and the community to conversion. This call is not just to those joining the church for the first time, but it is a lifelong continuing summons to transformation of life to every member of the community. Catechesis calls for a holistic change which affects the cognitive, affective, and behavioral dimensions of life. It is a continuing call to recognize that life is a death-resurrection process in which the community and each member experience both the joys and pains of rebirth in Christ. Catechesis calls to conversion, but conversion is the gift of the Spirit.

Conversion is a turning away from selfishness and sin and a turning to justice and love. It is a continual dying and rising with Christ. Some churches see conversion as a sudden movement in life, an epiphany, an extraordinary event that compels one to accept Jesus as Lord almost instantaneously. Traditionally in the Catholic Church conversion has been seen as a slow, continuing, unending process of change. It demands that we put our trust in God and not in ourselves and recognize that it is the Mystery who is *for* us and not we for ourselves. In catechesis it is the Mystery who calls us to itself and invites us to conversion.

Conversion is a concrete experience, a transformation in life. As a religious conversion it requires a recognition and an acceptance of the transcendent/immanent God. As a Christian conversion it is the recognition that Jesus is Lord, that he is the Incarnate One whom God raised from the dead. Christian conversion is a movement from the primacy of the individual for itself to the acceptance of our relationship and responsibilities within the church and within our society. It causes a shift in the way we live out our lives, a change that makes us live with justice as "love's absolute minimum."[11] Such a conversion affects the intellect as new meanings are analyzed and accepted. The converted individual or community understands that no one has a monopoly on the truth, but that through the presence and power of the Spirit, truth resides in and is articulated by the new community into which it enters.

Most of all conversion is a change of heart. The *General Directory for Catechesis* notes that "faith and conversion arise from the *'heart.'*"[12] It is a movement of the heart from not even noticing others to loving them, to reaching out to those who are in need and recognizing them as brothers and sisters of the Mystery who is *for* us. Christian conversion commits us to Christ and to one another. In so doing it expands our loving, relates us to all of creation, leads us to acknowledge God's loving and compassionate presence with us always and everywhere, and gives us a renewed vision of reality. With conversion everything changes.

Catechesis is a work of the church, an ecclesial action, in which the whole church calls itself to conversion and to renewed Christian life. In catechesis the church renews its faith, faith not simply as response to truths, but faith as an existential act of acceptance of and commitment to the Mystery. In catechesis the church accepts responsibility for its sins, repents, and turns again through the power of the Holy Spirit and the love of Christ to God. Catechesis renews the life of the whole church.

Conversion is a renewal of faith. According to the *General Catechetical Directory*, "Faith is the acceptance and coming to fruit of the divine gift in us."[13] This divine gift is grace, God's own life in us. Grace expresses itself through faith. Christians are able to respond in faith to the self-communication of the Mystery *for* us because the Mystery enables them to do so. The Mystery gives people the initial faith through which they respond to the unconditional love which the Mystery pours out on them. The mystery enables conversion to happen.

Christian faith expresses itself in commitment to the life and teaching of Jesus. It expresses itself in an enthusiasm *(en theos)* for God, in action and in words, but mostly in living as a committed person-in-community. The response of faith is a free action of the person or community and cannot be imposed by anyone. The catechist cannot program a faith response, nor can she expect one, for both the individual and the community are free to accept or reject the gift of faith. Catechists are facilitators and animators, midwives and teachers but they are not producers of faith.

The Primary Form of Catechesis

The church directs its call to conversion primarily to adults because adults are "persons who are capable of an adherence that is fully responsible."[14] They can say "yes" to the Mystery and can respond freely to the embrace of that Holy Being who offers them unconditional love. Children are not ready to do this in a fully responsible way. Hopefully, catechesis will bring them into membership in the church in such a way that when they reach maturity they will see that the church helps them make sense of the world and of their lives. They will want to be part of it. They will feel lost without its embrace. It will be their home.

In its official documents the church has for the past thirty years spoken of the necessity to make catechesis with adults its priority form of catechesis. The *General Catechetical Directory* (1971) states that "catechesis for adults, must be considered the chief form of catechesis. All the other forms are in some way oriented to it."[15] The United States Bishops' Pastoral Message on Catholic Education, *To Teach as Jesus Did* (1972), notes that "the continuing education of adults is situated not at the periphery of the Church's educational mission but at its center."[16] Pope John Paul II wrote that the catechesis of adults "is the principal form of catechesis, because it is addressed to persons who have the greatest responsibilities and the capacity to live the Christian message in its fully developed form."[17] The revised *General Directory for Catechesis* (1997) repeats the words of the earlier document about adult catechesis as the chief form of catechesis and goes on to add that "this implies that the catechesis of other age groups should have it for a point of reference and should be expressed in conjunction with it."[18]

While the Catholic Church in the United States has made some progress in its efforts to develop catecheses for adults, the development is still in its early stages. Adult catechesis happens sporadically in some parishes when it happens at all. The *Notre Dame Study of Catholic Parish Life* conducted in 1983–1985 concluded that in parishes the religious education of the young is the highest catechetical priority.[19] The second highest priority was the religious education of preteens. By the time one reached the fifth in the list of "priorities" one found that parishes were concerned about adult religious education or catechesis.

For too long the church has placed its emphasis on the catechesis of children and has in fact neglected to catechize adults. When it did catechize adults, it instructed them by using educational methodologies appropriate for children. This is not surprising since the study of andragogy is a twentieth-century development. We can no longer use an outdated pedagogy with adults. We need to learn how to catechize adults and then adapt that process to the catechesis of children, the uninitiated, and youth. And we need to be quite clear about why we are catechizing at all.

The Components of Catechesis

The United States *National Catechetical Directory* describes catechesis as an action that is made up of four tasks or components. According to the directory these four components are (1) building the community, (2) sharing the church's stories and beliefs, (3) doing justice, and (4) praying together. Again and again the directory refers to the four components of catechesis, indicating that catechesis is incomplete without any one of the four "tasks."[20] This directory builds on the 1972 pastoral message on Catholic Education by the United States bishops called *To Teach as Jesus Did*. In that message the bishops wrote:

29

The educational mission of the Church is an integrated ministry embracing three interlocking dimensions: the message revealed by God *(didache)* which the Church proclaims; fellowship in the life of the Holy Spirit *(koinonia)*; service to the Christian community and the entire human community *(diakonia)*. While these three essential elements can be separated for the sake of analysis, they are joined in the one educational ministry.[21]

The pastoral message of the bishops was very well received in the United States church, and the motto "Community, Message, Service" became enormously popular in renewing Catholic school and parish catechetical programs for children. The *National Catechetical Directory, Sharing the Light of Faith*, built on the pastoral message and added a fourth element or component: prayer. When that directory was published, I, as a member of the national catechetical directory committee, wrote: "Consultation for the directory reminded us that catechesis also prepares for and leads to prayer. These are the *four* dimensions of the *one* ministry: community, message, social ministry, and prayer."[22] The directory committee also decided to write the components in the form of verbs so they would have a more dynamic quality: *building* community, *sharing* the message, *doing* justice, *praying* together.

The most recent official catechetical document, *General Directory for Catechesis* (1997) describes four "fundamental tasks" of catechesis. These four are described in an article entitled "Fundamental tasks of catechesis: helping to know, to celebrate and to contemplate the mystery of Christ." The four tasks are (1) promoting knowledge of the faith, (2) liturgical education, (3) moral formation, and (4) teaching to pray.[23] Article 86, entitled "Other fundamental tasks of catechesis: initiation and education in community life and to mission," names education for community life and missionary initiation as two additional tasks. In its description of these additional tasks the revised directory reinforces the ecumenical dimension of catechesis.

While the two directories may seem to promote different tasks, an examination of the tasks indicates that the United States and the

Vatican directories are in remarkable unity: They have simply used different language and to some extent a different emphasis, in their description of the catechetical act.

Four Tasks in Sharing the Light of Faith		*Six Tasks in General Directory for Catechesis*
(1) building the community	*relates to and*	(5) education for community life
		(6) missionary initiation
(2) sharing the Christian message	*relates to and*	(1) promoting knowledge of the faith
		(2) liturgical education
(3) doing justice	*relates to*	(3) moral formation
(4) praying together	*relates to*	(4) teaching to pray

Catherine Dooley points out: "The *General Directory for Catechesis* asserts that all these tasks are necessary and interdependent, 'When catechesis omits one of these elements, the Christian faith does not attain full development' (No. 87). Each of these tasks demands a commitment to the evangelization of the world."[24] *Sharing the Light of Faith* also saw the four components or tasks as making up the one act called catechesis. With the *GDC* we are reminded to give more attention to building community through our missionary efforts and to strengthen the ecumenical dimensions of building community.[25]

Recent catechetical publications and commentaries on the directories show that there is a widespread assumption at least in the United States that the catechetical act involves proclaiming Christ's message, building community, doing justice, and praying together. Because the use of the four components has been incorporated into catechetical ministry in the United States, I will continue to use the four-component schema in this book. However, I will also give more specific attention and emphasis to the missionary and ecumenical dimensions recommended in the recent *General Directory for Catechesis.*

These four components are essential aspects of the act of catechesis because they describe the very life of the church into which new members are being initiated and to which older members are continually recommitting themselves. The Acts of the Apostles presents the early Christian community in this way:

They devoted themselves to the teaching of the apostles and to the communal life, to the breaking of the bread and to the prayers....All who believed were together and had all things in common; they would sell their property and possessions and divided them among all according to each one's need. Every day they devoted themselves to meeting together in the temple area and to breaking bread in their homes. They ate their meals with exultation and sincerity of heart, praising God and enjoying favor with all the people. And every day the Lord added to their number those who were being saved. (Acts 2:42–47)

The life of the community focused on praying, doing justice, believing (the teaching of the apostles), and building up the community. These four actions together, as a whole, distinguished the Christian community. It is because these four actions are the components of Christian community life that they are components of catechesis.[26]

The four characteristics of the Christian community are the four actions that catechists use in catechesis to call the community to conversion. Catechesis keeps the community in touch with its beginnings and with its tradition. It does so by calling the community to reflect, critically, on the message and teaching of Christ, to examine how it is doing justice, to question how it builds up the community, and to join in ritual prayer which praises and thanks the Mystery *who is for* us.

Women and the Ministry of Catechesis

Recent studies of ministries in the Catholic Church indicate that the majority of the church's ministers are women. *The Notre Dame Study of Catholic Parish Life in the United States* notes that the church frequently puts forth "a female face."[27] It states:

over 80 percent of the CCD teachers and sponsors of the catechumenate are women.... Among those who lead or participate in adult Bible studies or religious discussion,...over 75 percent are women; among those who are active in parish renewal and spiritual growth over 70 percent are women; among those who join with prayer groups 80 percent are women. Even with

32

recreational programs and youth ministries we find that nearly 60 percent of those involved are women.

Even in parish councils the women are almost a majority: 48 percent are women and 52 percent are men. Of all forms of the ministry of the word women are more involved than men in evangelization, catechesis, and liturgy. It is only in the study of theology that women are less represented, and that is because until the last half of the twentieth century women were seldom accepted into theological schools or seminaries.

Fr. Philip Murnion describes present parish personnel as having a feminine dimension. He states that "this is not just a matter of how many women are now in formal positions of parish ministry, though that is of enormous importance." Rather it is a question of how the feminine dimension affects the community and what this means for other ministries in the church. Murnion's study indicates that 85 percent of new parish ministers are women, only 15 percent men.[28]

Women have long been dominant as catechists in parishes but it is only since the Second Vatican Council that it became ordinary for women to be directors of parish programs. In the past the newly ordained or young priest directed the program for children, though he may not have had any formal training in child psychology or education. In 1985 the *Notre Dame Study* found that 80 percent of the catechists in CCD programs *and* the *RCIA* were women. If the study examined only CCD programs it would find a much higher percentage of women serving as catechists. In 1994 *Toward Shaping the Agenda: A Study of Catholic Religious Education/Catechesis*[29] found that 87 percent of the 1,025 respondents who staffed CCD programs were women.

While this book is about the ministry of catechesis rather than a particular form of catechesis such as the catechesis of children, I have written it knowing that most of those who catechize in the church in the United States are women. I have worked with them, taught them, listened to them, watched them, and been both astonished and inspired by their commitment, their knowledge, and their skill. They make a major contribution to the continuing life of the church in the United States and all over the world.

Because of the number of women involved in catechetical ministry and because of the recognition that too many women feel oppressed by the church, I have, when it seems appropriate to do so and when it relates to catechesis, addressed some of the concerns of women and men who seek equality among all of us in the church. I have particularly addressed the question of inclusive language and formation of the church's normative and classic doctrinal texts in a patriarchal culture in the chapters on the Bible (chapter 7), the church's life and teaching (chapter 8) and liturgical catechesis (chapter 9).

The next chapter describes how the church progressed from an instructional model of catechesis at the beginning of the twentieth century to the possibility of multiple models of catechesis by the end of the 1960s. The history of this change emerged from the grass roots, and it is from the grass roots that several renewed approaches of catechesis developed, one of which is *Symbolic Catechesis.*

In Summary

The source of all ministries in the Catholic Church is the church's experience of the unconditional love of God for all of creation. People have felt and recognized this care and the covenant it expresses for millennia. They know that the love of the Mystery for us is undeserved and gratuitous, and their response is to love as well as they can. Some members of the community express their response through ministry.

The church's ministries emerge from its mission: to build the reign of God. These ministries take the form of the ministry of the word, the ministry of service, and the ministry of worship. Catechesis is a form of the ministry of the word, a ministry that calls the community and individuals within it to conversion.

FURTHER READINGS

Dooley, Catherine, and Mary Collins, eds. *The Echo Within: Emerging Issues in Religious Education*. A Tribute to Berard L. Marthaler, O.F.M., Conv. Allen, Tex.: Thomas More, 1997.

La Cugna, Catherine Mowry. *God for Us: The Trinity and Christian Life*. San Francisco: Harper, 1991.

Moran, Gabriel. *Catechesis of Revelation*. New York: Herder & Herder, 1967.

————. "Religious Education after Vatican II." In *Open Catholicism, The Tradition at Its Best: Essays in Honor of Gerard S. Sloyan*, ed. David Efroymson and John Raines, 151–66. A Michael Glazier Book. Collegeville, Minn.: Liturgical Press, 1997.

Warren, Michael, ed. *Sourcebook for Modern Catechetics*, vol. 1. Winona, Minn.: St. Mary's Press, 1983.

CHAPTER 2

The Story of Renewal

My mother, Mary O'Connor, was born in Chicago in 1908. As her life progressed she moved ever farther westward in Chicago from St. Mel's Parish to Resurrection Parish to St. Giles Parish in a western suburb. As she grew, her life changed not only geographically but also culturally. She moved from a neighborhood that was totally Irish Catholic to a suburb that welcomed people of different nationalities and many faiths.[1]

My mother's faith also grew and changed. The church of her childhood was far different from the church she knew as a senior citizen. Sometimes the changes bewildered her. Most of the time she welcomed them. She embraced the liturgical renewal with enthusiasm and expressed a desire to know more about the Bible. She particularly welcomed the ecumenical renewal, for she had many friends who belonged to other churches. Her participation in Sunday Mass brought her in contact with the liturgical, biblical, theological, and ecumenical renewal of the twentieth century, but like most adult Catholics in the United States, she never personally experienced the catechetical renewal.

When my mother was a child she received her "religious instruction" from the sisters in her parish school, St. Mel's. Her textbook was a catechism, the so-called *Baltimore Catechism.*[2] Her religious instruction and that of most children ordinarily stopped after they received the sacrament of confirmation at the age of fourteen.

The goal of this religious instruction was to teach the children doctrine, that which was true, with the understanding that once children *knew* what was true, they would *do* what was right (the good), and doing what was right would eventually lead to *union with God* in heaven. The schema was:

Teaching (giving information from the catechism, truth)
brought formation (right behavior, the good)
which led to the ultimate reward (union with God).

This methodology was quite a departure from the way in which the apostolic church catechized. In the early church catechesis was a process that included interaction with the community, oral instruction, acts of justice, communal prayer, and moral reform. The community followed the fourfold pattern of Christian living described by Luke in the Acts of the Apostles (2:42–44). As the centuries progressed, the institutionalized catechumenate became the process through which the community initiated its new members.

The fourth-century schema of St. Augustine influenced the catechesis of the Middle Ages. In his treatise *The First Catechetical Instruction* Augustine instructed the catechist, Deogratias, in a four-step methodology:

1. Tell the story
2. Explain the doctrine in the story
3. Ask questions to check understanding
4. Exhort to right behavior[3]

"Telling the story" in Augustine's schema included telling both stories of the Bible and stories of the church's history.

From the time of Augustine to the fifteenth century when the printing press was invented, catechesis was primarily oral. The so-called catechisms of the Middle Ages were instructions or sermons given at particular feasts or seasons. The liturgical year, which focused on the liturgical seasons and feasts and the lives of the saints, was the context for these instructions. Cathedrals with their stained glass windows, statues, gargoyles, and other visual arts were the "textbooks" which lent themselves to dramatic storytelling and to the oral catechesis of the bishop.

The Development of Catechisms

Although some catechetical works were written before the fifteenth century, they were addressed primarily to the literate clergy and to other educated adults. After the invention of the printing press in the mid-fifteenth century and the subsequent rise in literacy books became more important. While a Latin translation of the Bible is considered to be the first book printed by movable type, it was not long before catechism-type texts were also printed.[4]

In 1529 Martin Luther published two catechisms, the German Catechism and the Small Catechism.[5] The German Catechism, generally known as the Large Catechism, was a book that explained to the clergy how they could address the needs of the people for practical Christian living.[6] The Small Catechism was a book written for "ordinary pastors and preachers," urging them to "help me to teach the catechism to the people, especially those who are young."[7] The Small Catechism with its series of questions and answers became a prototype of future catechisms for children.

In 1554 the Jesuit Peter Canisius published a catechism entitled *A Compendium of Christian Doctrine Developed by Means of Questions, for Use by Christian Children.* Canisius divided the catechism in two parts: Part 1 on "Wisdom" followed the organization of Augustine's catechetical handbook entitled *Faith, Hope, and Charity.*[8]

What we *believe* (faith) is in the Apostles' Creed;
what we *hope* for is in the Lord's Prayer;
the way we *love* is in the Commandments; and
the sacraments as a way to come to wisdom and to keep justice.

Part 2 examined sins that destroy justice and good works that come from faith and hope.[9]

Canisius wrote his compendium of Christian doctrine *(summa)* to be used by teacher, pastors, and preachers during the years the Council of Trent was in session. Two years later, in 1556, Canisius published an abbreviated version, called the *Short Catechism,* "for small children and the uneducated," which included fifty-nine questions and answers for children to memorize.[10]

The catechisms of the Reformers (the Protestants) and the Counter-Reformers (the Catholics) had a major impact on the way in which the church initiated new members into the community. The Reformers and Counter-Reformers each emphasized the differences between them. As a result, after the Reformation, what had been known as "catechesis" throughout the earlier centuries became "religious instruction," primarily the religious instruction of children. This instruction focused on the difference between Protestants and Catholics, and it became instruction with a book, the catechism, rather than understanding the church's stories.

The Council of Trent (1545–1563) ordered the writing of a catechism as a resource for the clergy. Published in 1566, the *Romanus Catechismus,* popularly known as the *Catechism of the Council of Trent,* is the only catechism ever commissioned by an ecumenical council. The preface notes that the Reformers had been active in writing voluminous works that "deceived with incredible facility the simple and the incautious."[11] One purpose of the *Roman Catechism* was "to meet the mischievous activity of such men, and to rear the edifice of Christian knowledge on its only secure and solid basis, the instruction of its authorized teachers."[12] The authors intended this text for the use of the clergy to help them in their sermons and their instruction of children and youth.

The *Catechism of the Council of Trent* was organized into four parts that have become known as the "four pillars" of the catechism: the creed, the sacraments, the ten commandments, and prayer. The preface said that the "manner of communicating it [the doctrine] is of considerable importance" and encouraged paying close attention to the age, capacity, manners, and condition of the learners.[13] This catechism was composed in running prose, not in question-and-answer form, and was the basis for many catechisms written by priests and bishops in the post-Reformation period.

In the nineteenth century the question of the preparation of a new catechism for the entire church was raised again by a council. The First Vatican Council (1869–1870) considered the need for a new catechism and voted to authorize one but never implemented this decision. In the twentieth century the Second Vatican Council

(1962–1965) debated whether to prepare a catechism and decided to publish a directory instead. A directory differs from a catechism in that it presents general guidelines for catechesis, but is not a compendium of Christian doctrine.

From the sixteenth century until the middle of the twentieth century, religious instruction through a catechism was the ordinary way of instructing children and adult converts. But during the twentieth century a remarkable organic renewal of catechesis developed, which changed this pattern. This chapter narrates the story of this renewal by focusing on people who greatly influenced it: Bishop John Lancaster Spalding; Pope Pius X; Josef A. Jungmann, S.J.; Joseph Colomb, S.S.; and Johannes Hofinger, S.J. This survey cannot give a full picture of the many persons and events which effected renewal, but it can give an overview that will show the developmental and organic growth of insights that brought us to the beginning of the twenty-first century.

Bishop *John Lancaster Spalding* and the Baltimore Catechism

If one book shaped the Catholic Church in the twentieth century in the United States, that book has to be the *Baltimore Catechism*. Although its actual title was *A Catechism of Christian Doctrine*, it was known as the *Baltimore Catechism* because of its close association with the Third Plenary Council of Baltimore. Published in 1885, it was used in the United States throughout much of the twentieth century.

In the nineteenth century the question of a uniform catechism was a vexing one for the bishops. Some thought the writing of a catechism was a prerogative of the diocesan bishop. Many had written their own catechisms. Other bishops, primarily those concerned about uniformity and church discipline, favored the adoption of a single catechism, even if that meant using a catechism originally written for another country, such as Butler's Catechism, issued by the Synod of Maynooth for Ireland, in 1882.

At a special session on November 11, 1884, a catechism committee met to consider the bishops' concern for a new catechism.

On November 29, the bishops formally asked the committee to prepare a catechism. On December 6, eight days later, the committee distributed a preliminary draft of a catechism to the bishops for their approval. Because the council was about to close, the bishops took the proofs home with them with the understanding that they could forward changes or revisions to John Lancaster Spalding, bishop of Peoria, Illinois. Spalding, described by journalist-historian Charles Morris as "an indefatigable, unremittingly purple, Catholic pamphleteer,"[14] implemented the council's recommendation for a catechism. He worked with Monsignor Januarius de Concilio, formerly a professor of theology at Seton Hall's Immaculate Conception Seminary and then rector of St. Michael's Church in Jersey City, New Jersey, whom the bishops asked to prepare the manual.[15] With de Concilio, Spalding wrote, compiled, and directed the publication of the *Baltimore Catechism*.

The bishops had directed Spalding to send a draft of the catechism to them for their suggestions and then to report on it at the next annual meeting of the conference of archbishops. After the archbishops' examination and approval Spalding was to have it published as the official catechism of the United States, which all priests and teachers throughout the country would use.

Spalding, a dynamic and self-confident man, did not follow the recommended procedures. He expected long and possibly fruitless discussions about the content of the catechism. On February 23, 1885, he wrote to Archbishop Gibbons, saying, "I have received suggestions from all the archbishops concerning the catechism and have made such changes as seemed desirable."[16] On April 6, 1885, John Cardinal McCloskey gave the catechism his imprimatur and James Cardinal Gibbons approved the text. On April 11 the catechism was published. The official title page says: "Prepared and Enjoined by Order of the Third Plenary Council of Baltimore," not "approved by" that council.

The *Baltimore Catechism* was a small book, seventy-two pages, with 421 questions in thirty-seven chapters. It was not universally well received when it was first published. An anonymous critic writing in *Pastoral Blatt*, a monthly periodical from St. Louis, found the work to be pedagogically unsuitable and theologically inadequate. He found its treatment of God and the angels weak, its one question about the resurrection unworthy of that mystery,[17] and censured it for generally ignoring the work of the Holy Spirit in the church. While the *Baltimore Catechism* was endorsed in some dioceses, from its beginning it encountered serious resistance from both instructors and bishops.[18]

Ten years after its publication dissatisfaction with the *Baltimore Catechism* continued. In 1895 the archbishops of the country met and decided to poll the other bishops in order to determine if they should revise the catechism. The poll showed that the bishops of the country favored a revision.[19] The revision, however, was delayed. When the catechism finally was revised almost fifty years later in 1941, largely the work of Francis J. Connell, C.SS.P., the revision met with little favor. When all but older Americans say they studied the *Baltimore Catechism* as children, they do not mean the 1885 text but this revision, usually accompanied by supplementary materials.

The catechism was neither christocentric nor trinitarian. Nor was it biblical. Even when revised, it did not incorporate the liturgical insights of the time. Most importantly, it did not show any priorities among the doctrines. It did, however, promote both unity and uniformity, as the bishops wished.

In the renewal of catechesis in the United States in the twentieth century the *Baltimore Catechism* (1885) may be seen as a benchmark for the beginning of the century, and *Catechism of the Catholic Church* (1994) as a benchmark for the ending of the century. What happened between the publication of these two books was a significant renewal in the church's understanding of the nature of catechesis.

1900–1936. Pope Pius X and the Catechetical Movement: Focus on Methodology

The twentieth century can easily claim to be the most active catechetical century since the apostolic age. Each decade brought new questions and new insights that moved the church from its understanding of religious instruction as the rote learning of children to catechesis as critical inquiry into the relationship of life and faith by adults.

On August 4, 1903, shortly after the century began, Giuseppe Sarto, patriarch of Venice, was elected pope and chose the name Pius X. The new pope had spent many years as a parish priest, and his primary interests were pastoral. During his papacy he called for a renewal of the Confraternity of Christian Doctrine throughout the world.[20] The Confraternity was a lay organization begun in the sixteenth century to provide religious education to all who were deprived of such education.

The revival of the Confraternity of Christian Doctrine laid the groundwork for catechetical renewal in this century. Pope Pius X reawakened an organization that had been quiescent. In the United States many dioceses reinstituted the Confraternity and assigned parish priests to develop parish chapters. Parishes approached their religious instruction programs with a new enthusiasm

Pope Pius X's encyclical *On the Teaching of Christian Doctrine* required parish priests to "instruct the boys and girls, for the space of an hour from the text of the Catechism on those things they must believe and do in order to attain salvation."[21] This regulation revived the religious instruction offered to children attending the public schools. The encyclical also stated that the priest should encourage and prepare "lay helpers" for teaching the catechism, bringing numbers of lay women and men into this work. The second regulation initiated a program of instruction for these volunteer lay teachers that was one of the most effective adult catechetical programs in the history of the church.

During the First World War (1914–1918) military chaplains noted that many soldiers, when away from their villages and families, did not practice their faith. Often they did not attend Sunday Mass, nor did they frequent the sacraments or keep the commandments. When asked questions about their faith, the soldiers either could not respond or their responses were inaccurate. In the 1920s the chaplains determined that the religious instruction of the children was responsible for this inadequacy and recommended reform in the methods of imparting instruction. This gave added impetus to the methodological reform introduced by educational theorists who were promoting the "learn by doing" methodology. These theorists suggested that children learn not only by hearing but also by doing. The question became, What methodologies will best improve the teaching of the doctrines of the faith?

A new methodology called the "Munich method" was developed. This method included learning by doing and consisted of three steps: presentation, explanation, and application. The lesson began with

> the *presentation* of a story, usually a biblical story,
> went on to *explain* the doctrine that interpreted the story, and
> then *applied* the doctrine to life.

Critics said that the Munich method implied passive learning and focused on biblical stories rather than life experiences. It was introduced into the United States by Joseph J. Baierl, of St. Bernard's Seminary, Rochester, New York, in a series of texts called *The Creed Explained* (1919). This work, popularized by Anthony Fuerst of St. Mary's Seminary, Cleveland, and Rudolph G. Bandas of St. Paul Seminary in Minnesota,[22] never achieved wide acceptance, but it opened the way for other methodological reforms.

Other ways of improving methodology developed in the late 1920s and the 1930s. Teachers began to introduce drama, dance, and even drawing into religious instruction. They recommended hymn singing and liturgical celebrations. Method reformers encouraged concrete rather than abstract language with the children. They urged active rather than passive learning. And finally, they called for a reorganization of the catechisms.

In summary, the first three decades of the twentieth century focused on improving the methodology of religious instruction. The reform called for more participation from the children. It used additional materials to supplement the catechisms. It recognized that the understanding of doctrine was not enough and that the goal of religious instruction ought to be not simply *understanding* but the Christian *formation* of the child.

While this renewed goal emerged from evaluation of local parish programs, it was articulated by leaders in the dioceses and took many years before it was implemented on the parish level. Communications at that time were certainly not as instantaneous as they are now, and the presumption often was that change was not needed.

During this time most theologians, parish priests, and teachers took it for granted that the language in which the church expressed its doctrines of faith was unchangeable. In 1936 Josef Andreas Jungmann, S.J., seriously questioned that presupposition.

1936–1960. Josef Andreas Jungmann, S.J., and Joseph S. Colomb, S.S.: Focus on Content

Two men, Josef Jungmann from Austria and Joseph Colomb from France, had an extraordinary influence on the renewal of catechesis in the second third of the twentieth century. Their work brought to the church new insights about the nature, goal, and process of catechesis. The works of these two priests was discussed and debated by religious education leaders in Europe for twenty-five years. In 1960 their work was affirmed at an International Catechetical Study Week in Eichstatt, Germany.

Josef Andreas Jungmann (1889–1976)

Josef Jungmann was born in 1889 in South Tirol, Austria. Twenty-four years later he was ordained a priest for his home diocese, Brixen, and he began his pastoral ministry in villages of the South Tirol area. His experiences in those villages led him to recognize what he described as "the vast gulf between the joyful good news of the gospel and the legalistic fearsome piety of the people of his parish."[23]

In 1917 Jungmann entered the Society of Jesus. The Society, aware of his pastoral interests, sent him to Innsbruck to study in order to prepare him to teach catechetics and liturgy. Jungmann's pastoral interest in catechetics led him to write a dissertation entitled "Catechetical and Kerygmatic Texts of the First Three Centuries."

In 1925 he began teaching catechetics at Innsbruck. During these years of teaching Jungmann did further research on catechetics and revised and reworked his dissertation, *Die Frohbotschaft und unsere Glaubensverkündigung,* which he published in 1936. It was abridged and translated into English twenty-six years later as *The Good News Yesterday and Today.*[24]

With the publication of *Die Frohbotschaft* Jungmann reintroduced the word catechesis, and he challenged catechetical leaders to reassess the renewal movement. He questioned a basic theological premise of the time by proposing what was then unthinkable: *that the content of catechesis needed to be renewed.* Jungmann supported the emphasis placed on methodological reform in the teaching of religion but said that a change in methodology was not enough. He stated that "the main root of today's religious malady is…an extensive misunderstanding or nonunderstanding of the Christian message."[25] Jungmann said that the Christian message needed to be reinvigorated with the life and dynamism it possessed in the apostolic church. The refrain that echoes throughout Jungmann's critique is that

> it is not enough to show the necessity and reasonableness of the faith, nor enough to expound every point of doctrine and every commandment down to the very last division; but it is singularly important to achieve first of all *a vital understanding* of the Christian message, bringing together "the many" into a consistent, unified whole, that *there may be joyous interest and enthusiastic response in living faith.*[26]

The Good News is divided into three parts. In part 1, "The Situation," Jungmann observed that the peace, joy, and hope of the faith of the early church contrasted unfavorably with the faith of the most Catholics today. He noted that in the present, "all that is genuinely Christian, truly supernatural—the merciful plan of God revealed in the humanity of Christ, calling for man's inmost participation—all this has been largely lost from sight."[27] Jungmann described church life as impoverished due to a static theology that did not speak to people's lives, a liturgy divorced from the people, and a form of instruction that he described as "arid intellectualism."

He pointed out that what we needed was a "luminous center from which the whole of faith grows together unto clear unity."[28] That luminous center is Christ, for it is "from the radiance of *Christ* that God's merciful plan, as well as its concrete realization, is rendered immediately intelligible."[29]

Jungmann believed that deficiencies in the proclamation of the message could be traced back to the breakup of the central core of the proclamation. "It is Christ we proclaim," he wrote, and he noted that it is a wholly Christ-centered catechesis that we need. In religious instruction not only was Christ no longer viewed as the "radiant core" of the salvific message, but "in the heralding of Christ, the bringer of grace—the two decisive components, *Christ* and grace, became ever more and more separated."[30]

Because of Jungmann's writings, readers recognized that the message presented in catechesis ought to include not only creeds and doctrinal formulations, but also Scripture and liturgy. All three sources—doctrine, Scripture, and liturgy—were intimately and organically related to Christian life. Jungmann's basic premise was that catechesis should return to an examination of these sources of Christian faith and determine how they interact with one another and with a fourth source, the witness of daily life.

Jungmann also reoriented the goal of catechesis. He wrote that the real difference between theology and catechesis is that *"theology is primarily at the service of knowledge,"* while the *"proclamation of the faith, on the other hand, is entirely orientated toward life."*[31] Catechesis leads to "holiness." It is a process of "religious formation" "which will round out and perfect the world-view of the young by acquainting them with the supernatural order in which we actually are."[32]

Jungmann's critique of theology was controversial. It provoked such negative responses from some theologians that the Jesuit General, Ladislaus Ledochowski cautioned Jungmann about this catechetical work, and then withdrew Jungmann's book from the market.[33] In response Jungmann changed his focus from the study of catechetics to the study of liturgy and became the premier liturgical scholar of the twentieth century.[34]

The Good News as presented by Jungmann was a masterful work. Its continuing acceptance by catechetical leaders testifies to their recognition that Jungmann had both identified a basic defect in religious instruction and presented a program in catechesis that promised to give new life to their endeavors. G. Emmett Carter, later archbishop of Toronto, wrote that "the shift in emphasis from method to content in the catechetical renewal has been brought about almost single-handedly by Fr. Josef A. Jungmann, through his book *The Good Tidings and Our Profession of Faith*."[35] This was an extraordinary and a costly accomplishment.

Joseph Colomb, S.S. (1902–1979)

Born in 1902 in the Diocese of Lyon, France, Joseph Colomb did much of his initial religious education ministry in his home diocese. A Sulpician priest, he received a degree in philosophy from the Catholic Faculty of Lyon and was director of the theological college at the University of Lyon from 1928 to 1945. In 1945 he was appointed associate director of religious education for that archdiocese. One of his first actions was to begin a school for catechists.

In the decade before Colomb moved to the diocesan office, catechetical renewal in France had focused on the "activities method" evidenced in the work of Mlle. Françoise Derkenne and Marie Fargues.[36] Their work raised questions about the need to adapt catechetical instruction to the age and cultural or social conditions of the children. In subsequent writings Colomb developed their insights, which were based on principles of developmental learning.

Colomb insisted on a return to the sources of faith in catechesis: the Scriptures, the liturgy, and doctrine, but instead of calling the fourth source "witness," he called it "human experience." Colomb called upon catechists to awaken the spiritual sense of the child by drawing out the Christian meaning of their human experiences. This work is difficult, said Colomb, for it presupposes that the catechist "has a very highly developed sense of the spirit, liberty and responsibility which makes up the greatness of natural [man]. It presupposes a truly human, thoughtful experience of this greatness."[37]

Colomb emphasized that understanding is dependent on experience. He wrote:

> I cannot understand a book about mountains or valleys if I have never seen these things with my own eyes in my own country, if I have not the *experience* of what is a mountain or a valley. Book knowledge and oral knowledge presupposes a *personally experienced* knowledge. If this is lacking, or if the book knowledge does not fit with it, then the book bears no meaning for me; it may be learnt by heart, it may provide words, it does not enter into the living person. Any full understanding is built upon some experience; it makes this experience more conscious and prepares the way for further experiences.[38]

He went on to ask, "How can anyone understand a lesson on prayer who has never prayed?" or, "If I have no experience of a parish community, what good can I get out of a lesson on the parish?" He said that, because all knowledge relates to experience, the catechist needs to adapt the program "to the religious experience of the child and answer the questions the child would put if he had permission."[39]

For Colomb the experience of parish community is part of the *content* of catechesis. He believed that the task of the catechist is to bring the child's attention to those privileged daily experiences of life. Such experiences included celebrations of family prayer, feasts, liturgy, and also the "good works" of the community. Colomb wrote that "it is on the child's *religious experience* that we must build, not on the textbook."[40]

A second major contribution of Colomb was his reexamination and restatement of the goal of catechesis. Colomb pointed out that the act of faith is a response to *God*, not a response to *objective statements*. He emphasized that faith is the acceptance of God as present through signs or symbols that manifest or reveal God's presence. These signs reveal a hidden God whom the Holy Spirit enables us to recognize. These signs or symbols are both internal and external. The Holy Spirit within us enables us to respond to the external signs of God's presence.

Colomb described the goal of catechesis as a living and dynamic faith in God. This revision of the goal was both astonishing and dismaying to those who emphasized that faith was the acceptance of unchangeable dogmatic truths. Colomb reestablished two poles of faith, the *fides quae*, the faith that we believe (doctrine) and *fides qua*, the act of faith by which we believe (commitment). Colomb described the act of faith this way:

> The act of faith is situated on the plane of the spirit and liberty. Critical reason protects it against the irrational, emotive, instinctive and pathological. It is the supreme act of the conscious and free being, the personal act par excellence, by which one offers oneself to God, thus choosing one's fate. It is the act which completes the human being by opening him to the dimensions of God.[41]

Colomb recognized that faith is a gift from God. "There is," he wrote, "in our soul a call towards the Father, which is of a supernatural order, which is already the grace of Christ, already the light of the Word." According to Colomb all persons are called to the Father through the word Christ speaks. This word awakens us, enlightens us, reveals God to us. The exterior word, Christ, meets the interior word of the Spirit and "faith springs from this encounter."[42]

Colomb recognized that faith is a gift, but he saw it also as the supreme act of the conscious and free being. "We must," he insisted, "really educate the free person to fight for his faith, to choose."[43] For that reason

> our catechisms must absolutely go beyond memory and customs (although these must receive their share), beyond the intelligence (although we must see that the child understands); all must be imbued with liberty offered for the acceptance, for choice (in the measure in which that has a meaning for the child).[44]

Colomb encouraged catechists to speak to the whole person: intelligence, heart, and will. Through this methodology, he believed that faith would be strengthened, for faith is the adherence, conversion, and commitment of the whole person, intelligence, heart, and will. Colomb also restated the goal of catechesis to be "a living faith," that faith that is commitment to Christ as Lord.

While the French school of catechetics (Colomb) did not always agree with the German school (Jungmann), both schools had many common understandings about the catechetical act. First, both of them believed that it was not enough to renew the method of catechesis, but that the *content* ought also to be renewed. The church should draw on its primary sources of faith: the Bible, the liturgy, and the church's doctrine and life. Colomb emphasized that life experience was a fourth source or sign of faith. Second, both agreed that the goal of catechesis ought to be the strengthening of faith, although they differed to a degree in their description of faith. Finally, both schools returned to the language of the early church, the language of catechesis, and in so doing they moved religious instruction from an educational to a ministerial base. Their work, developed over the 1930s, 1940s, and 1950s, became accepted throughout the world in the 1960s.

1960–1968. *Johannes Hofinger and the Catechetical Study Weeks: Focus on Integration and Synthesis*

An indefatigable Jesuit named Johannes Hofinger set out to proclaim the benefits of Jungmann's *kerygmatic* catechesis to the world. He organized International Catechetical Study Weeks held on five different continents during the late 1950s and the1960s. To these Study Weeks he invited catechetical leaders from the five continents and gave them the opportunity to study, discuss, affirm, or reject premises of catechetical renewal. Some participants in the Study Weeks were later bishops or *periti* (consultants) at the Second Vatican Council. They brought to the Study Weeks theological and pastoral insights of the council, and to the council the catechetical insights of the Study Weeks.

Hofinger was an organizer, a theologian, and a person committed to the renewal of catechesis. He had a profound effect on this renewal because of the Study Weeks and also because of his teaching, speaking, and writing. A student and admirer of Jungmann, Hofinger first came to the United States in 1955 to Immaculate Heart College in Los Angeles and later went to the University of

51

Notre Dame to speak about *kerygmatic* catechesis. While in the United States he met Sister Maria de la Cruz Aymes-Couche, S.H., who later described him as "an incarnation of the 'kerygmatic' approach, exemplifying in his life the Gospel message of the Good News and giving to catechetical ministry a theology relevant to people hungry for the word of God."[45]

Hofinger coauthored with Sister Maria de la Cruz the *On Our Way* catechetical series for children in grades one through six.[46] This series presented a revolutionary new face to catechesis. It incorporated the recommendations of Jungmann in its pastoral approach to catechesis and in the use of the four sources. Through the *On Our Way* series the authors introduced the reforms of Jungmann to parishes in the United States.

However, it was Hofinger's sponsorship of the International Catechetical Study Weeks that had the greatest effect on catechetical renewal. Initially, Hofinger planned a Study Week on liturgy and the missions to be held in Nijmegen, Holland, in 1959.[47] He invited over two hundred missionaries and missionary bishops from around the world to this conference. Participants were to consider pastoral questions about the topic. The liturgical experience of the missionaries, their interest in how other missionaries had experienced sacramental life in the missions, the richness of the discussion, the clarity and focus of the speakers all contributed to a most successful meeting, so successful, in fact, that Hofinger decided to have another meeting on the topic of catechesis.

Eichstätt 1960: The Four Sources

In 1960 Hofinger invited participants to a second Study Week in Eichstätt, Germany, on the topic of catechetics and the missions. Bishops, missionaries from five continents and internationally recognized specialists in catechetics came from all over the world to Eichstätt. Most of the participants were European by birth, though a minority were from other continents. Hofinger himself describes the participants as those from the "home countries" or from the "mission lands."[48]

The Eichstätt Study Week has been described as "a landmark in the history of modern catechetics."[49] It brought together the kerygmatic approach of the Jungmann school and the developmental catechesis and pedagogy of signs of the French. Ten years later Luis Erdozain described Eichstätt as "the explosion of a movement still trying to define itself."[50] At Eichstätt the convergence of the German and French principles of renewal brought forth international acceptance of Jungmann's "kerygmatic catechesis" and Colomb's understanding of a "life of faith" as its goal. Alfonso Nebreda described the debates between the French and German catechists in this way:

> Anyone who was involved in the behind-the-scenes happenings at Eichstätt would recall the rather dramatic clash between the German and French experts. The German team…came to the Congress with a ready-made set of conclusions which accurately mirrored the specifically German kerygmatic approach, conspicuously connected with the history of the new German catechism. But when they proposed it as a workable draft to be accepted as conclusions of the meeting, the French group…frontally opposed it as unacceptable. After rather prolonged and hectic discussion, a compromise was reached of which one of the main characteristics was precisely the adoption (as part of the conclusions) of the then current emphasis on that privileged tetrad of signs[51]

Despite the differing approaches at the Study Week, the conclusions of Eichstätt stated that "catechesis embraces a fourfold presentation of the faith: through liturgy, Bible, systematic teaching and the testimony of Christian living."[52]

Eichstätt was both an end and a beginning. In ratifying the four-signs approach to catechesis on an international level, the congress ended the narrow vision of catechesis as only instruction in doctrine. In accepting the four signs as content and recognizing that catechesis seeks the response of a change of heart, it initiated a new search into the nature of conversion and of the catechetical act. Both of these topics were considered at successive congresses.

Bangkok 1962: Adaptation and Adults

Two years after the Eichstätt meeting catechetical leaders assembled in Bangkok, Thailand, from October 31 through November 3, 1962, to study ways in which the principles of modern catechetics accepted at Eichstätt could be applied to the missions.[53] The move from Europe to Asia, where Catholics were a small minority of peoples of other religions, had a profound effect on the participants, most of whom were from Europe even if they served as missionaries in Asia.

Hofinger reminded the participants that while the original aim of the Eichstätt meeting was to address the problems of missionary catechetics, the discussion had led instead to an analysis of the basic principles of catechetical renewal. The problem of applying these principles to missionary catechesis remained, and Hofinger asked the Bangkok assembly to address the mission questions.

Since missionaries ordinarily catechize adults rather than children, the participants at Bangkok initiated a dramatic shift from emphasis on the catechesis of children to the catechesis of adults. They also shifted from concern about the content of catechesis to concern about those being catechized. These shifts represented a change of focus from the content of catechesis to the subjects of catechesis. This anthropological approach (concern with peoples' questions) represented a major shift in the reform process.

The shift to the person/community focus led the participants to discuss how to catechize people who were not Christian, and this led to a recognition of different stages of conversion called preevangelization, evangelization, and catechesis proper.[54] Theodore Stone wrote that "the guiding principle of pre-evangelization is anthropocentric, because we must start from the nonbeliever and carefully respect his spiritual situation."[55]

This emphasis on the subject, particularly the adult subject, brought the participants at Bangkok a step further than Eichstätt. They acknowledged that it was not sufficient to renew the content of catechesis to include the Bible, doctrine, liturgy, and human experience. Catechesis in both non-Christian and Christian countries was to take its beginning from the *life experience* and *culture* of the people, primarily adults, being catechized. Catechists need to understand and take into consideration the culture and experience of the adults being catechized. Without doing so, the catechesis would be incomplete.

Katigondo 1964 and Manila 1967: An Anthropological Orientation

The Pan African Study Week held at Katigondo, Uganda, August 27–September 1, 1964, and the Asian Study Week held in Manila, April 16–30, 1967, continued to expand and refine the meaning of the subject-centered and adult focus of catechesis. In Katigondo, the first Study Week to be held after the promulgation of the *Constitution on the Sacred Liturgy (Sacrosanctum Concilium)*, the delegates emphasized the need to adapt the liturgy and liturgical catechesis to the culture of the people. The conclusions of that congress noted that

> the liturgy has an inherent and indispensable catechetical function of illumination and liberation. It exercises this function mainly through symbolism and community action and, in order to do so effectively, requires adaptation to the cultural responses of the participants.[56]

The participants clearly recognized the intimate relationship of catechesis with liturgy and of both ministries with culture, and of the need for adaptation of the ministry according to the nature and age of those being catechized.

The movement toward a subject-centered orientation of catechesis begun at Bangkok and expanded at Katigondo reached a new climax at Manila. The discussions, debates, and documents that emerged from the Second Vatican Council, particularly the *Pastoral Constitution on the Church in the Modern World (Gaudium et Spes)*, and the *Decree on the Church's Missionary Activity (Ad Gentes)*, both promulgated on December 7, 1965, had a profound influence on the proceedings.[57]

In the Manila meeting the two main currents within the catechetical movement, the kerygmatic approach and the subject-

55

centered approach, were seen not as conflicting but as complementary. Luis Erdozain remarked that the anthropological orientation appeared to be "the unexpected fruit of the seed sown by the kerygmatic renewal."[58] The kerygmatic movement insisted on a deeper understanding of the word of God. The subject-centered movement recognized that this word of God is never found in a pure state, but in the heart of the person and community. Insofar as God speaks to humankind, one must seek out humankind in its cultural situation.

The primary question that emerged from this new vision of a subject-centered catechesis was: How does one carry out such a catechesis in pastoral practice?

Medellín 1968: Cultural and Communal Catechesis

By the time the delegates assembled for the Sixth International Study Week in Medellín, Colombia, August 11–17, 1968, the church in Latin America had begun a reassessment of its position in society. The publication of Pope John XXIII's encyclicals *Mater et Magistra* (July 15, 1961) and *Pacem in Terris* (April 11, 1963), and Pope Paul VI's encyclical *Populorum Progressio* (March 16, 1967), plus the impact of the documents of the Second Vatican Council, caused the church to engage in a struggle of radical reform of its own structures and its position in society. It was in that environment of revolutionary social change and church reform that the Study Week began.

While the catechetical leaders who attended the congress came from many nations and continents, the majority of the 196 participants were Latin Americans already participating in the process of social and church reform. For that reason and because the meeting was held the week before the International Eucharistic Congress at Bogota, Colombia, which Pope Paul VI was to attend, the Study Week took on a special tone of urgency. As Terence J. Sheridan, the editor of the Study Week's proceedings, remarked:

> It was the fact that the Sixth International Catechetical Study Week was held in a continent boiling with unrest and in an atmosphere of near revolution that called forth the most out-

spoken declarations about the position of the Church and of catechetics. In none of the other five international meetings had there been such sincere dialogue. Modern catechetics benefitted from this attack on its relevance and came well through its baptism of fire.[59]

That the Study Week took place in a land that was experiencing "the widening gap between rich and poor, the overfed and the starving," and because "it was attended by priests, and not a few bishops, burdened with the thought that their people were deprived of the necessities of life," brought the participants at the Study Week to the determination that it was not enough to talk about reading the "signs of the times."[60] They recognized the need to make a political analysis of the life situation of the people and to engage in action, transformative action. This transformation included a change in theological thinking. The sociologist François Houtard wrote that at Medellín

> there was evident a refusal to accept the dichotomies: natural-supernatural, Church-world, evangelization-social action.... Consequently, the idea of a "purely religious catechesis" made no sense, any more than that of a social revolution which is not related to the work of salvation.[61]

The calm environment and judicious discussion of Eichstätt were gone. A sense of urgency permeated the conference. And the *conclusions* of the Medellín Study Week demonstrate the spirit and thought of the participants. The conclusions include the following ideas: (1) the beginning point of catechesis ought to be the life situation of the *group;* (2) in catechesis the culture, the society, and the church need to be interpreted and critiqued; (3) the plurality of life-situations throughout the world demands a diversity of catechetical forms; (4) the *method and content* of catechesis cannot be separated. The method of catechesis *is* a content. The participants were committed to a renewed form of catechetical ministry. The General Conclusions state that "the task of catechesis is a fundamental aspect of the mission of the Church. To fail [in catechesis] would be...tantamount to treason, both to man to whom the church must bring salvation and to the Gospel, which she has received."[62] And they were convinced that there is no one single form of catechesis. They wrote

> We want to stress the demands of pluralism in the joint pastoral effort. The situations in which catechesis evolves are very diverse; from those of the patriarchal type, where traditional forms are still accepted, to those of the most advanced contemporary urban civilizations....It is impossible in view of this, to think in terms of a universal catechesis of the monolithic type.[63]

The participants also connected catechesis with evangelization, writing in the conclusions that "the pastoral activity of the Church must be eminently evangelizing so that a reality of faith is not presupposed until after the necessary verifications."

However the dominant theme of Medellín is that God is present in human affairs and human activities. There is, say the conclusions, a complex unity, differentiated and dynamic, which exists

between human values	and the relationship of God;
between the projects of humankind	and the salvific project of God realized in Christ;
between human history	and the history of salvation;
between the progressive realization of Christianity within time and	its eschatological fulfillment.[64]

Catechesis is more than a repetition of the Christian message. It is an interpretation of the life situation of human communities in the "light of Christ dead and risen."[65]

The participants at Medellín knew there needed to be more cooperation in the sharing of information and experience about catechesis among nations. They made "an earnest appeal" to French Cardinal Jean Villot, Prefect of the Congregation of the Clergy, to utilize the conclusions reached by the delegates of the Study Week at Medellín in discussions and deliberations of the committee preparing the *General Catechetical Directory* mandated by the *Decree on the Bishops' Pastoral Office in the Church*.

The participants at Medellín articulated an understanding of the nature of catechesis that evolved over decades. While in the first third of the century catechetical leaders focused on renewing the method of catechizing and in the second third renewing the content of catechesis, by the time of Medellin they recognized that *method and content cannot be separated.* Catechesis, or the interpretation of life in the light of the Gospel, is an integrated process. The *process of catechesis is itself content.* At Medellin the participants integrated the insights of the century into a new vision of catechesis.

Renewal in the United States

Even as the catechetical renewal was developing in Europe through the leadership of Josef Jungmann and Joseph Colomb, and as the renewal movement became international through the Study Weeks planned by Johannes Hofinger, catechetical renewal was taking place in different but related ways in nations throughout the world.

Father Edwin V. O'Hara, in the United States in the 1920s, recognized the catechetical needs of children living in rural areas and founded the first Catholic religion vacation schools. Later as Bishop O'Hara of Great Falls, Montana, he reactivated the Confraternity of Christian Doctrine to meet the religious education needs of children in his dioceses. In 1934 the United States bishops at their annual meeting established a national office for the Confraternity and created a committee of bishops chaired by Bishop O'Hara to supervise the national office and the development of the Confraternity. At its first meeting the committee decided to open a national center of the Confraternity of Christian Doctrine in Washington, D.C. The activation and renewal of the CCD, particularly under the direction of Joseph B. Collins, S.S., who led the CCD for twenty-five years, had an enormous impact on catechetical renewal in the United States.

In 1957 Fr. Gerard S. Sloyan was appointed head of the Department of Religious Education at the Catholic University of America in Washington, D.C. Sloyan, an early supporter in the United States of the renewal of the liturgy, attended a 1956 meeting in Antwerp sponsored by the *Lumen Vitae Centre* in Brussels, Belgium, which shortly after opened a one-year course offering successful candidates a *diplome*. At Antwerp he met Georges Delcuve; Joseph Colomb; François Coudreau, S.S.; Piet Schoonenberg, S.J.; and other catechetical leaders, a number of whom he convinced to write chapters in his *Shaping the Christian Message*, a text that brought the European renewal to the United States.[66] As department head at the Catholic University of America, Sloyan brought the European influence of Jungmann and a knowledge of educational and catechetical development in the United States to a generation of graduate students in winter and summer study. In the decade of the 1960s under Sloyan's leadership the university granted both M.A. and Ph.D. degrees in theology, Bible, and catechetics to hundreds of sisters, brothers, and priests who brought the fruit of their study to other universities, to their dioceses, parishes, schools and CCD programs. Also, through his writings, particularly *Shaping the Christian Message*, and its follow-ups *Modern Catechetics* and *Speaking of Religious Education*,[67] articles in the early issues of *The Living Light* and *PACE* and later through promotion of the English translation of Jungmann's *The Good News*, Sloyan brought both the history and theory of catechetical renewal to this country. In this way and through many excellent writings the catechetical reform that began in Europe spread to the grass roots of the Catholic Church in the United States.

Other Catholic colleges and universities began to offer courses in catechetics theology, biblical and liturgical studies in order to foster the renewal called for by the Second Vatican Council. In 1957 Marquette University was beginning a program under the direction of Bernard Cooke, S.J., another leader in the effort to renew parish ministries through education. Later Fordham University, Boston College, the University of Notre Dame, and Loyola University, Chicago, were among those universities supporting the renewal effort. These institutions provided courses during the summer for Catholic school teachers. Frequently their faculty members were among the most prominent speakers at diocesan and national conferences.

In the spring of 1964 Fr. Russell Neighbor, director of the National Center for Religious Education-CCD, with the encouragement of Sloyan initiated the publication of the journal *The*

Living Light. Mary Perkins Ryan, who was a leader in both the liturgical and catechetical renewal in this country, was its first executive editor and Neighbor, as director of the National Center was its editor in chief. *The Living Light* became the first major Catholic catechetical journal in the United States. Berard Marthaler, O.F.M., Conv., succeeded Ryan as executive editor in 1974.[68]

Shortly after the closing of the Vatican Council, Gabriel Moran, F.S.C., a doctoral student at the Catholic University of America published his dissertation on the relationship of catechesis to revelation. Moran wrote it during the time the Second Vatican Council was preparing its *Dogmatic Constitution on Divine Revelation*, which was promulgated in 1965. Moran's work, published in 1966 as two trade books, *Theology of Revelation* and *Catechesis of Revelation*, incorporated many of the insights of the council on revelation, particularly the dynamic nature of revelation as God's self-communication.[69]

Moran's books had a wide circulation and a profound effect on catechetical renewal in the United States. Students, primarily women religious, brothers, and priests read and were energized by the freshness of his approach. Moran took religious instruction out of the revelation-as-concept model and replaced it with a catechesis that grew out of revelation as God's self-communication. He emphasized the need for a christocentric, biblical, doctrinal, liturgical catechesis. He introduced generations of Catholics to the profound reality of God's personal communion of knowledge and love within the believing community. He stirred not only minds but hearts, reminding his readers that God is always immanently present, reaching out in love to all.

Moran gave the ministry of catechesis a foundation in the theology of revelation. For him the loving, personal and communal, sacramental or symbolic self-giving of God was the beginning point for all catechesis, all teaching of religion, and all theology. Moran united what was for most Catholics a profoundly new theology of revelation with the renewed catechetical theory; his contribution to catechetical renewal in the United States is immeasurable.[70]

In Summary

The movement from the *Baltimore Catechism* to Medellín is extraordinary, but its history demonstrates an organic, creative, well-debated, and faith-filled development. By and large it was a grass-roots movement that began with people who had pastoral experience and who recognized the urgent need to listen to the aspirations and hopes of the people in the parish. Pius X spent many years as a parish priest. Joseph Jungmann was highly influenced by his Tirol upbringing and his parish work. Joseph Colomb worked for much of the time in a diocesan office. Johannes Hofinger lived and served in China and the Philippines. And the participants of the Study Weeks came to the conferences with urgent pastoral questions.

The renewal moved from renewing the place of religious instruction in the parish through the Confraternity of Christian Doctrine,

> to renewing the methodology so that it responded to the children,
> to renewing the content so that we returned to the sources of faith,
> to reformulating our goal,
> to recognizing the need to focus on adult catechesis,
> to the insight that we needed to focus on the subject being catechized,
> to realizing that the cultural situation in which our people live
> is a source of catechesis.

The major achievement of the reform was that it brought about a recognition of the essential unity between faith and life. This insight permeates all of the official catechetical documents promulgated in the last third of the century. Now we shall take a look at some of those documents and examine how they affirm the grass-roots reform.

FURTHER READINGS

Bryce, Mary Charles. "The *Baltimore Catechism*—Origin and Reception." In *Sourcebook for Modern Catechetics*, ed. Michael Warren, 140–45. Winona, Minn.: Saint Mary's Press, 1983.

Jungmann, Josef. *The Good News Yesterday and Today.* Translated (abridged) and edited by William A. Huesman. New York: W. H. Sadlier, 1962.

Marthaler, Berard. *The Catechism Yesterday and Today: The Evolution of a Genre.* Collegeville, Minn.: Liturgical Press, 1955.

Moran, Gabriel. *Theology of Revelation.* New York: Herder & Herder, 1966.

———. *Theology of Catechesis.* New York: Herder & Herder, 1966.

Warren, Michael, ed. *Sourcebook for Modern Catechetics*, vol. 1. Winona, Minn.: St. Mary's Press, 1983.

———. *Sourcebook for Modern Catechetics*, vol. 2. Winona, Minn.: St. Mary's Press, 1997.

CHAPTER 3

The Story of
Affirmation 1971–1997:
Church Documents on Catechetics

The spirit of renewal among Catholics in the United States during and immediately after the Second Vatican Council energized many parish ministers and led them to look forward to reforms that would lead to a more dynamic church ministry and life. Directors of catechetical ministry and catechists anticipated the official affirmation of the catechetical renewal, particularly with its emphasis on adult catechesis. They looked forward to the catechetical directory which the council called for and which they hoped would affirm the renewal process and give catechists both credibility and direction in their parish ministry.

While many catechetical documents have been issued since the council, the following seven documents describe most fully the church's renewed understanding of the nature of catechesis: the *General Catechetical Directory* (1971), the *Rite of Christian Initiation of Adults* (1972), *On Evangelization in the Modern World* (1975), *On Catechesis in Our Time* (1979), *Sharing the Light of Faith* (1979), *Catechism of the Catholic Church* (1994), and the revised *General Directory for Catechesis* (1997). No brief summary can do justice to any of these documents; therefore, in this chapter a brief summary of each document's purpose and focus will be presented, as well as the ways in which each has contributed to catechetical renewal. The following questions will be asked of each document:

1. When and why was it written?
2. Who wrote it and for whom was it written?
3. What is its purpose?
4. How does it contribute to catechetical renewal?

1971: *The* General Catechetical Directory

When and why was it written? The Second Vatican Council's *Decree on the Bishops' Pastoral Office in the Church* directed that "general directories concerning the care of souls be compiled for the use both of bishops and parish priests."[1] These "directories" were to guide them "in the discharge of their particular pastoral function." Among the directories called for was a catechetical directory in which "the fundamental principles of this instruction and its organization will be dealt with and the preparation of books relating to it."[2]

In 1971, directories were a relatively new literary form in the Catholic Church; however, in 1964 the church in France published a catechetical directory entitled *La Directoire de Pastoral Catéchètique*.[3] The Italian bishops published Italy's catechetical directory, *Il rennovamento della catechesi*, in 1970, shortly before the publication of the *General Directory*.[4] Both of those directories influenced the writing of the *General Directory*. They were pastoral in tone and offered guidelines rather than directives.

The *General Catechetical Directory (GCD)* was published on Easter Sunday, April 11, 1971. The Sacred Congregation for the Clergy, which prepared the document, convened an International Catechetical Congress in Rome September 20–25, 1971, to discuss the directory and its place in the church.[5]

Who wrote it and for whom was it written? The task of implementing the council mandate for a directory was given in June 1966 to the Congregation for the Clergy, chaired at that time by Cardinal Jean Villot. As noted earlier, Cardinal Villot participated in the Study Week at Medellín, and at that conference the congress recommended that Villot utilize the conclusions reached at Medellín in the preparation of the catechetical directory. Under Villot's direction an international commission of eight persons met in Rome in May 1968 to plan the directory.[6] This commission was responsible for writing the directory, though it consulted regularly with the Congregation for the Clergy, and also with the Congregation for the Doctrine of the Faith, and the Congregation for the Sacraments.

The directory states in its preface that "it is chiefly intended for bishops, Conferences of Bishops, and in general all who under their leadership and direction have responsibility in the catechetical field." It is a guide for leaders and professionals in the ministry of catechesis. In the first year after its publication, between thirty and forty thousand copies were sold in the United States.[7] It is obvious that the document had wide appeal to leaders in the field.

What is its purpose? The purpose of the directory, according to its foreword, "is to provide the basic principles of pastoral theology....by which pastoral action in the ministry of the word can be more fittingly directed and governed."[8] The document is primarily a policy statement of principles of catechesis. The work of applying the principles is left to the bishops.

How does it contribute to catechetical renewal? The tone of the directory is pastoral, positive, and even poetic. Readers found it appealing and interesting. It is interesting to note that the directory begins not with doctrine or discipline but with a description of contemporary human society. It follows the methodology it recommends: offering first a description of the present human situation in which catechesis takes place.

A major contribution of the directory is that it establishes the documents of the Second Vatican Council as the foundation of a renewed catechetical ministry. Fourteen of the sixteen council documents are referred to in the text, and there are approximately 150 such references in the 134 articles of the directory.[9] In addition, its submission to Episcopal Conferences throughout the world ensured that it would not present a narrow description of catechesis.

Other strengths are:

- It presented the foundation of catechetical ministry as God's self-communication in revelation and humankind's response in faith.
- It brought the insights of Jungmann, Colomb, and the Catechetical Study Weeks—particularly Medellín—to the universal church.
- It established as the goal of catechesis a strong, living, and conscious faith.
- It presented the symbols of revelation: the Bible, the church (its life and teaching), and the church's liturgy as the source for interpreting the meaning of life and the signs of the times.
- It recognized that adult catechesis "is the chief form of catechesis," and that there are a plurality of forms of catechesis.
- It presented human experience as central in catechesis and stated that such experience helps "make the Christian message more intelligible."[10]

One weakness is that it did not emphasize the justice dimension of catechesis. However, the United States catechetical directory expanded on the *General Directory's* presentation of justice and included working for justice as an integral dimension of catechesis.

The *General Catechetical Directory* presents catechesis as a ministry of the word which gives voice to the living tradition of the church. The goal of this ministry is to "stir up a lively faith which turns the mind to God, impels conformance with his action, leads a living knowledge of the expressions of the tradition, and speaks and manifests the true significance of the world and human existence."[11] Through catechesis the church brings the gospel to all people. Catechesis seeks and calls for conversion, and it is directed primarily to adults because it is adults who are capable of an adherence that is fully responsible.[12]

The *GCD* moved the church from an instructional model of catechesis into an anthropological model which focused on the experience of the people and their faith. It changed catechesis from a one-dimensional task (instruction) to a multidimensional ministry in which the catechist and the community integrated four tasks into the one ministry of catechesis: building community, sharing the church's stories and beliefs, working for justice, and praying together.

1972: The **Rite of Christian Initiation of Adults**

When and why was it written? The Second Vatican Council called for a restoration of the catechumenate for adults when it stated in the *Constitution on the Sacred Liturgy (CSL):*

> The catechumenate for adults, divided into several distinct stages, is to be restored and brought into use at the discretion of the local Ordinary. By this means the time of the catechumenate, which is destined for the requisite formation, may be sanctified by sacred rites to be celebrated at successive stages.[13]

The document went on to say: "Both rites for the baptism of adults are to be revised; not only the simpler rite but also, taking into consideration the restored catechumenate, the more solemn rite." Pope Paul VI promulgated the *Rite of Christian Initiation of Adults (RCIA)* in 1972. In 1974 a provisional translation was approved for use in the United States. The bishops of the United States approved an official edition of the rite, translated by the International Committee on English in the Liturgy, in 1986 and mandated its use in parishes beginning September 1, 1988.

Who wrote it and for whom was it written? The Vatican Congregation for Divine Worship prepared the rite. It was written for all Catholic communities throughout the world. It describes the church's catechetical and liturgical processes of preparing and initiating adults or children of catechetical age into the church.

What is its purpose? The rite fulfills the directions of Vatican Council II that the catechumenate for adults be divided into stages and restored.[14] The rite recognizes that initiation requires conversion, and it sets "distinct steps" of progress for those seeking membership. The *Rite of Christian Initiation of Adults* offers a catechetical process completed by liturgical rites which then lead

to a new catechesis followed by a new liturgical rite until the cate-
chumen experiences the rites of initiation and then the mystagogical catechesis which follows it.

How does the RCIA *contribute to catechetical renewal?*

- Both *Sharing the Light of Faith: National Catechetical Directory for Catholics of the United States* and the *General Directory
  for Catechesis* written almost twenty years later state that the
  RCIA is a model of catechesis and provides a norm for all
  catechesis.[15] The revised *General Directory for Catechesis*
  (1997) reiterates that

  > The model for all catechesis is the baptismal catechu-
  > menate when, by specific formation, an adult con-
  > verted to belief is brought to explicit profession of
  > baptismal faith during the Paschal Vigil.[16]

- It transforms private instruction for converts by the parish
  priest into catechesis for inquiring adults in the midst of a
  faith community. The change from instructional language
  to catechetical language describes a profound change in the
  way in which the church perceives what it is doing when it
  initiates new members into the community.
- This *RCIA* describes initiation into the church as a public
  journey of conversion through stages in which the inquirers
  and catechumens are supported by the faith community.
  Conversion and initiation are not "private" affairs to be
  conducted by the priest and the "convert." They are public,
  community expressions of faith.
- The *RCIA* as a model of catechesis presumes a gradual
  process of initiation which moves through periods of conversion marked by rites that are sometimes called "steps" or
  "doorways."
- The *RCIA* presents conversion as an ongoing and continuous
  turning toward God and away from sin. This process cannot
  be hurried, timed, or programmed so that the periods fit into
  an academic year schedule or into the lenten season.

- Each of the four catechetical periods includes experience of and reflection on the church's symbols, Scriptures, and prayer texts.
- It recognizes that "it does not do justice to catechesis to think of it as instruction alone."[17]
- Initiation revolves around conversion, and for Christians conversion focuses on Jesus as the Christ.
- The whole of the initiation process has a paschal character. Every catechesis focuses on the paschal mystery in our lives, both as individuals and as a community of faith.
- While many ministers of the community participate in the initiation process, and while the local assembly is the primary agent in this process, the catechist has a significant role to play in the life of the initiating community.
- The rite indicates how important it is for catechists and liturgists to work together.

The model of catechesis presented in the *RCIA* represents the best of the renewal of catechesis in the twentieth century. It incorporates the insights of the catechetical Study Weeks from Eichstätt to Medellín. The final revision published in 1988 is in harmony with the principles and guidelines of the *General Catechetical Directory*, both the original version of 1971 and the revised version of 1997.

1975: On Evangelization in the Modern World

When and why was it written? On December 8, 1975, the tenth anniversary of the closing of the Second Vatican Council, Pope Paul VI promulgated one of the most extraordinary papal documents of the twentieth century. The apostolic exhortation called *On Evangelization in the Modern World (EMW)* describes the depth of the renewal needed by the church's ministers if they are to bring the gospel to the world.

This apostolic exhortation, written ten years after the close of Vatican Council II, is a response to the 1974 Synod of Bishops, which discussed evangelization as a ministry in the church. The bishops of that synod requested that the pope reflect on their synodal deliberations and present guidelines for evangelization to the church as a whole.

Who wrote it and for whom was it written? To some extent *On Evangelization* summarizes the deliberations of the synod, but it also gives evidence of the teaching and unique spirit of Paul VI. The pope says he wrote the document to *confirm* those who are evangelizing and to *encourage* them in their mission. He wants evangelizers "in this time of uncertainty and confusion" to accomplish their "task with ever increasing love, zeal and joy."[18]

What is its purpose? Rich in imagery, this meditation presents Pope Paul's reflection on how the church at the end of the twentieth century can most effectively proclaim the gospel through the ministries of evangelization, preaching, and catechesis.

How does it contribute to catechetical renewal?

- Paul VI recognized that "the hidden energy of the Good News" seemed to be missing today. What can the church do, he asks, to bring about the transformation of humankind, a transformation called for by the gospel in all its beauty and evangelical power.
- Pope Paul makes clear that he sees evangelization as more than the proclamation of the gospel to unbelievers. He describes both preaching and catechesis as two forms of evangelization. They are both evangelizing ministries.
- The pope points out that the church itself is in need of evangelizing.
- Evangelization is described as bringing "the Christian message" to people of this time."[19] It is "proclaiming the Gospel to all people,"[20] or proclaiming the coming of God's reign.[21] Evangelization "constitutes the central mission of the church."[22]
- Finally, Paul VI states that evangelization "means bringing the Good News into all the strata of humanity, and through its influence transforming humanity from within and making it new.[23]

71

According to Pope Paul, both preaching and catechizing are forms of evangelization, rather than being in contrast to evangelization. They both seek interior renewal or conversion. They are both the proclamation of Christ's good news. They are essential ministries in the church's mission. They are both expressions of faith and shapers of faith. And they are both done with an enormous respect for those being evangelized.

Pope Paul's references to the necessity of evangelizing cultures, beginning with the experience of the person, echoes the *General Catechetical Directory*. He states that

> what matters is to evangelize culture and cultures (not in a purely decorative way as it were by applying a thin veneer, but in a vital way, in depth and right to their very roots), in the wide and rich sense which these terms have in *Gaudium et Spes*, always taking the person as one's starting point and always coming back to the relationships of people among themselves and with God.[24]

The pope reminds us that it is social structures that so often oppress people and that catechists and evangelists need to recognize that social structures are human constructs that can and, if necessary, must be changed. This echoes not only the directory but also the conclusions of the Medellín Study Week.

1979: On Catechesis in Our Time

When and why was it written? Pope Paul VI was not satisfied to have only a synod on evangelization; he called the bishops together again in 1977 for a Fifth International Synod on "Catechetics in Our Time, Especially to Children and Young People." This synod was held in Rome from September 30 through October 29, 1977. As the synod ended, the bishops prepared a paper called a "Message to the People of God," which expressed the main ideas of their deliberations.[25] They requested that the pope consider their statement as he prepared his apostolic exhortation in response to the synod.

Who wrote it? And for whom was it written? After the closing
of the synod, Pope Paul began writing the papal exhortation which
ordinarily follows a synod. His death on August 6, 1978, inter-
rupted that writing, which was then taken up by his successor Pope
John Paul I. After Pope John Paul I's death, the apostolic exhortation on catechetics was written by his successor, Pope John Paul II,
and was called *On Catechesis in Our Time (CT)*. The author begins
by stating:

> Pope John Paul I, whose zeal and gifts as a catechist amazed us
> all, had taken them in hand and was preparing to publish them
> when he was suddenly called to God....I am therefore taking
> up the inheritance of these two Popes in response to the
> request which was expressly formulated by the Bishops at the
> end of the Fourth General Assembly of the Synod and which
> was welcomed by Pope Paul VI in his closing speech.[26]

The document was promulgated "to the Episcopate, the Clergy and
the Faithful of the Entire Catholic Church," on October 16, 1979.

What is its purpose? Pope John Paul II stated the purpose
when he wrote:

> I ardently desire that this Apostolic Exhortation to the whole
> Church should strengthen the solidity of the faith and of
> Christian living, should give fresh vigor to the initiatives in
> hand, should stimulate creativity—with the required vigi-
> lance—and should help to spread among the communities the
> joy of bringing the mystery of Christ to the world.[27]

The pope also stated that he was writing the document "in order to
fulfil one of the chief duties of my apostolic charge. Catechesis has
always been a central care in my ministry as a priest and as a bishop."[28]

How does it contribute to catechetical renewal? Pope John
Paul II presents his views on catechesis clearly and forcibly in *On
Catechesis in Our Time*.

- It emphasizes that catechesis is christocentric; it seeks to
  understand the meaning of Christ's words and actions.

73

Christocentric means that the "definitive aim of catechesis is to put people not only in touch but in communion, in intimacy, with Jesus Christ."[29] It "also means the intention to transmit not one's own teaching or that of some other master, but the teaching of Jesus Christ."[30]

- It presents Christ's teaching not as "a body of abstract truths" but as the communication of the living mystery of God."[31]
- Pope John Paul II affirms the *General Catechetical Directory* as the foundational catechetical document of our time.[32]
- He reinforces the idea of four tasks that make up the whole of the catechetical act.
- One unique emphasis of Pope John Paul regarding catechesis is that it needs to be "systematic." By systematic he means "not improvised but programmed to reach a precise goal."[33] He states, "Nor is any opposition to be set up between a catechesis taking life as its point of departure and a traditional, doctrinal and systematic catechesis."[34]
- Pope John Paul presents catechesis as intimately related to evangelization, describing catechesis as "a moment or aspect of evangelization."[35]
- He emphasizes the need to respond to cultural and developmental differences among the people.
- He calls for a catechesis for all in the church, excusing no one as he writes, "It must be repeated that nobody in the Church of Jesus Christ should feel excused from receiving catechesis. This is true even of young seminarians and young religious, and of all those called to the task of being pastors and catechists."[36]

Overall, *On Catechesis in Our Time* reflects both the *General Catechetical Directory* and Paul VI's *On Evangelization in the Modern World*. Its style reflects the unique person who wrote it, Pope John Paul II, giving more emphasis to educational and systematic catechesis than has been found in previous documents.

1979: Sharing the Light of Faith: National Catechetical Directory for Catholics of the United States

When and why was it written? The *General Catechetical Directory* provided basic principles and guidelines for catechesis throughout the world. It did not attempt to apply those guidelines to particular cultures or nations. Instead it directed national and regional episcopal conferences to prepare directories for their own regions or nations.

Preparation for a national catechetical directory for the United States began in 1971, when the administrative board of the National Conference of Catholic Bishops asked Bishop William E. McManus, chairman of the Bishops' Committee on Education. to create a plan for the development of a National Directory for the United States, which culminated in the publication of *Sharing the Light of Faith* in 1979.

Who wrote it and for whom was it written? The bishops approved a plan for preparing a directory in 1972 and called for two committees to supervise its development. The first committee, called the Bishops' Committee of Policy and Review,[37] was to set policy for preparing the directory and to review the work of the second committee, called the National Catechetical Directory (NCD) Committee. This second committee was to be the working committee that would write the directory. The bishops gave the committee "decision-making responsibility" in the preparation of the national directory.

In 1974 Msgr. Wilfrid H. Paradis and Sister Marcella Frye M.H.S.H., director and associate director of NCD development, and Archbishop John F. Whealon, who was a member of the Bishops' Committee on Policy and Review and an *ex officio* member of the Directory Committee, initiated a consultation to select the National Catechetical Directory Committee, which was eventually composed of four bishops and eight other members. The bishops were Archbishop Whealon, Bishops William D. Borders, Mark J. Hurley, and Kenneth J. Povich. Other members included Mary Baylouny; Celia Ann Cavazos, M.C.D.P.; Thomas C. Lawler; James

Lyke, O.F.M.; Joan O'Keefe; Cosmos Rubencamp, C.F.X.; Reverend William A. Wassmuth; and this author, Anne Marie Mongoven, O.P. Committee members represented different geographical sections of the United States and many different constituencies. Members of the committee included volunteer catechists, parents, diocesan directors of religious education, parish directors of catechetical programs, Catholic and public school teachers, a campus minister, and a leader in the National Conference of Diocesan Directors of Religious Education.

Sharing the Light of Faith begins with a preface that describes the directory's audience as "those responsible for catechesis in the United States." It describes its audience as

> parents and guardians exercising their responsibilities as the primary educators of children; professional and paraprofessional catechists at all levels; men and women religious; deacons and priests involved in this ministry; and members of diocesan and parish council education committees or boards with catechetical duties. The NCD is also of basic importance to writers and publishers of catechetical texts and other materials for catechesis.[38]

The *General Directory's* audience was the bishops of the world. The national directory aimed at a different level of responsibility. A continuing question during the process was how do we write a document for both parents and professional leaders in the parish?

What is its purpose? The directory itself notes that it was "prepared in response," to the *General Catechetical Directory*. It is "an official statement of the National Conference of Catholic Bishops of the United States" which offers guidelines for parish catechesis including the catechesis of adults, youth, and children. The document states: "This NCD seeks to help the entire Catholic community grow in unity, love, and peace. Its purpose is correspondingly evangelical and missionary, looking toward an increase in the vitality and holiness of Christ's body which is the Church."[39]

How does it contribute to catechetical renewal? It contributes to catechetical renewal in the United States in many ways.

- Chapter 2 is extraordinarily rich in its description of catechesis. It describes catechesis as "a form of the ministry of the word which proclaims and teaches. It leads to and flows from the ministry of worship, which sanctifies through prayer and sacrament. It supports the ministry of service, which is linked to efforts to achieve social justice...."
- It reinforces the *General Directory* by stating that the purpose of catechesis is to enrich the faith life of the community.
- The directory presents catechesis as "a lifelong process for the individual and a constant and concerted pastoral activity of the Christian community."[40]
- It emphasizes, as did earlier documents, that adult catechesis is the chief form of catechesis.
- *Sharing the Light of Faith* describes the "signs of faith" as biblical signs, liturgical signs, ecclesial signs, and the natural signs. These signs are "manifestations" which "point to a deeper reality: God's self-communication in the world."[41]
- The United States directory made a major contribution to the church's insight on the nature of catechesis with its inclusion of an entire chapter on the place of social justice in catechetical ministry.

In March 1979, Archbishop Jean Jadot, apostolic delegate in the United States, addressed a religious education conference for the Charlotte and Raleigh dioceses of North Carolina. In that address Jadot stated that chapter 2 in the United States directory, "The Catechetical Ministry of the Church,"

> may, in time, be considered the greatest contribution of the *National Catechetical Directory*. The principal reason for this judgment shared my many, is the rich description it gives of catechesis, its purpose and its goals.[42]

That description of catechesis singled out by Jadot clearly distinguishes catechesis from religious instruction.

Sharing the Light of Faith represents a culmination of the renewal movements in the church during this past century. It sets forth not only a renewed and reinvigorated form of catechesis, but it also incorporates advances in biblical, liturgical, and theological studies and the human sciences. That incorporation gives witness to the integral relationship catechesis has to those other areas of study.

1994: *The* Catechism of the Catholic Church

When it was first published the *Catechism of the Catholic Church* was a best-seller. The number of copies sold in the United States reportedly exceeds two million. It has been translated into more than twenty languages, and more than eight million copies have been sold worldwide. What is the cause of such widespread popularity? Why was the catechism written? How should it be used? What is the relationship of this or any catechism to the ministry of catechesis? Because the catechism is not *about* catechesis but is instead a reference book for the catechist and the community, it will be examined differently, by describing briefly the history and process of its development and its place in the catechetical process.

Although the church's catechetical tradition began in apostolic times, catechisms *as textbooks for the people* are a fairly recent addition to the Catholic tradition. It was the invention of the printing press that changed the experience of church teaching from the oral word of the teacher to the written word of the catechism.[43] Yet even to this day the Council of Trent is the only general council that commissioned a catechism. This catechism, generally known as the Roman Catechism, was written, as noted earlier, to assist the clergy in their instruction of the people through sermons. It was an "antidote" to the teaching of Martin Luther through his catechisms.

The First Vatican Council (1869–1870) spent more time discussing the pros and cons of writing a new catechism than it did on any other pastoral topic. Michael Donnellan notes: "From the first day of debate, however, polarization of opinion set in, as the underlying issue surfaced of bishops' rights vis-à-vis Roman centralization."[44] The proposal for a catechism became part of the unfinished business of the council that was suspended because of the Franco-Prussian War.

Ninety-two years later the Second Vatican Council picked up the debate on the merits of preparing a catechism for the church. After considerable debate, the council did not recommend a catechism, but instead it endorsed a catechetical "directory," which presented pastoral principles for catechesis. Not every bishop agreed with that decision. There was tension between those bishops who favored uniformity of doctrinal expression as a means of promoting church unity and those who believed that different cultures demand different forms of faith expression. This tension outlasted the council.

In 1977 at the synod on "Catechesis in Our Time," the question of whether to write a catechism arose again. At that time, the bishops were unable to come to a consensus either on the utility or the contents of a catechism. In his exhortation which followed the synod, Pope John Paul II encouraged the preparation of "genuine catechisms which will be faithful to the essential content of revelation and up-to-date method, and which will be capable of educating the Christian generations of the future to a sturdy faith."[45]

In 1985 an Extraordinary Synod convened to celebrate the twentieth anniversary of the Second Vatican Council. At that synod Cardinal Bernard Law of Boston proposed a new catechism. He called for "a commission of Cardinals to prepare a draft of a conciliar Catechism to be promulgated by the Holy Father after consulting the bishops of the world." He went on to say that national catechisms would not fill the need for clear articulation of the church's faith and asked for a universal catechism instead.

While Pope John Paul II strongly supported Cardinal Law's request for a new catechism, his vision of a catechism differed in some significant ways from that of the cardinal. First, he describes it as a catechism for the *universal* church rather than a *universal* catechism. In other words, it is not the *only* catechism.

The pope noted in his apostolic exhortation *Fidei depositum*, which accompanied the publication of the catechism, that the Synod of Bishops desired a catechism that would be "a point of reference for the catechisms or compendiums that are prepared in the various regions."[46] To emphasize this Pope John Paul states: "This catechism is given to them [church's pastors] that it may be a sure an authentic reference text for teaching catholic doctrine and particularly for preparing *local* catechisms."[47]

The pope describes this new catechism not only as a "sure and authentic reference text for teaching catholic doctrine," but also as a reference for the preparation of national or local catechism. He notes that this catechism is not intended to replace local approved catechisms. Rather, the pope points out that the catechism "is meant to encourage and assist in the writing of new local catechisms, which take into account various situations and cultures, while carefully preserving the unity of faith and fidelity to catholic doctrine."[48]

The prologue of the catechism repeats the thought of Pope John Paul II when it states in article 24 that, "by design, this Catechism does not set out to provide the adaptation of doctrinal presentations and catechetical methods required by the differences of culture, age, spiritual maturity, and social and ecclesial condition among all those to whom it is addressed. Such indispensable adaptations are the responsibility of particular catechisms, and, even more, of those who instruct the faithful."[49]

The publication of the *Catechism of the Catholic Church* is, by the authors' own description, seen as the *beginning* of a catechetical process, not the conclusion. The catechism itself claims that it must be adapted before it can be used with most of the people. If cultural adaptation is as important as Pope John Paul II indicates it is in his writings, a single catechism for all United States Catholics will not suffice. The differences in age, culture, stages of faith, and intellectual ability of our people need to be respected. Our rural communities have different concerns from our inner city or suburban communities. The many Latino and Asian ethnic communities as well as the many communities of European descent in the United States have different needs and different cultural biases. Young adults of Generation X view life differently from the baby boomer generation or senior adults. Peoples' situations in life, their questions, concerns, understandings, and vision of life move them to ask different questions about the faith. The pluralistic views of our multicultural Catholic communities need to be respected and responded to through catechesis and catechisms.

After the publication of the *Catechism of the Catholic Church*, the bishops of the United States through the National Conference of Catholic Bishops appointed an Ad Hoc Committee of archbishops and bishops to oversee the use of the catechism. This Ad Hoc Committee initiated an Office for the Catechism to implement the committee's policies. This office has focused its work on the evaluation of published catechetical series for children and is now beginning to set criteria for catechetical series of adolescents.

The *Catechism of the Catholic Church* sets forth the teaching of the Catholic Church. But it must always be seen as related to the *General Directory for Catechesis*, which presents the pastoral context for catechesis. That directory section states: "The *Catechism of the Catholic Church* and the *General Directory for Catechesis* are two distinct but complementary instruments at the service of the Church's catechetical activity." They should be seen as indispensable to one another.

1997: *The* General Directory for Catechesis

When and why was it written? This document is a 1997 revision of the *General Catechetical Directory*, published in 1971. The preface tells us that "the thirty-year period between the conclusion of the Second Vatican Council and the threshold of the third millennium is without doubt most providential for the orientation and promotion of catechesis."[50] It mentions several ways in which the vigor of catechesis has "reemerged" during this time, stating that, "the course of catechesis...has been characterized everywhere by generous dedication, worthy initiatives and by positive results for the education and growth in the faith of children, young people and adults."[51] The document goes on to say that while the renewal of catechesis has generally been quite positive, it also has some shortcomings, and both the vigor of the renewal and the shortcomings have brought about this revision.

The preface emphasizes continuity with the immediate past, pointing out the many efforts that the church has made to renew catechesis, particularly through the work of Pope Paul VI and Pope John Paul II. It refers to the publication of the *Rite of Christian Initiation of Adults* as especially useful for catechetical renewal, and it commends the many General Assemblies of the Synod of Bishops for their contributions to this renewal. It notes also that the publication of the *Catechism of the Catholic Church* calls for a revision of the 1971 directory.[52]

Who wrote it and for whom was it written? The Congregation for the Clergy was responsible for the preparation of the *General Directory for Catechesis*. It called upon a "group of Bishops and experts in theology and catechesis" to prepare the document and states that "Episcopal Conferences and several experts were consulted as were the principal catechetical institutes and centers."[53]

The directory "is addressed principally to the Bishops, and,…to those who have responsibility for catechesis."[54] Interestingly, it also notes that the revised directory is to "be of use in forming those preparing for ordination to the Priesthood, in the continuing formation of priests and in the formation of catechists."[55] This was not mentioned in earlier documents.

What is its purpose? The directory states its purpose in two different ways. First, it points out that its object is "to provide those fundamental theologico-pastoral principles drawn from the Church's Magisterium, particularly those inspired by the Second Vatican Council, which are capable of better orienting and coordinating the pastoral activity of the ministry of the word and, concretely catechesis."[56] Second, it also states that "the immediate end of the Directory is to assist in the composition of catechetical directories and catechisms."[57] This second end was not so clearly stated in the earlier document.

How does it contribute to catechetical renewal?

- The first three chapters of part 1 set forth a fuller description of catechesis as a ministry of the word that emerges out of the revelation of God.

- The document describes catechesis as a "moment" in the process of evangelization. The process of evangelization includes not only the proclamation of the gospel to those who are not believers but "Christian witness, dialogue and presence in charity, the proclamation of the Gospel and the call to conversion, the catechumenate and Christian Initiation, and the formation of the Christian communities through and by means of the sacraments and their ministers."[58]
- The revised directory in harmony with previous church documents recognizes the goal of catechesis as conversion and the strengthening of faith.
- It repeats that "catechesis for adults...must be considered the chief form of catechesis."[59]
- It describes catechesis is "an ecclesial act"[60] and states that catechesis accomplishes its goal through interrelated tasks, which it describes as promoting knowledge of the faith, liturgical education, moral formation, teaching to pray, and initiation and education in community life and mission.
- The revised directory presents the signs of catechesis as "sources" of the "Source," who is Jesus Christ.
- Finally, the *General Directory for Catechesis* gives more emphasis than did the earlier document to the need to seek inculturation of the gospel message and to respond to the cultural identity of those being catechized.

Describing catechesis as a moment in the process of evangelization is a major contribution. The English word *evangelization* has within itself a dynamic and a vigor that seem to be lacking in the English word *catechize*. Perhaps it is the history of the *catechism* as an abstract, dry, and somewhat burdensome textbook for many children that stigmatizes *catechize*, but the recognition that catechesis is a moment in the process of evangelization gives an added vigor and energy to the notion of what catechesis truly is. This is not simply a semantic change but another way of describing the breadth and depth of the catechetical process.

The biblical renewal in catechesis sought by Josef Jungmann has indeed come, and perhaps it was so exciting for the catechetical community to engage the word of God through Scripture that it sometimes isolated the Scriptures from what the church has learned in its history. This directory cautions against that possibility.

The *General Directory for Catechesis* describes the "fundamental tasks" of catechesis as helping the community "to know, to celebrate and to contemplate the mystery of Christ." This will be done by promoting knowledge of the faith, liturgical education, moral formation, teaching the catechized to pray, education for community life, and missionary initiation.[61] The directory challenges us by stating: "When catechesis omits one of these elements, the Christian faith does not attain full development."[62] The revised directory presents a rich and full vision of the nature of catechesis and challenges the entire Catholic community to participate in it.

In Summary

The catechetical renewal that began at the beginning of the twentieth century with Pope Pius X's changing the age of first communion for children progressed through the first two-thirds of the century from a renewal of methodology, to a renewal of content (Jungmann) to a change in goal and in approach to people of different ages (Colomb). In 1960 Johannes Hofinger inaugurated the Study Weeks, which moved from international acceptance of the four sources in Eichstätt, to adaptation in Bangkok, to adult catechesis as the primary form of catechesis in Katigonda and Manila, and finally in the 1960s to a recognition that catechesis must respond to the social and cultural situation of the communities in which it happened. The process of catechesis is itself content.

The story of grass-roots renewal was followed by affirmation from the official church through a series of documents and synods that set forth the best of the renewal insights. This renewal is not yet completed. The recently published *General Directory for Catechesis* calls for a renewal of national directories, which will mean new studies and new insights and new understandings about the best way to do evangelizing catechesis.

To imply that catechetical renewal was one uninterrupted spiral forward would, however, misrepresent the reality of catechetical renewal. It is true that from the beginning of this century through the 1970s there was a rather uninterrupted movement forward. But in the 1980s a coordinated resistance to the renewal movement surfaced.

This movement expressed itself in its concern for the effectiveness of the catechesis of children. A 1988 study did indicate an ambiguity on the part of bishops and priests regarding the primary purpose of catechesis. When asked to agree or disagree with the following statements regarding "the general purposes of Parish Programs" of religious education, bishops and priests appear to be in harmony.

Question	Bishops Agree %	Priests Agree %
Main purpose is to help people grow in faith into adult Christians	99. 0	99.0
Main purpose is to communicate sound doctrine to children and youth	75.9	68.4[63]

Only 76 percent of the bishops and 68 percent of the priests agreed that communicating "sound doctrine" was the main purpose of catechesis. Even with these somewhat surprising numbers, priests in different regions of the country did not agree. In the west only 56 percent of priests agreed about the centrality of communicating sound doctrine.

There is an obvious conflict among us about the purpose of catechesis for children.

The following chapter examines the theology of catechesis that has emerged from the renewal as expressed and ratified through these seven documents.

FURTHER READINGS

Catechism of the Catholic Church. Washington, D.C.: United States Catholic Conference, 1994.

Connell, Martin, ed. *The Catechetical Documents: A Parish Resource*. Chicago: Liturgy Training Publications, 1966.

Dooley, Catherine. "The General Directory for Catechesis and the Catechism: Focus on Evangelizing," *Origins* 28 (4 June 1997): 33–39.

Horan, Michael P., and Jane F. Regan. *Good News in New Forms: A Companion to the General Directory for Catechesis*. Washington, D.C.: National Conference of Catechetical Leadership, 1997.

Marthaler, Berard. *Catechetics in Context: Notes and Commentary on the General Catechetical Directory Issued by the Sacred Congregation for the Clergy*. Huntington, Ind. Our Sunday Visitor, Inc., 1973.

————. *Sharing the Light of Faith: An Official Commentary*. Washington, D.C.: United States Catholic Conference, 1981.

Mongoven, Anne Marie. *Signs of Catechesis: An Overview of the National Catechetical Directory*. New York: Paulist Press, 1979.

Morris, Thomas H. *The RCIA Transforming the Church: A Resource for Pastoral Implementation*. Rev. ed. New York: Paulist Press, 1997.

————. *Rite of Christian Initiation of Adults*. Study Edition. Chicago: Liturgy Training Publications, 1988.

Walsh, Michael J., ed. *Commentary on the Catechism of the Catholic Church*. Collegeville, Minn.: Liturgical Press, 1994.

CHAPTER 4

A Theology of Catechesis

Sometimes we wonder how the teaching of the church in an ecumenical council really affects us or changes our lives. A catechist once asked me if I would stop talking about conciliar teaching and speak about practical or pastoral concerns. After all, he said, councils don't really affect the people in the pews.

I wonder. I think that the catechist would acknowledge that the Second Vatican Council changed the way we worship (unless he wasn't born before 1960!), and it changed our relationship to the Bible. It changed the way we minister and gave us new insights into who can minister. It altered our relationships with other churches and with members of the Jewish community. But did the teaching of the council change the way we catechize? And, if it did alter our understanding of catechesis, how did it do so?

The basic and underlying theology which supports all theology is the theology of revelation and faith. It is the church's teaching on these two topics that leads theologians to refer to the theology of revelation and faith as "fundamental theology." And in the second Vatican Council the church's understanding of revelation and faith, as presented in the *Dogmatic Constitution* on *Divine Revelation (Dei Verbum)*, is a development of the teaching of Vatican Council I. This foundational development alters our understanding of catechesis.

The council changed the way we think about all of reality when it renewed and reoriented the church's teaching on the meaning of revelation. A community's understanding of how and when and what God reveals focuses the life of the community or the individual. If, for example, a believer understands that God reveals laws, then the law of God will be his or her principal guide in life. If believers understand revelation as concepts or insights, then they will discover to whom that knowledge has been given and try to live according to the information and insights God has revealed. If believers consider revelation primarily as the self-communication of God through symbols of God's presence such as the Bible, the church, its teaching, life, and worship, and all of creation, then they are likely to perceive these symbols in a new way. What is the church's teaching on revelation and how does it affect our understanding of the nature of catechesis?

Avery Dulles points out that Vatican Council I (1869–1870) "came closer than any previous church Council to setting forth an authoritative Catholic view of revelation."[1] However, Vatican I's description of revelation is limited in scope because the chief purpose of its debate was not to set forth the church's teaching on revelation but to respond to certain erroneous teachings of the time.[2] That council never intended to present a comprehensive, balanced theology of revelation.

The Second Vatican Council developed and broadened the church's teaching on revelation in the *Dogmatic Constitution on Divine Revelation,* the only one of the sixteen documents of Vatican II that was discussed and/or revised throughout all four sessions of the council. The development of this document restored the church's focus on revelation as the dynamic self-communication of God in wisdom and love to humankind. Revelation is not doctrine, though doctrine is revelation, but revelation is primarily the self-communication of the Mystery to humankind. This Mystery is communicated through symbols of the church and of creation. God is present to the community through the church itself, through the Bible, through the doctrine and life of the church, including its worship. And God is present through all of creation, through the signs of the times. It is these symbols of revelation and faith that ought to be the focus of catechesis.

The *Dogmatic Constitution on Divine Revelation* is the basic reference for a theology of catechesis, for it sets forth the fundamental theology that is the basis of Christian life. The constitution is the basic reference, rather than the catechism, as it is the primary reference from which the catechism draws its teaching. The catechism distills the teaching of the constitution. The *General Directory for Catechesis* acknowledges that the constitution is the foundation for catechesis also when it states: "*Part One*...roots catechesis above all in the conciliar constitution *Dei Verbum....*"[3] This chapter will describe the theology of revelation and faith presented in that constitution and show how symbolic revelation is the basis for a theology of catechesis.

A Theology of Symbolic Revelation

The council fathers at the Second Vatican Council approved the constitution *On Divine Revelation* by a vote of 2,344 to 6, and Pope Paul VI promulgated it on November 18, 1965. The final document bore little resemblance to the original draft, which was sent to the fathers in the summer of 1962 before the council began.

On Divine Revelation includes a preface and six chapters:

	Preface (art. 1)
Chapter 1	Divine Revelation Itself (arts. 2–6)
Chapter 2	The Transmission of Divine Revelation (arts. 7–10)
Chapter 3	Sacred Scripture, Its Divine Inspiration and Its Interpretation (arts. 11–13)
Chapter 4	The Old Testament (arts. 14–16)
Chapter 5	The New Testament (arts. 17–20)
Chapter 6	Sacred Scripture in the Life on the Church (arts. 21–26)

The constitution, though of major theological significance, is a short document.[4] Chapter 1, arguably the most important chapter in the constitution, was not added until late in the development of the document.[5] It is this chapter that most clearly describes the nature of revelation. An analysis of the preface and chapter 1 will set forth the theology on which a renewed catechesis is based.

The Preface

> [1]Hearing the Word of God reverently and proclaiming it confidently, this holy synod makes its own the words of St. John: "We proclaim to you the eternal life which was with the Father and was made manifest to us—that which we have seen and heard we proclaim also to you, so that you may have fellowship with us and our fellowship is with the Father and His Son Jesus Christ" (1 Jn 1:2–3). Following, then, in the steps of the councils of Trent and Vatican I, this synod wishes to set forth the authentic teaching on divine revelation and its transmission. For it wants the whole world to hear the summons to salvation, so that through hearing it may believe, through belief it may hope, through hope it may come to love.

The first words of *On Divine Revelation* present the writers of the document as listeners of the word. Cardinal Joseph Ratzinger describes this beginning as "one of the happiest formulations in the text."[6] He notes that it presents the "Word of God" over and above all other human expressions or teachings. It presents the council fathers and the whole church as people of faith, listeners who hear the word, who are enlivened by the word and who proclaim the word to others. The church receives its word from another.

The constitution's preface draws upon the First Epistle of John to describe the gospel the church proclaims: the Word became incarnate and dwelt among us and lives with us in our common fellowship. It notes that the whole church draws on the past to announce in the present the wonderful works of God. This is what the church is about and this is what catechesis does. The catechist is a bridge and a prophet who announces what the church has seen and heard in the past, and calls on the catechized to open their eyes and ears, to see and to hear what God has done and is doing for us now. The catechist reminds the catechized that we are all called to live in communion with the Divine Mystery.

The final sentence of the preface places the teaching of this council in continuity with the teachings of the church by establishing a relationship with the teaching of the Council of Trent

(1545–1563) and the First Vatican Council (1869–1870). This continuity is not simply "a rigid external identification" with the past, but it is a way of preserving the old even "in the midst of progress."[7] The last phrase of the final sentence of the preface expresses the wishes and hopes not only of the council but of all the church and of all catechetical ministers.

Chapter 1: Revelation Itself (Articles 2–6)

The constitution *On Divine Revelation* went through seven major drafts (A–G) before its final approval. It was not until the fifth draft that what is now chapter 1 was introduced. This brief chapter of only five articles presents the most profound teaching of the council. Its five articles describe what revelation is.

ARTICLE 2

[2.]It pleased God, in his goodness and wisdom, to reveal himself and to make known the mystery of his will (see Eph 1:9) which was that people can draw near to the Father, through Christ, the Word made flesh, in the Holy Spirit, and thus become sharers in the divine nature (see Eph 2:18; 2 Pt 1:4).

The first sentence of article 2 is a masterpiece not only because of what it says but also because of what it does not say. It says that God chose to reveal *"himself"* and *"the mystery."* There is no mention here of the "eternal decrees" of God's will. The Latin text for *the mystery* is *sacramentum*, which is a translation of the Greek *mystērion*. What God reveals is the *Mystery*, the Godhead itself. The idea of God "unveiling" the Godhead is reinforced by the trinitarian reference to Father, Son, and Holy Spirit.

Revelation is:
God's self-communication,
trinitarian,
to all,
the Mystery,
relational.

Catechesis invites the catechized to recognize God's self-communication as emerging from the great love of the *Divine Mystery for us*. This *Mystery* reaches out dynamically in goodness and wisdom to all of humankind. The Trinity is open to us, seeking our response in love. God is revealing the Mystery so that humankind may "draw near to the Father and become sharers in the divine nature." Revelation is an act of grace, a transformative action. It is dynamic and personal. It is ongoing and relational. It is salvific.

Revelation is dynamic, personal, communal, loving, seeking response, ongoing, transformative, saving, liberating.

> By this revelation, then, the invisible God (see Col 1:14; 1 Tm 1:17) from the fullness of His love, addresses men and women as his friends (see Ex 33:11; Jn 15:14–15) and lives among them (see Bar 3:38), in order to invite and receive them into his own company.

Revelation is not only a gift from God but it initiates a dialogue between God and men and women. God speaks to us as his *friends*. God lives among us, is with us always and everywhere, inviting us to be part of the trinitarian community of love. The use of the present tense for "addresses" was not accidental. This dialogue is ongoing.

Revelation is gift, dialogue, God speaking, friendship, always present, active.

> The pattern of this revelation unfolds through deeds and words which are intrinsically connected: the works performed by God in the history of salvation show forth and confirm the doctrine and realities signified by the words; the words, for their part, proclaim the works, and bring to light the mystery they contain.

God's revelation takes place in history and has taken place through works (e.g., exodus, incarnation) and words (e.g., prophets), which "are intrinsically connected." God speaks to us, lovingly, and we as God's people hand on the story of these works and these words from generation to generation.

Revelation is present, historical, prophetic, through works, through words.

The most intimate truth thus revealed about God and human salvation shines forth for us in Christ, who is himself both the mediator and the sum total of revelation. The *most intimate* truth about God is that *God is for us.* This deepest truth shines out in Christ, who is the fullness of revelation, now and always. Jesus is the fullness of revelation (truly divine) and mediator for us. The Latin word *compleō* (completely) translates into "sum total" or "fullness." Jesus, the Christ, is the completeness of God's self-communication.

Revelation is salvific, full in Christ, complete in Christ.

ARTICLE 3

[3.]God, who creates and conserves all things by his Word (see Jn 1:3), provides constant evidence of himself in created realities (see Rom 1:19–20). Furthermore, wishing to open up the way to heavenly salvation, he manifested himself to our first parents from the very beginning. After the fall, he buoyed them up with the hope of salvation, by promising redemption (see Gn 3:15); and he has never ceased to take care of the human race, in order to give eternal life to all those who seek salvation by persevering in doing good (see Rom 2:6–7). In his own time, God called Abraham and made him into a great nation (see Gn 12:2). After the era of the patriarchs, he taught this nation, through Moses and the prophets, to recognize him as the only living and true God, as a provident Father and just judge. He taught them, too, to look for the promised Saviour. And so, throughout the ages, he prepared the way for the Gospel.

Paragraph 3 is a cornucopia of images of God: creator, manifestor of self, giver of hope, promiser of redemption, caretaker of the human race, giver of eternal life, living and true God, teacher, provider, just judge, preparer of the gospel. God gives "evidence of himself," of the Divinity, through "created realities." All creation is a symbol of the Creator. God not only created but *conserves* these realities. God created this world *by his word*, through Christ. The world itself is christic. The world and all created realities reveal Christ and the Creator.

Creation reveals the Mystery.

Creation gives evidence of God.

Revelation is present, historical, caring, enduring.

The profundity of this teaching is extraordinary and of paramount importance for catechists, for it tells us that the transcendent God is immanently present in the world and in our lives. Historically, God acted through the patriarchs and prophets, through the people of Israel, never ceasing to take care of the human race. And this ceaseless care continues.

ARTICLE 4

4.After God had spoken many times and in various ways through the prophets, "in these last days he has spoken to us by a Son" (Heb 1:1–2). For He sent His Son, the eternal Word, who enlightens all humankind, to live among them and to tell them about the inner life of God (Jn 1:1–18).

This fourth article presents the climax of the church's teaching on revelation. It reminds us that God revealed the Divine Mystery through the prophets, but now "in these last days" God sent his Son "to enlighten all humankind, to live among them and to tell them about the inner life of God."

Revelation is full in Christ.
Jesus is the speech of God.

94

Hence, Jesus Christ, sent as "a man among men and women," "speaks the words of God" (Jn 3:34), and accomplishes the saving work which the Father gave him to do (see Jn 5:36; 17:4). As a result, he himself—to see whom is to see the Father (see Jn 14:9)—completed and perfected revelation and confirmed it with divine guarantees. Everything to do with his presence and his manifestation of himself was involved in achieving this: his words and works, signs and miracles, but above all his death and glorious resurrection from the dead, and finally his sending of the Spirit of truth. He (Jesus) revealed that God was with us, to deliver us from the darkness of sin and death, and to raise us up to eternal life.

Article 4 is the apex of this chapter. It presents the incarnate Jesus as the fullness of revelation. No other symbol of revelation is comparable to the fullness of God's self-communication through the Son.

Jesus is the fullness of revelation, the incarnation of the Mystery.

Jesus is the sacrament of the Father. "To see Jesus is to see His Father." Jesus is the perfect symbol of God. Jesus the Christ is both the completion and the perfection of revelation. He is both the revealer and the revelation (the Divine). He is also the fullness of faith (fully human). Other symbols lead to and point to the Father and the Spirit. Jesus does not simply lead and point to the divine Mystery. He is one with it.

Revelation is sacramental, christocentric, (Spirit-filled). Christ is both the Revealer and the One revealed.

Article 4 points out that through his whole life, through his words and deeds, his signs and wonders, but "especially through His death and glorious resurrection from the dead and final sending of the Spirit of truth," Jesus revealed the Father.

Revelation is present in the life, death, and resurrection of Jesus and in the sending of the Spirit.

95

The Christian dispensation, therefore, since it is the new and definitive covenant, will never pass away; and now no new public revelation is to be expected before the glorious manifestation of our Lord, Jesus Christ (see 1 Tm 6:14 and Ti 2:13).

The final paragraph of article 4 is an eschatological statement, that is, a statement about the fullness of time, the end time. It reminds us, as the *Constitution on the Church* states, that "the promised and hoped for restoration, therefore, has already begun in Christ. It is carried forward in the sending of the holy Spirit and through him continues in the church...."[8] It emphasizes again that Jesus is himself the fullness of revelation.

Avery Dulles noted that in the preparation of the constitution *On Divine Revelation* the question was raised as to whether the statement "that revelation closed with the death of the last Apostle" should be inserted into the document. Some bishops proposed that article 4, which focuses on revelation through Christ should be amended to include an explicit affirmation that revelation "closed with the death of the Apostles." The commission responsible for the "preparation of the schema refused, and replied tersely, 'The truth intended by this statement is already declared, when it is said that Christ completes revelation.'"[9] The Latin *compleō* means to fulfill rather than to close.

ARTICLE 5

In the next article in this short chapter, the council entered into a description of faith as a gift from God which is the human response to God's revelation.

"The obedience of faith" (see Rom 16:26; compare Rom 1:5; 2 Cor 10:5–6) must be our response to God who reveals. By faith one freely commits oneself entirely to God, making "the full submission of intellect and will to God, who reveals,"[10] and willingly assenting to the revelation given by God. For this faith to be accorded we need the grace of God, anticipating it and assisting it, as well as the interior helps of the Holy Spirit, who moves the heart and converts it to God, and opens the eyes of the mind and "makes it easy for all to accept and believe the truth."[11] The same holy Spirit constantly perfects faith by his gifts, so that revelation may be more and more deeply understood.

Article 5 reminds us that faith is a gift of grace and that it may be understood in two ways, both as "commitment" to God through Christ *(fides qua)* and as "the faith which we believe," truths of faith *(fides quae)*. These two forms of faith relate to the understanding of revelation as God's own self-communication to humankind, and to the truths that emerge from that experience of God's self-communication.[12]

Faith as commitment *(fides qua)* is the response to revelation as God's self-communication of the Divine Mystery. This faith also expresses itself in words and in actions, in beliefs and in a way of living. Beliefs are an essential expression of faith *(fides quae)*, for they conceptualize the faith experience of the community. They both express and communicate the faith community's meanings. They are symbols that express both adequately and inadequately the faith community's experience of the Divine Mystery.

Faith as the response to revelation shares in the qualities and characteristics of revelation. It is the human response of giving to the divine self-gift. It is personal, historical, communal, dialogical, sacramental, or symbolic. It has qualities or characteristics that closely relate to the qualities and characteristics of revelation.

Revelation and faith may both be described as:

relational	*communicating*	*conceptual*
transformative	*sacramental*	*biblical*
personal	*enlightening*	*christocentric*
communal	*truthful*	*trinitarian*
loving	*symbolic*	*Spirit-filled*
ongoing	*expressed through words*	*liberating*
salvific	*expressed through actions*	*constant*
dialogical	*present*	*creative*
historical	*informing*	*gift*
ecumenical	*experiential*	*symbolic*

Avery Dulles rightly points out that while faith is personal, our personal faith is really a sharing in the faith of the community. He writes: "Acceptance of revelation (that is, faith) is achieved and manifested within a living community of faith in which the insights of all the members are exchanged and subjected to mutual criticism, so that illusions can be detected and exposed."[13] It is the community which hands on its faith to its new members.

ARTICLE 6

The final article in chapter 1 summarizes the whole chapter in its first paragraph.

> 6By divine revelation, God wished to manifest and communi-
> cate both himself and the eternal decrees of his will concerning
> the salvation of humankind. He wished in other words, "to
> share with us divine benefits which entirely surpass the powers
> of the human mind to understand."
>
> The holy synod professes that "God, the first principle
> and last end of all things, can be known with certainty from the
> created world, by the natural light of human reason" (see Rom
> 1:20). It teaches that it is to his revelation that we must attribute
> the fact "that those things, which in themselves are not beyond
> the grasp of human reason, can, in the present condition of the
> human race, be known by all with ease, with firm certainty; and
> without the contamination of error."

The final paragraph of the first chapter demonstrates that the teaching on revelation developed at Vatican II emerges from and is consonant with the teaching of the church in the past.

This first chapter of *On Divine Revelation* describes revelation not simply as truths or eternal decrees but as the self-communication of the Mystery whom we call God. The Mystery is always here, always for us. The Mystery is always revealing, initiating, and inviting a relationship of love with humankind, and the response to this divine self-revelation is faith *(fides qua)*, which is itself a gift from the Divine. In trying to express or articulate the experience of God's self-gift to us, the church tells its story from Abraham through today and from its story it draws forth teachings, doctrines, or dogmas that it holds sacred as those meanings which express and communicate its experience of God.

Chapters 2–6 of On Divine Revelation

Chapter 2, almost as extraordinary in its teaching as chapter 1, points out that revelation is "sacramental" or "symbolic" and historical. What the church hands on through symbol is what it has been freely given and commissioned by Christ to hand on. Article 7 begins by reminding us that the apostles

> handed on, by oral preaching, by their example, by their dispositions, what they themselves had received…through the promptings of the Holy Spirit.

Article 8 describes what the apostles handed on:

> What was handed on by the apostles comprises everything that serves to make the people of God live their lives in holiness and increase their faith. In this way the church, in its doctrine, life and worship, perpetuates and transmits to every generation all that it itself is, all that it believes.

What the church is handing on through its doctrine, life, and worship is called *Tradition*. Tradition is dynamic, communal, and living. The church hands on the life of the community, including its life as a community of justice, a worshiping community, a teaching community, a believing community. A renewed understanding of *revelation* has led to a renewed understanding of Tradition.[14]

Ratzinger points out that the council discussed the fact that "not everything that exists in the church must for that reason be also a legitimate tradition."[15] So the church turns to the Sacred Scripture as a "criterion for an indispensable criticism of tradition, and tradition must therefore always be related back to it and measured by it."[16] The church looks to the Sacred Scriptures not only to keep the Christian event alive but as a norm by which to critique its own teaching, life, and worship in the present.

Chapters 3, 4, and 5 of *On Divine Revelation* present church teaching on "Sacred Scripture: Its Divine Inspiration and Its Interpretation," as well as principles for interpreting and praying with the Old and New Testaments. Chapter 6, "Sacred Scripture in the Life of the Church," encourages the reading of and preaching on the Bible even as it compares the "Table of the Word" to the "Table of the Lord."

On Divine Revelation describes the revelation of the Mystery happening in a "sacramental" or symbolic way. The Mystery reveals itself through the world, through "created realities," which are symbols of God's presence with us. The Holy Being revealed the Mystery through Abraham, the patriarchs, Moses, the prophets, and finally through Jesus, who is the perfect symbol of God, the fullness of revelation. The church brought into being by Jesus as a symbol of himself has been commissioned to carry on Jesus' work and to hand on what God has revealed to all generations. The church does this through the Sacred Scriptures, a preeminent symbol of the church's life and through the symbols of Tradition, the teaching, life, and worship of the church. The text of *On Divine Revelation* clearly points to specific symbols through which the Mystery reveals itself.

Avery Dulles describes revelatory symbols as "those which express and mediate God's self-communication."[17] It is these symbols that the community attends to and participates in in catechesis. They are *that through which* the community meets and engages the Divine Mystery. It is for this reason that a theological understanding of symbol needs to be described. And for that we turn to Karl Rahner and his theology of symbol.

A Theology of Symbol

Karl Rahner points out that a symbol is *that through which* a reality expresses itself.[18] He states that every being in order to become itself must express itself. The expression of the self is the "symbol." This symbol constitutes or "makes" the self. For this reason every symbol is intimately related to the reality it expresses. It is not the fullness of that reality, but it is an expression of the reality which makes the reality present to itself and to others.

In our society symbols are frequently downgraded as if they were not "real." A news reporter will say that something is "only a symbol." Or this is "only a symbolic action," meaning it does not count for much. Theologically, on the contrary, symbols and symbolic actions have profound meaning that is readily communicated, evocative, and somewhat ambiguous. The *Catechism of the Catholic Church* acknowledges the importance of symbols when it states:

> In human life, signs and symbols occupy an important place. As a being at once body and spirit, man expresses and perceives spiritual realities through physical signs and symbols. As a social being, man needs signs and symbols to communicate with others, through language, gestures, and actions. The same holds true for his relationship with God.[19]

Symbols Are Intrinsically Related to the Reality They Express

As *that through which* a reality is present, symbols participate in the reality they express. They are intrinsic to the reality they make present. For example, a person expresses his or her parenthood in a child. The symbol of the adult's parenthood is the child. When people are in love they symbolize themselves in words and actions that express their love. The words and actions are symbols of their love.

One way a nation symbolizes itself is in the ways it relates to the poorest and neediest of its citizens. Providing homes for the homeless and caring for the hungry and underprivileged are symbolic actions that express the nation. Slavery was at one time a symbol of the United States. Outlawing slavery became a symbol of the renewed nation. Symbols participate in and relate to the reality they make present.

Symbols Are Rich in Meaning

Symbols are carriers of meaning. Words are, of course, symbols that express meaning, but often a person's body language or gestures express meaning more fully than her words. Conflict

101

between actions and words communicates a sense of falsehood about the words being spoken. We simply do not believe the speaker. A person who by action discriminates against others but through words speaks for justice creates disbelief because the actions convey different, even opposite, meanings.

Symbols Evoke a Response

Symbols are evocative; they summon a response from those who encounter them. Symbols appeal to the imagination, which triggers a response from the totality of the person. The giving of a gift (a symbolic gesture) can evoke joy or surprise or even anger, depending on what the giving of the gift symbolizes. The giving of a flag to a wife or mother at a funeral symbolizes the country's gratefulness for the military service of the person who died and evokes pride or love from the one receiving the flag.

Symbols Are Concrete

Symbols are concrete, not abstract. The concrete moving of the body embracing or withdrawing is a way of expressing abstract meaning. We express grief in crying. We express happiness in a smile or a calmness or a "whoopee." Often our body moves and symbolizes our response before we have a chance to express the response in words. The idea of "ethnic cleansing" is an abstraction expressed in the concrete symbolic action of isolating or killing people of a particular ethnic group simply because they belong to that ethnic group.

Symbols Are Ambiguous

Symbols are ambiguous. While they evoke thought and give rise to meaning, often they evoke a multiplicity of responses because their meaning is ambiguous. They provide a "surplus" of meaning. This multivalent characteristic gives them a certain power in representing the Divine Mystery, for their richness provides both clarity and ambiguity, both meaning and a recognition that the meaning they give is inadequate. No symbol adequately expresses the Divine. Every symbol of the Divine engages us and offers us multiple and even conflicting insights. This leads us to say that our language about God is always "limited, image-bound or imperfect."[20]

Symbols Are Partial Expressions of a Reality

Symbols are not the same as the reality they make present (with one exception). They are intrinsically, even intimately, related to the reality they express, but they are only partial expressions of that reality. As a human being you express your outrage or your love through your body language and through verbal language, through gestures and words. Your primary symbol is your body. But no single bodily action or word expresses you fully. And most of your actions and words convey multiple meanings.

The only Symbol who fully expresses the reality he symbolizes is Jesus, who is the symbol of the Father. Describing Jesus as the *symbol of the Father* is stating that he is the *full* expression of the Divinity. Jesus and the Father (with the Spirit) are one united reality. When the Gospel presents Jesus as saying, "The Father and I are one," or "He who sees me sees the Father," the language tells us that Jesus, the truly human person, is also truly and fully divine. All other symbols are partial expressions of that which they express and make present.

Symbols Express Corporate as well as Individual Realities

Symbols express communal as well as personal realities. The United States of America as a country expresses and symbolizes itself through its leaders, through the president, the members of Congress, the military, the Peace Corps, and through its actions such as feeding the hungry, waging war, respecting free speech even when disagreeing with the speaker. It expresses itself in the acceptance of the death penalty and its policy on abortion. It symbolizes itself in the choice of its leaders.

Human Beings Are Symbol Makers

Among all the creatures on earth, the human being is the only symbol-making creature for he, she, or they *consciously* represent and express themselves through symbols. In this way human beings image and participate in the life of the Divine Being who is the symbol maker par excellence. People individually and communally express themselves in words and in actions and in so doing they become what they express themselves to be.

Symbols of Revelation

Revelation, the self-communication or unveiling of God to humankind takes place through symbols. These symbols are *that through which* God is present and loving to humankind. These symbols are not simply or only intellectual concepts, but they are multivalent; they participate in many characteristics of symbol. And as they are multivalent so they are ambiguous. What are these Christian symbols of the Divine Mystery?

The church, the people of God, is a primary symbol of God. It is the corporate body through which Christ is present in the world. It is intimately related to the reality it makes present, but it is not the same as that reality. It is filled with the Holy Spirit who gives it life, but it is not the Holy Spirit. It presents an ambiguous image because people see in it both traces of God and sinfulness. It evokes response and is rich in meaning.

The church symbolizes itself through the Sacred Scriptures and Tradition. By Tradition we mean the life, teaching, and worship of the church.

The Sacred Scriptures

The Sacred Scriptures are a preeminent symbol of the church. They are not simply a word from the past. They are the word which symbolizes, expresses, and makes present the relationship of God with the Jewish and Christian people in history. The Scriptures are paradigmatic and provocative for the church of the present.

Scripture scholars tell us that the Gospels are a unique form of literature. They are not essays. They are a passionate proclamation of the story of God's love. And the story told in the Gospels is the story of the Incarnate One who symbolizes through his humanity God's love for humankind not only in the past but also today, in the present.

The New Testament, like the Old Testament, is a love story. It is the story of God's remarkable and loving pursuit of humankind. The Gospels symbolize the good news proclaimed and preached by Jesus: that the Divine Mystery is always present for us, concretely, in our daily lives. God as *creator* is present to us, God as *Spirit* and *Comforter* is present to us, and *Christ our risen Lord* is always here *for* us.

People become Christians because the Christian gospel gives them hope and a view of the world that is both coherent and unimaginable. The gospel articulates peoples' innermost hopes and insights. It resonates with their lives. Men and women experience their best selves in the parables and teaching of Jesus, the Christ. People become Christians because the gospel resonates with the truth they already inchoately know.

The Church and Its Teaching, Life, and Worship: Tradition

Cardinal Ratzinger describes "Tradition" as the perpetuation, "the constant continuation and making present of everything that the Church is, of everything that it believes. Tradition is identified, and thus defined, with the being and the faith of the Church."[21] As noted earlier, Tradition is the "teaching, life, and worship" of the church. Through its teaching, life, and worship the church symbolizes Christ present today, yesterday, and tomorrow.

At the Second Vatican Council, Cardinal Albert Meyer of Chicago reminded the fathers that "not everything that exists in the Church must for that reason be also a legitimate tradition; in other words, not every tradition that arises in the Church is a true

105

celebration and keeping present of the mystery of Christ."[22] The church is not the fullness of that which it symbolizes. It is graced and also sinful. Whatever grace the church has and offers comes to it through the redemptive life of Jesus and the inspiration of the Holy Spirit sent by the Father and the Son to sustain and energize it.

The church symbolizes itself through its teaching, its doctrines, and dogmas. As the human community is a reasoning community, so the church as a human community seeks and shares meaning. One way the church expresses the meaning of its experience with the Divine Mystery is through its doctrines. The church's teaching word is meant to be a living and active word, a healing and challenging word, a word that gives life, and, in its varied expressions throughout the centuries, a word that built the church and filled it with joy.

Doctrines ought to be life-giving, for they are Spirit-filled. Doctrines emerge out of the church's experience and tell us that life is reasonable, God is loving, we are not alone, and we have every reason to hope for fullness of life. Doctrines can free us from oppression even in the midst of tyranny and cruelty. All doctrines are clothed in language that is inadequate, for no language can fully express the Mystery calling us to faith.

The church also reveals the Mystery as it worships. The worshiping community symbolizes Christ present with us through ordinary human actions which are given new meaning by the words that accompany them. In the water-bath the church gives birth, cleanses, renews, and energizes itself. As it eats and drinks bread and wine at a festive meal it symbolizes Christ present with us in every meal. When it sings and dances, proclaims and listens, embraces and forgives it appeals to our imagination to recognize the Mystery present in every ordinary human endeavor. The church massages fragrant oils into our forehead or hands and shows forth the holiness of the body and the person called to perform services to the community and the world. And these holy actions move the community out from the world of the church at worship to the world of the needy, where the church feeds the hungry, clothes the naked, instructs the ignorant, visits the imprisoned, cares for the sick, shelters the homeless, and does whatever else the poor and impoverished or oppressed need to have done for them. The symbols of the church urge us to see what Rahner calls "the more," the depth dimension of all reality.

Created Realities as Symbols of the Divine Mystery

On Divine Revelation describes the symbols of God in two ways: as created realities and as expressions of the church. Created realities include all of physical creation since it emerged from God as Creator, and the signs of the times. The signs of the times include all human interaction and symbolic actions—the arts, the sciences, technology, political and economic life, culture, international relations, daily life, death, war, and peace.[23] These realities carry meaning and symbolize God's self-manifestation to humankind. They show forth God's presence. Created realities are not God but are symbols of God. They reveal the uniqueness, brilliance, artistry, and love of the "more" who brought the universe into being, the Divine Mystery.

The theological foundation for catechesis and all forms of the ministry of the word begins with the church's teaching on revelation. The Holy Mystery is present always and everywhere communicating itself in knowledge and love through symbols. Revelation is not an unmediated or purely interior experience of God. Symbols of God, which we call revelatory symbols express and mediate God's self-revelation. In this revelation God comes to us as friend. God is *for* us. There is no niche or cranny of human life in which the Mystery is not present inviting us to communion with it. All of life is sacred. Nothing is profane. The Spirit is always with us. Grace is everywhere. Catechesis is the ministry of the church, which helps us recognize and respond to that loving presence.

A Theology of Catechesis

Catechesis is a ministry in which the church facilitates the community's growth in faith through its participation in the symbols of

God's self-revelation. The catechist assists the community to recognize the presence of God by leading it to discover, examine, consider, and live with (participate in) the symbols of revelation and faith. The catechist asks: If God is present, revealing the Mystery in our ordinary daily lives, in "the signs of the times," through the church, its Scriptures, and its Tradition, how are we to recognize that presence? How are we to know that the presence we recognize is authentic?

It will hardly be possible to recognize and respond to the symbols of God if we do not recognize the symbols through which we live out our own lives and relate with one another. Catechists help the community to recognize that in the midst of its work, its computing and its transporting, its teaching, its reporting and its farming, its buying and selling, its living and dying there is meaning. In all our activities the Mystery is *with* us and *for* us. Whether we are single parents struggling for the basic needs of our children, or adults who participate in the sickness and dying of their parents, or men or women who have lost their jobs, or families battered by floods or natural disasters, the Mystery is with us in our joys and tragedies, in these daily signs of the times. God is with us and God is for us and the church, which is Christ's body on earth, the Great Sacrament, is with us to help us understand and experience that loving Presence.

Symbolic catechesis focuses on symbols of daily life and symbols of God's presence. The community discovers them, examines them, explores their meaning, lives with them, listens to them, tastes them, embraces them, traces their history. The *General Directory for Catechesis* encourages this when it says that catechesis shall exhibit that knowledge which is typical of faith, which "is knowledge through signs."[24] Through encounter with the symbols of life and of faith we move from the visible to the invisible. We move, in response, to the Mystery.

This theology of catechesis recognizes the nature of the church as a sacrament or symbol of God's presence and recognizes the signs of the times as symbols of God's self-communication in love.[25] As we are surrounded by the revelatory symbols of God through the church, the Bible, the teaching, life, and worship of the church, so we are surrounded by symbols of God's self-communication in the signs of the times. In catechesis the catechist invites the community to recognize those symbols in their daily lives which manifest the presence of the Holy One and to interpret or understand them through their experience and knowledge of faith symbols. At the same time the catechist leads the community to discover how symbols of daily life enable us to understand symbols of faith.

The response to the invitation to correlate or associate faith symbols with daily life ought to be holistic, involving intellect and will, imagination, memory, body, heart, and spirit. It will be a faith response, personal and communal, living and dynamic, committing the totality of the person and the community to the Divine Mystery who is everywhere present and always *for* it. Catechesis is a challenge both for the catechist and the catechetical community. The catechist is a symbol of God's self-communication to the community. She or he is a human symbol which expresses the dynamic relationship of faith and revelation. The community, on the other hand, is also a symbol of faith. It symbolizes through its commitment and its hopes the presence of the Divine Mystery within it. Both catechist and community work together as graced searchers for meaning. The whole enterprise is holy.

The understanding that revelation is God's self-communication expressed through symbol broadens the nature of the catechetical act. If the goal of catechesis is to invite the community to conversion of life, to *metanoia*, as a response to God's self-giving, and faith is seen as a holistic act that involves all dimensions of the human person, then the catechist will invite the community to experience, know, meet, and live with the multiple symbols through which the Mystery reveals itself. And the catechist and community will interpret human life, both communal life and personal life, through those symbols. In this way catechesis becomes reflection on and participation in the symbols of the Mystery of God, a reflection that calls the community to conversion and faith.

In symbolic catechesis the community examines and understands the teaching of the church and recognizes them as gifts that help us live faithfully. If in the past there was a focus on the communication of correct doctrine and the minimizing of other dimensions of Catholic life, the renewal of catechesis tells us that communicating correct doctrine is only one part, albeit an essential dimension of catechetical ministry. The catechist seeks conversion, and conversion is not only intellectual (although it certainly is intellectual) but also affective and performative. Catechesis seeks the conversion of the whole person in community.

If we take seriously the understanding that human experience, particularly communal human experience, is a locus of God's self-revelation, then in catechesis we will take human experience much more seriously than we presently do. We cannot simply give lip service to reflecting on experience in order to get to the religious insights. The religious insights will have shallow meaning if the community has not seriously considered the life issue about which it is concerned.

Human experience does not stand alone as a symbol of God's presence in catechesis. We cannot take any experience, whether it is the death of a loved one, the destruction of a home, the marriage of a son or daughter, or the winning of the lottery, and simply examine it without relating it to the Mystery *for* us. Critical reflection on life's issues without regard to the religious dimension is of value and it may happen often in the community's life, but critical reflection that does not turn at some point to a recognition of the presence and the meaning of the Mystery in our lives is not catechesis.

Symbolic catechesis is a catechesis in which the faith community looks at its life, at its world, at common concerns and questions and tries to make sense of them in the light of its Christian faith. In symbolic catechesis there is no question you cannot ask. Every question manifests a search for God. In symbolic catechesis there cannot be a fear of overstepping boundaries in asking questions. Real concerns need to be expressed. Real doubts need to be recognized. Doubts are not anti-faith. They are faith seeking meaning. Sincere and real questions are not only valid but ought to be sought. The only way we can search for meaning is through questions, doubts, reconsiderations, gaining new insights, dialogue, being alone, being together, trust and prayer.

Through catechesis the community becomes aware of its own symbolic expressions of faith and attentive to the symbols that express and constitute the presence of the Divine in daily life. The community learns to turn to the Sacred Scriptures, the teaching, life, and worship of the church for meaning for understanding and for vision. The catechist leads the community to participate in and recognize church symbols as symbols of both revelation and faith.

The catechetical community engages the symbols of God's revelation that come to us through the experiences of daily life and achieves meaning and understanding by correlating and associating the experiences of daily life with the symbols of faith. Catechesis helps the community to recognize that God, *the Holy One* is revealing the Divine Mystery to us through these almost homely intimacies of daily life. This catechesis leads the catechist and the community to turn to the Mystery with a response of love. It leads them to look with reverence on all created reality and to recognize the symbols of faith as invitations to deeper relationships with one another, with the whole of the universe, and with the Mystery itself.

Catechesis is a ministry in which the catechist acts as an activator, facilitator, leader, and catalyst for the assembled community. The catechist leads the community to reflect critically on its life and then to interpret the meaning of life through the Scriptures, through sacramental rituals, through doctrine, through the church's living and acts of justice. This reflection involves a circular movement between life symbols and faith symbols in which faith gives meaning to life, and at the same time, life enlightens faith.

The goal of symbolic catechesis is to strengthen the faith of the catechetical community and each member within it. No one can program an experience of God nor growth in faith. Those are grace-filled gift moments. But the catechist can bring together the community and the community's symbols in such a way that the community recognizes the extraordinary character of its own life. The catechist who is able to recognize the extraordinariness of human life and of the human community will be able to facilitate growth in faith. That catechist is called to be a wise woman or man for the community.

111

Adults may ask: How can I live with any fullness and prayerfully when I am overwhelmed with the responsibilities of single parent-hood? Or what does it mean for me to be a care giver to my parent and at the same time a wife to my husband and a parent to my children? Or is it my (or our) responsibility to support those without jobs or the mentally ill who are on our streets? In catechesis the community examines in a variety of ways God's self-communication in love to this particular community and the faith of this community, which enables it to respond to God's love. The church's theology of revelation teaches us that the Divine Mystery is present to us, in unconditional love, supporting us in every endeavor, constantly seeking our faith. The Mystery is *for us.* How will we respond to it?

FURTHER READINGS

Catechism of the Catholic Church. Washington, D.C.: United States Catholic Conference, 1994.

Congregation for the Clergy. *General Directory for Catechesis*. Washington, D.C.: United States Catholic Conference, 1997.

Dulles, Avery. *Models of Revelation*. Garden City, N.Y.: Doubleday, 1983.

———. *Revelation Theology*. A Crossroad Book. New York: Seabury Press, 1969.

Haight, Roger. *Dynamics of Theology*. New York: Paulist Press, 1990.

Hilkert, Mary Catherine, O.P. "Experience and Tradition: Can the Center Hold?" In *Freeing Theology: The Essentials of Theology in Feminist Perspective*, ed. Catherine Mowry LaCugna, 59–83. San Francisco: Harper, 1993.

———. *Naming Grace: Preaching and the Sacramental Imagination*. New York: Continuum, 1997.

Latourelle, René. *Theology of Revelation*. Staten Island, N.Y.: Alba House, 1966.

O'Collins, Gerald. *Fundamental Theology*. New York: Paulist Press, 1981.

———. *Retrieving Fundamental Theology: The Three Styles of Contemporary Theology*. New York: Paulist Press, 1993.

Rahner, Karl. "The Theology of Symbol." In *Theological Investigations*, vol. 4. Translated by Kevin Smyth. New York: Seabury Press, 1974.

PART II

The Process of Symbolic Catechesis

CHAPTER 5

Symbolic Catechesis

One of the most important insights emerging from the historical and theological renewal of catechesis in the twentieth century may be that there is no single catechetical approach that is satisfactory for all people. Differing cultures, different levels of education, different stages of faith, different intellectual abilities, different life experiences all require different catechetical approaches. There is no one magic approach for everyone or every community. "Symbolic catechesis" is, however, an approach that is particularly apt for people of the twenty-first century. This chapter will describe both the structure and the approach of symbolic catechesis.

A Catechesis for the Twenty-first Century

Symbolic catechesis is a form of catechesis that associates or correlates the symbols of human events and experiences, the "signs of the times," with the symbols of faith: the Bible, and the teaching, life, and worship of the church. Faith symbols enable us to interpret life, and, conversely, life symbols help us to understand faith. Symbolic catechesis integrates life and faith symbols in a harmonious, dialogical, critical, and thought-provoking way. Such a catechesis involves the person and the community in a searching for truth and identity, not abstract truth but the truth of Christian life; not abstract identity but, concretely, identity as a Christian in this world today. And the search focuses not only on the question Who am I? but on Who are we as a Christian community?

Symbolic catechesis emerged out of the catechetical renewal of the twentieth century and "fits" the human side of the church in the United States in the twenty-first century. It is a flexible and adaptable approach for people of differing cultures, ages, education, ethnicity, race, and gender. It is in both continuity and discontinuity with the past, building on the renewal of the twentieth century and at the same time avoiding the excesses of the "arid intellectualism" that Josef Jungmann had pointed out. It presumes faith, incipient or mature faith, on the part of the members of the community. It is an approach in which diversity of ideas, experiences, and culture is welcome.

The goal of symbolic catechesis is the strengthening of faith commitment among the members of the catechetical community. Faith commitment grows and develops through the actual living out of Christian life, which includes (1) the deepening of relationships among the community members, (2) the broadening of insights and understandings regarding the stories and teachings of the church, (3) the experience of doing justice as integral to daily life, and (4) worshiping with a community of believers. The process of symbolic catechesis involves the members of the catechetical community living out the elements of Christian life together.

How can this happen? How can a community of five or six parishioners taste what it means to be Christian by living out their Christian life in an adult catechetical process? Both the structure and the process of symbolic catechesis make this possible. The structure of symbolic catechesis is the four components upon which it is built; the process of symbolic catechesis is the way in which these four components are brought together as an integrated whole, and the relative emphasis given to each component.

While most catechetical approaches have the same goal and most catechists recognize their relationship to the church, not all approaches are of equal value. Though it is not easy to evaluate effectiveness when the object being measured is the conversion of a community of people, there are indications that particular catechetical approaches meet some peoples' needs more adequately than others. This means that we may need to evaluate our approaches and identify which ones meet the needs of our diverse populations.

Such an evaluation will show that symbolic catechesis is an effective approach for many individuals and communities in the United States church in the twenty-first century.

Symbolic catechesis is an appropriate approach for the beginning of the twenty-first century for three reasons. First, at a time when "American law and politics trivialize religious devotion,"[1] when some of the intelligentsia belittle or are antagonistic to religious faith, constantly separating it from public policy, commerce, and education, symbolic catechesis confesses that religious faith transforms life and the way in which people perceive the world. In symbolic catechesis the community remembers its history and recognizes that the Divine Mystery is always present with it and for it. Symbolic catechesis acknowledges that people encounter the sacred in the events of daily life. It states clearly and unambiguously that faith and life cannot be separated. Culture and religious faith are not two realms of life. Faith integrates and transforms life. It makes life whole.

Second, at a time when the culture focuses on the differences that exist among peoples and often divides people rather than unifying them, symbolic catechesis focuses on the unity that exists among the diverse members and communities of the faithful and tries to strengthen this union. It understands the church as being a communion of the faithful who are united by the gospel, nourished by the sacraments, particularly the Eucharist, and always called to work for a just society. Symbolic catechesis emphasizes through word and through witness that the church, the body of Christ, is one. It brings diverse people together. This church is the home of the poor and the wealthy, the educated and uneducated, the powerful and those who are powerless. Symbolic catechesis recognizes that this diverse church is the principal symbol through which God enlightens and graces humankind. It acknowledges that the church is sinful as well as holy even as it calls the community to holiness and repentance. Symbolic catechesis presents the church as a community of extraordinary diversity where all are welcomed.

Third, symbolic catechesis is a particularly apt approach because its very structure involves a living out of Christian life. The structure includes the four primary components of Christian life described in Acts: (1) the teaching of the apostles (sharing our meaning and beliefs); (2) the communal life (building community); (3) the breaking of the bread and the prayers (praying together); and (4) having all things in common (doing justice) (Acts 2:42–44). These four actions are four constitutive components of Christian life, and together they are the structural elements of symbolic catechesis.

This structure and process of symbolic catechesis emerged out of the study of catechetical renewal and a variety of catechetical experiences with adult communities of faith over several decades. It is a catechetical approach that appeals to the cognitive, affective, and performative or ethical dimensions of human life. It draws on the best of educational theory and cultural studies regarding how to minister to both adults and young people. It has a natural appeal for most adults because it presumes their questions, concerns, and experiences are significant sources for developing a living faith.

Today most catechetical approaches, but not all, include the four components of "building community, sharing the message, doing justice, and praying together." However, the ways they integrate the components and the priority they give to each component differ. Therefore, the catechetical process differs also.

The Process of Symbolic Catechesis

The process of symbolic catechesis resembles a symphony. The orchestra (community) plays the music in its own unique way, directed or guided by a conductor (the catechist[s]) who is one with the orchestra. The music has four movements, loosely connected, each with its own variation of the same experience. The experiences are the life events of the community and the life-death-resurrection of Jesus and the story of the church he founded. In each movement the community approaches the experiences from a different perspective. The movements are:

1. Reflecting on a common experience
2. Interpreting the experience through a faith symbol

3. Moving outward from the experience to acts of justice
together
4. Praying together about the experience

In each movement the community develops bonds of faith and love and becomes more of a unified integrated community of faith. Occasionally the third movement may become the first movement and the other movements follow the experience of acts of justice.

These four movements are framed by a gathering experience at the beginning (a prelude) and a sending forth experience (a coda) at the end. A graphic presentation of the process looks like this:

Gathering (prelude)
1. Reflecting on a common human experience
2. Correlating the experience with a faith symbol
3. Moving outward from the experience to acts of
justice together
4. Praying together about the experience
through rituals
Sending forth (coda)

The gathering begins when the catechist(s) begins to prepare the place where the small group will meet, and as the people begin to leave their homes and move toward the meeting place. As the people arrive at the parish the catechist meets the people at the door, welcomes them, calls them by name, introduces them to one another, if necessary, and does whatever she can to make them feel comfortable and at home. When it is time to begin, the catechist gathers the group and with a short but carefully prepared prayer, about four lines, moves into the first movement. The prayer reorients the community's life. It may begin with the sign of the cross, followed by, "Let us pray," and a moment of silence in which the community turns away from the whatever preoccupied it and turns toward a more reflective stance. The words of the prayer announce that we live in a sacred world in which God, the Holy Mystery is with us, and we are searching for help, for understanding, for release from a particular life concern. It ends with trinitarian praise.

121

The first movement, reflecting on a common experience, gently nudges the community into dialogue by initiating a conversation on an experience that concerns or interests all the participants. In the second movement the community considers that experience from the viewpoint of a faith symbol, such as the Bible or the church's life, teaching, or worship. The third movement takes the community from introspection to a consideration of the needs of others. The climax of the symphony, the fourth movement, is the ritual prayer where the community joins together as one and offers praise and glory to the Divine Mystery who the community recognizes is present with it in this meeting.

In symbolic catechesis every word and action lead to this final prayer, where the community consciously and deliberately joins itself to the Mystery. The ritual prayer is not simply a closing or an add-on, but it is that experience toward which the whole session points. In the ritual prayer the community synthesizes its catechetical experience and together as a community it seeks to recognize and respond to the presence of the Mystery who is always with it offering unconditional love and acceptance.

A symphony is a communal enterprise. The players work together watching the director carefully and following her lead. All the musicians and the director, as one, bring the musical score to life. The director does not play a musical instrument, but she or he enables the sounds of many musicians to harmonize. All the musicians need one another and all recognize that they can play well not only when they perform well as individuals but when as a group of individuals who rely on each other. As in an orchestra, relationships among the individuals in the catechetical community change. As they discuss and converse, pray and listen, do acts of justice together and ask their questions, appreciation for others grows, the need for mutual support becomes obvious, and responsibility for one another becomes more apparent. The group is growing into a stronger faith community.

Movement 1: Reflecting on a Common Human Experience. In symbolic catechesis the community of faith guided by the catechist examines or analyzes a particular common human experience. It seeks through communal study in a context of prayer and justice to understand the nature, value, and effect of this experience on individuals and their communities (family, friends, coworkers, neighborhood, etc.). The community asks: How is this experience (joblessness, illness, poverty, aging) affecting our lives ? How is it affecting others with whom we are interacting? What is the moral or ethical challenge of this experience?

It does this knowing that there are no simple answers to such an analysis and that there seldom is a one-to-one correspondence between a life experience and a faith symbol. The community is seeking meaning, and the pursuit of insight may take a long time, or many catechetical sessions. But insight comes through participation in the symbols of life and of faith and in their mutually critical correlation.

T.S. Eliot wrote, "We had the experience but missed the meaning."[2] We have all experienced a sudden illumination in particular experiences, and often we missed the meaning or did not reflect on the meaning beyond the sudden illumination. But it is the meaning that enlightens us and carries us forward in life. Why am I alive? What does it mean to be a mother or a father? Or what does my younger sister's death mean? We constantly seek meaning and insight, and at the same time we walk away from it. "We had the experience but missed the meaning."

Symbolic catechesis is a search for the meaning of life and of faith and of their relationship. Whether it is a question of the meaning of the Holocaust or the welcoming of thousands of new immigrants to our city, the birth of a new child or the death of a dear friend, the community asks whatever questions it has, freely, without fear, and seeks some understanding about that issue. In this process there is no unaskable question. There may be questions without totally satisfactory responses.

In symbolic catechesis the questions of the community are central in the catechesis. The catechesis is organized around the people's questions, focuses on them, derives from them. It presumes that people live in society and in a number of communities within that society and that every individual question is related to a societal concern. Ordinary people think about and are concerned about questions regarding the meaning of their lives as members of a family, or an ethnic group, or a fellowship, or community organization, or church. A 1982 survey conducted by the Gallup Organization demonstrated "that 90 percent of the public claimed to have thought about 'living a worthwhile life' at least a fair amount (or a lot) during the preceding two years." Eighty-three percent of these people thought about "basic values in life." Eighty-one percent thought about their "relation to God," and 70 percent thought about "developing your faith."[3] People want to consider together the deeper questions of life.

If the people's concerns focus on a religious question, a question about the Bible, or questions about church teachings on issues such as the death penalty or the value of human life, or sexuality, or peace and war, then the catechist should begin with that concern. If the community gathers because it is concerned about the closing of a factory and the loss of jobs, or problems with drugs and adolescents, or how to deal with retirement, those are the questions that will be addressed. The questions of the people, whether about daily life or faith, are the focus of the gathering, and these questions need and deserve to be thoroughly examined. They are not simply a "jumping-off" place that will lead to a theological topic. The human question or concern has value in itself. It will be that which brings the people together.

When the common interest of the community is a religious topic such as the liturgical season of lent, or Bible study, or preparing the children for a sacrament, then that "religious" concern or issue is the experience that the community probes and analyzes. This concept will be developed more fully in chapters 7 and 9 on the biblical and liturgical symbols of faith. In all cases the catechesis is inductive, beginning from an experience and moving to the second movement of interpretation and reflection on a faith symbol. The process described below will be the same for all age groups, but on occasion the experience to be considered will be the religious question with which the people are concerned.

In adult catechesis done on an occasional basis, the parish director of catechesis begins planning the catechesis by recognizing the interests and concerns of the people in the parish. Hopefully the parish will do a needs assessment, which will help the parish leaders recognize the concerns of the people. Many times these concerns are readily known by parish pastoral ministers, but these leaders do not relate what they know to parish catechesis. For example, the geographic area in which the people live may be a high crime area or an area where many people are out of work. It may be a wealthy suburban community or a neighborhood of elderly people. Those characteristics already tell the catechist or director of catechetical ministry something about what the concerns and interests of the people are. Parish leaders need to listen to their people's concerns and respond by setting up "conversations" on the topic of their interest. This will mean that the catechist may need to become familiar with the implication of such concerns and be able to relate them to Christian faith.[4] But that is, after all, the work of the director of catechetical ministry and the parish team.

Symbolic catechesis differs from most other "experiential" approaches in that it honors human experience as a *locus* of revelation and begins with a reflection on a human issue not as a lead-in to a theological topic but simply because this particular human experience is a concern of the community. In symbolic catechesis the human experience leads us to whatever faith symbols relate to the experience. The experience leads us not only to reflect on symbols of faith but to live with them and by them.

In symbolic catechesis the community, led by the catechist, analyzes, evaluates, considers, critiques, and studies the experience, concern, or issue that brought it together. In the beginning of the session it does this without reference to religion or the use of religious language. If the concern is how one copes with life as a care giver to an elderly or sick parent, the catechist may lead the community by asking one or several questions similar to the following ones:

"Will you share with us your story of what you do as a care giver?"

"What is the most rewarding experience of being a care giver?"

"What is the most difficult thing for you as a care giver?"

125

"How would you describe your relationship to the person for
whom you care?"
"How has being a care giver affected your relationships with
family or friends?"
"Why did you become a care giver?"
"Who helps or supports you in your care giving?"
"How long do you think you can continue to do this?"

These or similar questions enable the members of the group
to understand what it means to be a care giver and how this service
affects the care giver's life as well as the life of the person who
receives the care. Through this discussion, members of the catechetical community recognize that others share their experiences
and concerns. The participants can tell their stories and ask their
questions without fear of negative judgment. They will hear from
the questions and concerns of others how this common experience
affects them. The participants will, because they share a life experience, reflect and perhaps question the way in which the culture
views their common experience.

In symbolic catechesis the catechist invites, leads, and commends to the catechized that they examine and reflect on the experience which is their present concern and which has brought them
together. This analysis will not be superficial but will be a probing,
critical analysis and an honest dialogue about how their common
experience affects their lives. What does this experience say to each
of those who share it? What does it say to us as a community? What
does our family or our culture say about this experience?

Symbolic catechesis is not counseling. It is an examination of a
human concern but not a clinical examination of that concern. It is
a search for meaning in the context of faith. If someone needs counseling or professional guidance, the work of the catechist is to assist
the individual in finding the professional help that is needed.

In a process of correlation or association, the community
relates its concern to the church tradition or faith symbols and seeks
to understand its question in light of its faith. The community
relates the Tradition to the concern and as it does so learns about

both its question and the Tradition. In this process light is shed on both life and faith.

Movement 2: Correlating the Experience with a Faith Symbol. Human experience does not stand alone in catechesis. In catechesis we do not take any experience, whether it is the death of a loved one, destruction from a natural disaster, the marriage of a son or daughter, or the winning of the lottery, and simply examine it without relating it to a symbol of faith. Critical reflection apart from faith is certainly of value, but critical reflection that does not turn at some point to a recognition of the presence of God's revelation through the church is not catechesis.

Symbols of Christian faith include all actions, truths, rituals, and people by which the church expresses its faith in Jesus as Lord. The biblical symbols are normative and preeminent symbols in the faith community we call church. The Bible is, as Karl Rahner often observes, "the church's book." The Bible describes the experiences of our Jewish and Christian ancestors, was written by our ancestors, and accepted, proclaimed, preserved, and canonized by the church. Doctrinal symbols, particularly the creeds, the history of the church, and the witness of Christian heroes and heroines are also symbols of faith. Liturgical symbols, particularly the liturgical assembly with its actions and words in the celebration of the sacraments, express the church's faith and summon us to transformation. These symbols may befriend and authenticate the cultural interpretation of an experience (e.g., caring for the sick), letting us know that it leads to personal and community freedom. Or they may confront the cultural meaning (assisted suicide), indicating that the cultural meaning leads to subjection or dehumanization. Faith symbols help us explore the meaning of ordinary daily experiences.

Symbolic catechesis is a ministry in which the community seeks to understand how our lives relate to our faith and how our faith gives meaning to our lives. The community may not be able to articulate fully the teachings of the church, but as a Christian community it professes that Jesus is Lord, that God is Trinity and that the Trinity is *for* us. It is the church, the people of God, the body of Christ, both human and divine, a community of saints and sinners.

As church it is one, but obviously not perfectly one; it is holy but not fully holy; catholic, but it does not yet embrace all peoples; apostolic in that it accepts the witness of the apostles as normative for Christian belief, but still struggles to understand that belief. It is seeking deeper faith, fuller hope, love beyond understanding.

The first movement of symbolic catechesis is an analysis of a life experience. The second movement involves a consideration of a meaning of that life experience by *correlating* or associating that experience with a symbol of faith from the Bible and/or Tradition.[5] The question is: How do this experience and this faith symbol relate? There is not what Gregory Baum calls a "one-to-one correspondence" between the symbol and the experience. There is, if we free our imaginations to respond to the symbol, probably a surprising relationship between the experience and the faith symbol. Symbolic catechesis is the church in small groups seeking to understand daily life and faith by examining together the symbols of both life and faith.

Ordinarily the catechist is the one who introduces the faith dimension and invites the community to consider what the church has to say to us about a particular experience. She may bring to the community a biblical story or passage, a doctrinal statement, the story of the life of a Christian who shared their experience, or a liturgical celebration to help them discover what meaning faith gives to life. For example, with a community of care givers the catechist may invite the community to consider a Gospel story that demonstrates the need for and availability of supportive and care giving relationships. She may choose a passage that speaks to the importance of every individual human life and of God's care for those who are troubled. She could reflect on the story of Lazarus with care giver Martha's statement of rebuke to Jesus, "Lord, if you had been here, my brother would not have died" (Jn 11:21). Or she might consider the weariness of the care givers in her group and reflect with them on one of the sayings of Jesus, such as "Come to me, all you who labor and are burdened, and I will give you rest" (Mt 14:28).

On the other hand, she could consider a theological understanding or doctrinal teaching as a way of understanding the experience. For example, initially the fourth commandment reminded the

Israelites crossing the desert that they could not simply desert their elders who were having trouble continuing on the journey, but that they were to care for them and help them complete the journey. Taking care of the elderly has been a responsibility of the faith community for millennia. How does this story fashion us as care givers of a parent? What response does this story evoke in us individually and/or as a community of faith?

Or the catechist may turn to the works of mercy as Christian expressions of the grandeur of a humankind created in God's image. Depending on the circumstances of those being cared for, she could turn to the church's "Pastoral Care of the Sick" in the liturgical rites.[6] The examination of the church's attitude toward its sick members is described in the "General Introduction to the Pastoral Care of the Sick," and this document might be part of the interpretation or correlation. If it seems appropriate, the question of "assisted suicide" and the church's teaching regarding the rejection of that action as a form of euthanasia might be a way to understand and respond to the concerns of the community. The catechist and the community will take time to reflect critically on the faith symbol and to determine how it relates to their particular life experience. The community cannot seek simplistic solutions or ready-made answers, but they can with reverence, study, and prayer consider the meaning that the faith symbol gives to the experience. This very act is tradition, a "handing on" of the symbols of faith.

The catechist draws on whatever biblical, theological, liturgical, historical, or biographical symbols she believes will assist the catechized to comprehend their concern. This correlation of life and faith can take many directions, and the direction it takes will depend on movement 1, in which the catechized analyze their experience. Hopefully the catechist will know those in the catechesis well enough to have some idea of the primary questions they may ask. Since the catechist may not always know what turn the initial conversation of the community will take, she needs to be prepared to relate several different faith symbols to the experience in the correlation conversation.

No single catechesis will completely respond to any question nor solve any problem, but participation in and correlation of faith symbols can enlighten and give hope to the catechized. It can bring them insight. It may help them to see that the church is concerned about their daily lives and that it offers the wisdom and experience of its life to the individual and the community. Sometimes the teaching of the church clearly fits the needs of the catechized, but peoples' needs are so different that there is seldom one response that fits everyone. More will be said about this in chapter 8 on the use of doctrine in catechesis.

Symbolic catechesis focuses on human issues and concerns before pursuing religious topics. But after considering the meaning of the human issue, it turns to the faith symbols and assesses critically how this faith symbol relates to the issue. The community moves from its experience to a biblical story and suddenly sees the story in a new light, it sees it related to ordinary daily experience. The community follows this same process when it correlates its experience with church teaching. The process draws men and women from the world in which the church sometimes seems irrelevant, to a three-dimensional church of meaning which is with them as comforter and liberator and brother and sister in the midst of its pain and loss, or its joy and hope. Human concerns and faith symbols are not unrelated. They inform one another. Our experiences lead to faith and our faith leads to a recognition of the meaning and glory of human life. Our experiences tell us that life has moments of supreme joy and deep pain, and our faith tells us that the Mystery is with us lovingly even in the most silent and perhaps painful moments of our life. Catechesis enables us to welcome the Mystery in our lives.

Movement 3: Moving Outward from the Experience to Acts of Justice Together. The reflection on experience and the correlating of the experience with symbols of faith are the first two movements of symbolic catechesis. The third movement brings the community to look beyond itself to others who are in need. Every time the church gathers it looks out beyond its own concerns to the needs of others. When the Synod of Bishops at the Second General Assembly spoke of justice, they were unequivocal:

> Action on behalf of justice and participation in the transformation of the world fully appear to us as a constitutive dimension of the preaching of the Gospel, or, in other words, of the church's mission for the redemption of the human race and its liberation from every oppressive situation.[7]

Action on behalf of justice is an integral expression of Christian faith. Justice is not optional for the Christian community.

Doing justice, releasing the captive, feeding the hungry, sheltering the homeless is the Christian's ordinary way of life. Being Christian means being just. The Gospel of Luke records Jesus' understanding of his life as one of doing justice. Jesus says:

> The Spirit of the Lord is upon me,
> because he has anointed me
> to bring good news to the poor.
> He has sent me to proclaim release to the captives
> and recovery of sight to the blind,
> to let the oppressed go free,
> to proclaim the year of the Lord's favor. (Lk 4:18–19)

The Spirit is with Jesus. He is the "anointed one," the Messiah, who has come to inaugurate the reign of God. And this reign will be one in which "glad tidings" are brought to the poor, captives are liberated, the blind see, and the oppressed go free. At the beginning of his ministry Jesus proclaimed that the end time had come: "Repent, and believe in the gospel" (Mk 1:15). God reigns whenever we repent, accept conversion, and act justly. For Christians there is no option. Justice is at the heart of Christian life.

As the incarnation of God, Jesus is the fullness of revelation. He reveals the Mystery through his life committed to building God's reign, a reign of mercy and justice, of peace and love. Jesus' ministry demonstrates his dedication to those who are in need, the marginalized, the outcasts, the poor, the grieving. The Gospels are a magnificent mosaic of the words and actions of Jesus for those who are oppressed or shunned in any way. He reached out to

Samaritans. He chose women for friends and disciples. He ate with tax collectors and associated with prostitutes. He embraced the children. He preached the word of compassion and generosity for all who are powerless.

In preaching the reign of God through both his actions and words Jesus brought down upon himself the vindictiveness of those whose priorities did not include care and compassion for the poor and oppressed. By his message Jesus intimidated and threatened the powerful. He posed a danger to their world of riches and power. Jesus' preaching of the coming reign of God, in which those who hunger and thirst for justice would be satisfied, brought him to his death.

Jesus' commitment to building the reign of God continued in the apostolic church. From the beginning it concerned itself with the care of its widows and orphans. Luke tells us in Acts that "there was not a needy person among them, for as many as owned lands or houses sold them and brought the proceeds of what was sold. They laid it at the apostles' feet, and it was distributed to each as any had need" (Acts 4:34–35). And when the Greek Christians complained that their widows were neglected, the twelve chose deacons to serve them.

The concerns of the poor and powerless were not marginal for the Christian community. Christians shared whatever they had among themselves and with others. They modeled themselves on Jesus, who not only was the one without a place to lay his head but the one who conspicuously cared for those whom the culture marginalized. From the beginning, when the community shared all things in common according to each one's need, the church has seen itself as a missionary community whose responsibility extends beyond itself. It is the nature of the community to move outward in justice and mercy.

This third movement in symbolic catechesis is not simply a reminder that each one of us ought to be just and to decide to do something for others in the next week. This movement urges the community *as a community* to so some concrete action that will relieve the suffering of people. One question is: What structures of society breed injustice and how can we change those structures?

The catechists urge the community *as a corporate ecclesial body* to reach out in love and compassion.

Doing justice may mean setting up kitchens for feeding the hungry. Ideally it would be setting up a system where no one need be hungry. It may mean building homes with Habitat for Humanity. Doing justice means giving clothing to Goodwill or to the St. Vincent de Paul Society, but it also involves working to change the system that demeans people so that they do not have adequate clothing. The catechist will need to decide if the catechetical community is ready to extend practical justice to individuals or communities who are in need, or is ready to try to change the system that causes inequities.

In symbolic catechesis the community does justice. It decides to do it and it carries out its decision. It may decide to do what seems like a small action, for example, setting up a schedule where care givers can be released from their responsibility for a day a month or a day a week, or maybe even an hour a day. Or it may decide to do something about the housing regulations and rules in its community, rules and regulations that keep the poor from finding a decent place to live. The most important thing is that the catechetical community always be urged to involve itself in works of justice, recognizing that for Christians, for Catholics, this is not an optional work. It is required.

The United States Catholic Church has been a leader in recognizing that reaching out in mercy and love to others is an integral dimension of catechetical ministry. Chapter 7 of *Sharing the Light of Faith*, "Catechesis for Social Ministry," states that "catechesis for justice, mercy, and peace is a continuing process which concerns every person and every age."[8] And it reminds catechists that "catechesis concerning justice, mercy, and peace should be a part of the catechetical process. It should include efforts to motivate people to act on behalf of these values."[9]

Many of us have not yet learned how to do this well in our catechesis. Some catechists never had this kind of experience in their own catechesis so it is a bit awkward for them to initiate it with others. It seems "added on." But it cannot be "added on." It needs to be an integral dimension of the catechesis. It will become so when catechists recognize that doing justice together is not an optional exercise in catechesis, just as the doing of justice together is not an optional action for a Christian community.

Movement 4: Praying Together about the Experience Through Rituals. One day while participating in a parish catechetical session I heard the catechist say, "Let's close with a quickie prayer." And so she did. The people were hardly out of their chairs before the prayer was over. On several occasions I have been present to hear the catechist say, "We don't have time for a closing prayer tonight. I'll see all of you next week." Or the closing prayer has not been prepared and the leader does not invite the community to participate. Frequently there is no ritual nor are there ministries in the closing prayer. Most of the time, the priest or catechist simply says a short prayer, if a prayer is said at all. Seldom is the ritual prayer of the group significant.

With symbolic catechesis this changes. The communal ritual prayer of the group is a priority. It is the climax of the entire session or meeting. It is that toward which all other actions point. Everything that goes before it prepares for it, for in the communal prayer the integration of community building, the searching for meaning through faith symbols and the doing of justice become one. Here a synthesis takes place. The catechesis comes to completion as the community prays together.

The reason the closing prayer is a priority is that communal ritual prayer is a priority in the life of the Christian community. It has been through the ages a primary characteristic of both Jewish and Christian life. Jesus introduced himself in the synagogue during prayer. He read from the prophets during that service. During his lifetime he came to Jerusalem to celebrate the great Jewish ritual feast of Passover.

Jesus' community of disciples participated in communal synagogue prayer and met together regularly for their own ritual of "the breaking of the bread." Christians celebrated the life-death-resurrection of Christ in the paschal meal they called the breaking of the bread. They kept the day of resurrection as a sacred day of prayer, and as the decades and centuries passed, the community kept the year sacred through seasons of prayer: Advent, Lent, Easter, Pentecost, and Ordinary time. These seasons carry the community through cycles of time which commemorate the life-death-resurrection-glorification of Jesus the Lord. And it was not only seasons but even hours of the day that the church consecrated with communal ritual prayer. It gathered early in the morning for "morning prayer" and closed the day with "evening" and later "night" prayer. Praying together through ritual is integral to Christian life. We cannot really conceive of a Christian faith community without ritual prayer.

In symbolic catechesis the community begins the meeting with an introductory prayer that sets the tone for the evening. An example of an opening prayer in a session on care giving would be:

> Caring God,
> Your care for us is unconditional and unlimited.
> Help us to be loving care givers to those for whom we care.
> We ask this in the name of the Father, and of the Son, and of
>   the Holy Spirit.
> Amen.

This prayer moves the community from activity to quietness, or from action to thoughtful reflection on some event or concern of daily life.

The closing or climatic prayer is a longer and fuller prayer. It will bring together the insights and questions of the session or meeting, not in a didactic linear way but through simple words and ritual actions that lift the heart and stir the imagination. Prayer happens only when the community is familiar with its form and so can enter into it freely, not concerned about what will happen next. C. S. Lewis wrote at the beginning of his book on prayer:

> Every service [or prayer] is a structure of acts and words through which we receive a sacrament or repent, or supplicate, or adore. And it enables us to do these things best—if you like, it "works" best—when, through long familiarity, we don't have to think about it. As long as you notice, and have to count the steps, you are not yet dancing but only learning to dance. A good shoe is a shoe you don't notice. Good reading becomes possible when

135

you need not consciously think about eyes, or light, or print or spelling. The perfect church service would be one we were almost unaware of; our attention would have been on God.[10]

Familiar ritual prayer, where we don't have to think of the steps but can recognize and respond to God's presence with us, frees us to praise and give thanks and repent and ask for what we need.

Because Christians have often prayed the Liturgy of the Word, they don't have to think about the structure. As Lewis says, "it fits." It is familiar. At the same time the structure allows for innovation and change. It does not slavishly follow a pattern that induces boredom. It has much that is familiar and a little that is new.

A closing ritual prayer that follows the structure of the Liturgy of the Word will include the following parts:

Liturgy of the Word
Gathering hymn or instrumental music
Opening prayer
First reading (if having two)
Response (silence or psalm verse)
Alleluia (sung)
Second reading (Gospel)
Ritual action before or after homily
Homily (optional)
Petitions
Our Father
Sending forth

The prayer will usually include a ritual action related to the catechesis and the reading.

In the communal ritual prayer the catechist integrates what happened earlier in the session into the prayer. The opening prayer from the beginning of the session could be the beginning of the ritual prayer. It would recall the beginning of the session and all that has happened since the prayer was first said. It would, hopefully, have a fuller meaning when prayed the second time.

A biblical reading will follow the opening prayer. Only one reading is necessary. When a biblical passage is used in the second movement, that same biblical passage may be proclaimed during the prayer. For example, if the reflection on care giving used the story of Lazarus with Martha's statement, "Lord, if you had been here, my brother would not have died," it could be proclaimed in the prayer. Or if the community reflected on the saying of Jesus, "Come to me all you who labor and are burdened, and I will give you rest," that biblical passage would be proclaimed in the prayer. The point is to use the same biblical passage or a portion of it in the prayer as was used during the catechesis, because it will now have enriched meaning for this particular community. The proclamation of this biblical passage is not meant to be a cognitive summary of what the passage says. Rather, the proclaimed biblical passage will, it is hoped, stir the imagination, trigger the memory, and bring the community together with the Lord in its praise or lament, its thanksgiving or petition.

A homily follows as a response to the reading. The catechist could give a short three- to five-minute homily, though a member of the group might preach if he or she is able to prepare it and relate the reading to the group's concerns. Again, the homily will not be a summary of the community's conversation but it will offer insight, just one insight, which flows from the session and which the members of the community can take home with them as a word of faith, hope, and love. Keep it less than five minutes.

The petitions that follow the homily will include prayers for justice in which those in need will be remembered. In these prayers we identify ourselves as church and pray for the whole church, looking out beyond ourselves to the universal church and the world. In a session on care giving this is a time to pray for those to whom the care givers give care, for all those who are in need of care but have no one to care for them, and for other care givers. It is a time when the community looks out beyond itself and prays for people throughout the world who are in need. The Our Father with its seven petitions completes the prayers of petition.

A ritual action such as a blessing by the catechist or a sharing of the sign of peace and love may be inserted at some point in the prayer. Usually this action comes as a response to the readings, either before or after the homily. There are many ritual actions that may be appropriate at different times: the embrace of peace, the blessing with water, foot washing, a simple anointing for mission. If the reading does not suggest a particular ritual action, the catechist(s) needs to decide which action best fits this community at this time. If this was a community of care givers, I would consider how they care for the physical needs of their clients or how they use the sense of touch in their caring and would then probably have a ritual action in which I would anoint their hands with perfumed oil. While doing the anointing I would ask the Holy Spirit to strengthen them for their service.

Silence is always a part of Christian ritual prayer. A rhythm of silence and word or silence and action pervades the church's prayer. This rhythm gives members of the community an opportunity to recognize the presence of the Mystery in their lives, and it gives the community time to respond to this presence. This communal prayer is, hopefully, a time when this group of people experiences as a community the presence of the Mystery with them.

The ritual prayer calls for different ministries and different ministers. All who are present and participating make up the assembly. The leader or presider comes from the assembly and leads it in prayer as a conductor leads the orchestra. A lector proclaims the word. A cantor leads the sung response to the reading. A homilist interprets the proclaimed word. Another person ministers by leading the intercessory prayers. The presider gathers the community together in the beginning and at the end blesses them and sends them forth to serve others. All ministers emerge from the assembly in order to serve it. In the prayer, the prose of the catechesis becomes the poetry of prayer.

Everything in the catechetical session that preceded the prayer is brought to the prayer. And in the experience of prayer the community's pain and joy, fear and hope are integrated in an environment of peace and acceptance, of praise and thanksgiving. Hopefully, in its closing prayer the catechesis reaches its fullness. No one can program an experience of the Mystery, but if we attend to the quality of our prayer, it may become that special time when we recognize the Mystery with us. The prayer and the session end as do all Christian gatherings with the sending forth of the community to do justice.

The Process Is the Content in Symbolic Catechesis

Symbolic catechesis involves a process that is itself a living out of Christian faith. In the apostolic era the Christian was one within a community of people who professed Jesus as Lord, gathered on Sunday for "the breaking of the bread," prayed daily, served the poor and those in need, and accepted the evangelizing word preached by the apostles (Acts 2:42–46). They were one in faith, holy in prayer and works of justice, catholic in reaching out to everyone, and apostolic in professing the gospel the apostles preached.[11] Symbolic catechesis integrates these actions of being one, holy, catholic, and apostolic in its process. The process is the content of catechesis. The process of symbolic catechesis is itself a living out of Christian faith.

Symbolic catechesis builds up the four characteristics of the church (it is one, holy, catholic, and apostolic) in a specific way. It builds oneness by gathering individuals into a community, by studying together, by praying together, by doing justice together. It builds holiness by inviting the community to share its life and faith in prayer, in study, and in actions of justice. It fosters catholicity by motivating the community to look outside itself to others in justice and love and to recognize the witness of holiness in the lives of people of every ethnic and racial group. It strengthens the apostolic nature of the community by encouraging the community to share its stories, beliefs, values, and life with others. Whereas some catechetical approaches emphasize the building of a just society or the learning of doctrine, symbolic catechesis integrates the four movements of catechesis into a single integrated catechesis of life. It emphasizes *the living of Christian life*.

What draws adults together for symbolic catechesis are the life concerns they have in common and the faith that they share. For adults particular experiences, such as the death of a loved one, the

139

stress of rearing children, the loss of a job, moving to a new community far from family and friends, bring them to seek counsel or to turn to their faith for understanding and strength.[12] The question What is going on in my life, and how do I live with it? may not be articulated, but it leads people to join groups that are concerned about the same interests or concerns. For faithful people these issues often move them to join social or volunteer groups, but if their parish community seems at all interested in such concerns, they may turn to it.

Symbolic catechesis presumes Christian faith on the part of the participants, but not a particular stage of faith.[13] It is for those who have little knowledge and perhaps a tenuous commitment as well as for those who are strong participatory members of the faith community. It is an evangelical catechesis designed particularly for adults but suitable for people of all ages and all stages of faith. Each member of the community, whatever his or her stage of faith, supports the others and assists them to grow in faith.

Originally symbolic catechesis was designed for adults, though study and use indicate that with some modifications the process works well with children and young people. The process presumes a catechetical community of seven to fifteen persons. These persons meet weekly for four to six weeks at a time convenient for them to consider an interest or issue they have in common.[14] The catechist gathers the adults by advertising in the parish bulletin, by e-mail, posters, and announcements which invite all who are interested in a particular topic to come to a meeting. For example, the topic of interest might be caring for a sick or elderly parent, or single parenting, preparation for a sacrament, or interest in some book or books of the Bible. The announcement invites people who are interested to meet at a specific time and place. Ways of inviting people will be described more fully in chapter 6.

This is what the *General Directory for Catechesis* calls an "occasional" form of catechesis for adults. It does not continue for fifteen or twenty weeks, as do programs for children or youth, but continues for three to six weeks, according to the needs of the participants. The *General Directory for Catechesis* describes other forms of catechesis, all of which may be occasional: a vital study of Scripture, a Christian reading of events, liturgical catechesis, initiatives of spiritual formation, education in the faith.[15] Symbolic catechesis is a process in which the community considers a life experience, Scripture study, liturgy, moral questions, spirituality, or theology and relates the topic of its interest to its faith life. Frequently parishes offer occasional catechesis for adults during the weeks of Lent in order to give parishioners an opportunity to refresh themselves spiritually.

Symbolic Catechesis as the Building of Community

Christian faith is a communal enterprise. We come to faith through others and we share in the faith of the church. We hear about the church from others. We see the church in others. We become the church with others. We enter into the "household of Christ," and become part of the "household of faith" because others have invited us to be Christian with them.[16] The household of the faith began with Abraham and Sarah. It was through them and their descendants, through Jesus, the son of Mary, that our faith was handed on. Jesus bequeathed to us his community of disciples, the "household of Christ," which we call the church. It is into that household of faith from Jesus, through the disciples and the ever renewing church for two millennia, that the sacraments of initiation introduce us. We are born into the household of the human family and a particular family. We are baptized into the household of faith, the church.

This church shares its faith with us and gives us identity by handing on its life through its commitment, its insights, its values, its stories. It gives us language, a verbal language, a ritual language, and a performative or ethical language by which we can speak both to the Mystery who is *for* us and about the Mystery who is always with us. The church tells us that this Mystery is a Mystery of love, is in fact a trinitarian community of love always engendering life and always spiraling out beyond itself in a creating way. The church reminds us that we are made in the image of God and that the Holy Spirit dwells within us as love and light and wisdom.

141

One of the primary strengths of symbolic catechesis is that the process itself both discloses and builds relationships among the participants, it builds the church. This dimension is so strong that at one point I thought of calling the process "relational catechesis" rather than "symbolic catechesis." But "symbolic catechesis" is a more accurate name, since everything done in catechesis is a participation in a symbol of God's revelation.

Symbolic catechesis focuses on the community as a corporate body, the "body of Christ," as well as on the individuals as members of the community. The catechesis is not simply an individual, one-to-one dialogue among the participants. It is not a "Jesus and I" dialogue, but a "Jesus and Us" conversation. The community is united as one people in its commitment and vision of the nature of all reality. And it is this unity that the *community* draws on in its search for the Mystery. Symbolic catechesis brings together people who are one in faith, one in hope, one in love, and unified by a common quest. It is within the fullness of this community, which is never cut off from the larger parish community or the faith community throughout the world, that symbolic catechesis takes place.

Building the community is a major work of the catechist. It is a countercultural activity because the United States culture exalts the myth of the individual. The culture exalts the individual above the community. The "common good" takes second place to the good of the individual. People pull themselves up "by their own bootstraps." This myth and this attitude foster an insensibility toward others within the human community. The building up of relationships within the catechetical community of common faith, common values, and common beliefs relates both the individuals and the community to other communities. It strengthens familial and cultural bonds.

Building community means building relationships among the catechized, but it also means building relationships between the catechetical community and the parish, between the catechetical community and the world. The need to be conscious of our relationship with other Christians and with Jewish and Muslim people is an essential goal of catechesis. Symbolic catechesis

142

must be ecumenical, fostering reverence for other churches and religious faiths, examining how we differ and how much we have in common. It is of great importance that catechists speak of the Jewish community reverentially, as our brothers and sisters, our ancestors in the faith. As we avoid all kinds of sexist or racist language, so we must avoid any language that would be offensive to other churches or other religious faiths.

The catechist integrates the building up of the community into the four movements which together make up the catechetical act. In symbolic catechesis it is the community that reflects, correlates, and interprets the primary concern of the group. The community examines how well it is carrying out its responsibility for justice and love, and it is the community that prays together. The catechist as leader and resource person is a member of this community, and she constantly builds relationships among the members of the group. Symbolic catechesis is in every facet of its process a communal enterprise.

Symbolic catechesis offers groups of people a safe harbor in which they can come together to ask questions, seek meaning, share pain, express faith, do justice, pray together and in a word, *be church*. It does not give simplistic or even easy answers to every question, but it does build community relationships as it promotes an increase in faith among the participants. It recognizes the presence of evil in the world affecting our daily lives but it acknowledges the presence of God as being more powerful than all evil influences.

The integration of the four movements of catechesis into one catechetical act is at the heart of symbolic catechesis. Each act has its own focus, but all four are related. No one act is more important than another. It is the integration of all four into one that identifies symbolic catechesis. One way in which the community integrates the four movements is the recognition that all four movements involve consideration of the same concern of human experience. All four show how the Holy Mystery is with us and for us always.

In Summary

Symbolic catechesis is an approach that seems particularly well suited for the church in the United States in the new century. It does not hesitate to recognize and respond to the demands of cultural values and standards by ratifying them when they correspond to gospel values and by challenging them when they glorify and promote values opposed to the gospel. Symbolic catechesis recognizes the good in society and in a prophetic fashion it condemns that which is immoral or oppressive.

This approach takes seriously the understanding that human experience, particularly communal or shared human experience is a locus of revelation and self-communication. Our recognition of the presence of the Mystery of God in everyday life, in our relationships, our technology, and our commerce changes the way we interpret and understand these experiences. The Holy Spirit is always with us as church, and we turn to the church to help us understand and appreciate how the Mystery graces our world.

How does symbolic catechesis differ from other recent catechetical approaches? It is structured on the four dimensions of Christian life. It differs through its process, a process that includes experiencing the basic elements of Christian life together and synthesizing the catechesis in common prayer. All four of the characteristics of Christian life—that is, communal life, the teaching of the apostles, the works of justice, and community prayer—are each *equally important* dimensions of symbolic catechesis.

Although correlating the daily experiences of the people with the faith symbols of the church is an essential dimension of symbolic catechesis, it is not always the easiest thing for the catechist to do. The following four chapters will examine "the signs of the times," that is, the events of daily life as a place where God is present and active *for* us (chapter 6), the Bible as the preeminent faith symbol of the community (chapter 7), the teaching, life, and witness of the church as a faith symbol (chapter 8), and the liturgical life of the church as a faith symbol (chapter 9). The chapters will consider the natural, biblical, ecclesial, and liturgical symbols of God's presence and examine how they relate in catechesis and in life.

FURTHER READINGS

Catechism of the Catholic Church. Washington, D.C.: United States Catholic Conference, 1994.

Congregation for the Clergy. *General Directory for Catechesis*. Washington, D.C.: United States Catholic Conference, 1997.

Gallagher, Maureen. *The Art of Catechesis: What You Need to Be, Know, and Do*. With a Foreword by Archbishop Rembert G. Weakland. New York: Paulist Press, 1998.

Warren, Michael. "Communications, Communication, Communion," in *The Echo Within: Emerging Issues in Religious Education*. A Tribute to Berard L. Merthaler, O.F.M., Conv., ed. Catherine Dooley, O.P., and Mary Collins, O.S.B., 207–23. Allen, Tex.: Thomas More, 1997.

CHAPTER 6

Catechesis as a Critique of Life and Culture

Symbolic catechesis is a ministry in which the catechist invites the members of the community to conversion, to repentance, and to a change in their way of life. The catechist offers this invitation in the four movements of (1) reflecting on a common experience, (2) interpreting that experience through faith symbols, (3) moving outward to acts of justice, and (4) climaxing in praying together about the experience. Most catechists have been coordinating some of these movements. Other movements may be new to them. The more difficult movement for many catechists is the reflection on a common experience. How does one do that? What experiences are to be considered? This chapter will consider the life experiences or "signs of the times" and cultural experiences and values that are the subject of the first movement and describe how they become the subject of the catechesis. The final section will offer suggestions for pastoral planning, preparing, promoting, and processing.

Critiquing the "Signs of the Times"

The Gospel of Matthew tells us that "the Pharisees and Sadducees came, and to test Jesus they asked him to show them a sign from heaven. He answered them, 'When it is evening, you say, "It will be fair weather, for the sky is red." And in the morning, "It will be stormy today, for the sky is red and threatening." You know how to interpret the appearance of the sky, but you cannot interpret the signs of the times'" (Mt 16:1–3). The *signs of the times* "give hints of God's will in each age, but believers must be attentive to them." This saying, says Benedict Viviano, "is an invitation to the hermeneutics of history and as such a permanent challenge to the church."[1] It is a challenge whose meaning for the church was rediscovered by Pope John XXIII, Pope Paul VI, and the Second Vatican Council.

Pope John XXIII used this biblical passage to encourage the church to interpret what is happening in the world today. He urged Catholics to recognize the signs of the times and how they are influencing our time so that they could proclaim the gospel in language that not only is attentive to but also challenges today's world. Pope John wrote: "We make our own the recommendation of Jesus that one should know how to distinguish the signs of the times."[2] He repeated this recommendation in the opening address of the Second Vatican Council, saying: "Divine Providence is leading us to a new order of human relations which, by [men's] own efforts and even beyond their very expectations, are directed toward the fulfillment of God's superior and inscrutable designs….It is easy to discern this reality if we consider attentively *the world of today*…,"[3] by which he meant the signs of the times.

Pope John XXIII read daily events as "signs of the times" and in so doing developed the notion of what the "signs of the times" were.[4] In his encyclical *Peace on Earth (Pacem in Terris)*, written a few months before his death, the pope ended each chapter by suggesting ways to interpret signs of the times.[5] These paragraphs are called variously, "Characteristics of the Present Day," or "Signs of the Times," or "Modern Developments."

Some of the signs of the times described in *Peace on Earth* (1963) are (1) people are recognizing that disputes between states should be resolved by negotiation rather than by war;[6] (2) the working class has gradually gained ground in economic and public affairs; (3) women are now taking a part in public life, and they will no longer tolerate being treated as material instruments; and (4) human society has taken on a new appearance in social and political life, and there will no longer be nations that rule and nations that are ruled.[7]

Pope Paul VI followed John XXIII's pattern and in his encyclical *On the Church (Ecclesiam Suam)* called for the church to "enter into dialogue with the world in which it lives."[8] Some of the signs of the times that Pope Paul enunciated are the need for peace among nations and social classes, the destitution and famine that still plague entire populations, the advance of new nations toward freedom and independence, the current of modern thought over against Christian culture, the denial of the rights of free citizens and human beings, and the moral problems concerning the population explosion.[9] He anticipated the *Pastoral Constitution on the Church in the Modern World*, which states:

> In every age, the church carries the responsibility of reading the signs of the times and of interpreting them in the light of the Gospel, if it is to carry out its task. In language intelligible to every generation, it should be able to answer the ever recurring questions which people ask about the meaning of this present life and the life to come and how one is related to the other.[10]

The constitution develops this idea further:

> The People of God…try to discern the true signs of God's presence and purpose in the events, the needs and the desires which it shares with the rest of humanity today. For faith casts a new light on everything and makes known the full ideal which God has set for humanity….[11]

Article 44 makes discerning the meaning of the signs of the times the work of the entire community:

> With the help of the Holy Spirit it is the task of the whole people of God, particularly of its pastors and theologians, to listen to and distinguish the many voices of our times and to interpret them in the light of God's word, in order that the revealed truth may be more deeply penetrated, better understood, and more suitably presented.

What are the signs of the times? And how do the people of God critique them? How can catechists help them to do so?

One might think from the previous paragraphs that "signs of the times" included only major societal events. Major human events like wars between people of different religions, or floods and soil erosion caused by excess logging, the abuse and murder of children, the generosity of volunteers for charity organizations can be read more easily as signs of the times than personal or less cosmic events. But the council spoke of personal events also. It exhorted priests in the *Decree on the Ministry and Life of Priests (MLP)* to "be willing to listen to lay people, give brotherly consideration to their wishes, and recognize their experience and competence in the different fields of human activity. In this way they will be able to recognize along with them the signs of the times."[12]

In the *Declaration on Religious Liberty (RL)* the council noted that there were governments that gave people the freedom to practice their religion freely and other governments in which the "public authorities themselves try to deter the citizens from professing their religion." It stated that the council noted that it "gladly welcomes the first of these two facts as a happy sign of the time. In sorrow, however, it denounces the second as deplorable."[13] Through faith the council looked at a sign of the time and critiqued it.

That is what symbolic catechesis is all about, critiquing life and culture. In symbolic catechesis the community looks at the signs of the times that are evident in the community's life and critically reflects on those realities. It interprets them in the light of the symbols of faith, the Bible and church teaching, life, and worship. The community also recognizes that culture and life experiences help the community to critique faith symbols. A dialogue is going on between culture or life experiences and the faith of the community, and sometimes the culture or the life experience leads the community to reinterpret its faith symbols.

For example, today the church is speaking out against the death penalty or capital punishment. The United States bishops pointed out that "the value of human life is being undermined by the death penalty."[14] Yet in the past Christian emperors did not hesitate to use the death penalty, and the church itself used the death penalty for heretics. The church learned from its experience and culture in dialogue with the gospel. The moral rule is changing. This happens through the experience/culture/faith dialogue, which is a process that unites life and faith. Other examples of such change would be the church's teaching on religious liberty, on slavery, and usury.[15]

Theologian Edward Schillebeeckx points out that the "gulf between *faith* and *experience* is one of the fundamental reasons for the present-day crisis among Christians who are faithful to the church."[16] Thoughtful people cannot help but reflect on their experiences, which are for them the signs of their times. They consider significant societal events and ask, "What does this mean? Does my faith help me to make sense of what is going on? Or is my faith understanding in conflict with my common sense?" How can we close the gulf between our experience and our faith?

During the past century theologians began to probe more fully the relationship between experience and faith. Dermot Lane states that "one of the most significant developments in Christian theology in this century has been the recovery of experience as an integral element in the exercise of theology."[17] Donald Gelpi describes this recovery as the "turn to experience" by theologians.[18]

Before catechists can analyze the "signs of the times," or "life experiences," of people, they need to know the meaning of the word "experience" and to consider how individual and communal experiences are signs of the times.

The Meaning of Experience

We have already quoted T.S. Eliot's words: "we had the experience but missed the meaning."[19] We had the experience of giving birth, of falling in love, of getting a job, of being ill, of the unexpected death of a friend. As a community we experienced a flood, the election of a new president, a change in our pastor, the death of a beloved leader. A family experiences moving away from relatives to a place where they have no family, or the illness of a parent, the birth of a child, the death of a grandparent. Every day we as individuals and as members of communities have new experiences.

What do these experiences mean? Are they "signs of the times" in our lives? Why think about or try to interpret them? Thoughtful people reflect on their experiences because they believe that life itself has meaning. "Is that all there is?" is not just the name of a song sung by Peggy Lee; it is a question that comes from being human.

Before stating what the components of an experience are it seems necessary to say what experience is *not*. It is not an emotional outburst or the thoughtless and passive reception of sense data. It is not a mood brought about through artificial stimuli or drugs. Experiences are *conscious* interactions that have an intellectual component. In describing the nature of experience we shall follow the lead of theologians Edward Schillebeeckx, Dermot Lane, and Gerald O'Collins, each of whom presents experience as the product that arises out of the critical interaction between a human subject and another reality.[20]

In this interaction the subject, a thinking, feeling, discerning human being encounters an other reality. Lane writes: "The encounter is composed of a chain of events. These include a response or reaction from the subject as conscious subject toward reality. Following on this, reality is refracted or broken back upon the subject. This in turn evokes a process of critical reflection in the subject."[21] As we stand in the checkout line at the supermarket, we often are not conscious of the other people with us. When we consciously respond to or interact with one or more of them, we initiate an experience with them.

When I am experiencing, I *know* I am experiencing. Every experience has an intellectual component. The interpretation happens through language. Schillebeeckx describes an experience as a "speech event."[22] The language names what is happening during and after the encounter. The interpretation may be short or may continue long after the interaction has ceased. The continuing interpretation brings the experience into the present. Human experience has a cognitive component.

No experience happens in a vacuum. We bring to each experience our language, our past experiences, our view of the world, our culture, our hopes for the future, and the wisdom we inherited from our tradition. With all these components we enter into a dialogue with an outside reality. These components play a part in our interpretation of what is happening. Every new experience builds on past experiences, so that we always meet new experiences as a developing person or community.

Human experience is a complex reality. In each experience a person or community (an experience may be personal and/or communal) interacts with another reality, conscious of the interaction at the time it happens, and from that interaction draws conclusions, changes behavior, makes judgments. Experiences are always interpreted experiences, for reflection is an integral component of each experience. In each experience the subject's imagination, memory, intellect, emotions, and will—his or her whole being—are involved, and the experience is kept alive through the person or community's reflection.

Experiences are transformative; they change us. We experience becoming friends, or we experience marriage and our life changes. We have a child and life changes again. And with the experience of each new child there are more and more changes. We grow older, our health changes. We lose a job or get one. We experience vicariously through film and television or on the Internet the effects of hurricanes, the cruelties of war, the beauties of nature. We experience being cared for by others or caring for others. We experience the power of words in oratory or poetry. All day, every day we experience realities outside ourselves that affect us, and we are changed.

An experience is always concrete, not abstract. A person experiences being a care giver not in general but in caring for a specific person. A person experiences being a parent in the act of parenting a particular child or children. We experience death in our own dying or when someone we know dies. A person experiences success by succeeding at some definite task, or experiences failure by failing at some concrete action. In each experience we are wholly involved with a particular reality, a concrete other.

Experiences have differing degrees of impact. If a child dies, the impact on the parent's experience will ordinarily be deeper than the impact of the child's death on a stranger. Watching Stephen Spielberg's film *Saving Private Ryan,* with its lengthy depiction of the landing of American troops on the Normandy beaches in World

War II, may be a horrifying vicarious experience, but it cannot compare to the actual experience of landing on the beach. There is a different degree of immediacy.

Sometimes in a particularly significant experience I am more fully involved simply because of the degree of relationship between myself and the one with whom I am sharing the experience, or because of the nature of the experience and/or my consciousness of its importance. When a child is born, both mother and father have a higher level of involvement than do the medical professionals who attend the birth. Watching what happens to a person who has a drug overdose is not the same as having the drug overdose, but the experience of watching can also affect us.

In symbolic catechesis the community comes together to reflect on and interpret a societal or personal experience that the community shares. The catechist as leader, facilitator, and resource leads the community within the context of being a community of faith, justice, and prayer to interpret their own "signs of the times" through symbols of faith. Faith relates to life, and the catechist assists the community in bridging the gulf between faith and experience.

Discovering the Signs of the Times of Your Parishioners

We have all heard stories of CEOs of companies, presidents of universities, and pastors of parishes, who, shortly after their appointment, began to make changes. Within six months they had lost the confidence of the persons they were meant to serve. An important adage for directors of catechesis is this: Take time to know your people. Know your people before you do any planning. Know your people's needs. Every day learn something new about your people.

The story is told of a priest who was named a pastor for the first time. He moved into the parish and simply let things go on as they had before he came. He neither fired nor hired anyone. He attended staff meetings chaired by other members of the parish teams and participated primarily as a listener. He said he wanted to learn. Every day the new pastor took a walk for about an hour. He called it his "walking around" ministry. He walked up and down the streets of his parish, noticing what was going on or that nothing was going on, meeting people on the streets, stopping in the supermarket to greet people, pausing at the fire station to say hello, at the library to get a book. By the end of six months many of the parishioners knew him well enough to call him by name, and he knew more about the parish than some of the staff members who had been there for many years. His "walking around" was his ministry in the parish during his first year as pastor.

There are in the United States over nineteen thousand parishes (more parishes than post offices!), and every one of them is different from the others. The people are different, the tradition is different, the racial and ethnic mixes differ, and there are wide or narrow differences in the level of the people's education. Some parishes are wealthy, others poverty stricken. The level of attachment to the faith may be strong or hesitant, active or passive, dynamic or static. These are some "signs of the times" in the parish.

The *General Directory for Catechesis* notes that "the sower sends out his workers to proclaim the gospel through all the world and to that end shares with them the power of his Spirit. At the same time he shows them how to read the signs of the times and asks of them that special preparation which is necessary to carry out the sowing."[23] It goes on to say:

> The voice of the Spirit, which Jesus, on behalf of the Father, has communicated to his disciples, "resounds in the very events of history." Behind the changing data of present situations and in the deep motives of evangelization, it is necessary to discover "what may be genuine signs of the presence or the purpose of God" (*CMW*, 11; see also 4).
>
> Such analysis, however, must always be done in the light of faith. Availing herself of the human sciences, which are always necessary, the Church seeks to discover the meaning of the present situation within the perspective of the history of salvation.[24]

How does one discover "the presence or purpose of God" in the "events of history" in a parish? How does one catechize when there are so many differences even within a parish? How can anyone serve such a variety of people? How will the parish staff decide what "signs of the times" to consider this fall or next spring? A few principles will assist a director of catechetical ministry or a catechist to reach the people.

Know Your People. Every catechetical community, whether it is made up of adults, adolescents, or children, is composed of individuals who are on a journey of faith. The journey will extend throughout their lifetime, and each individual in the community will be at a different stage on the journey when you are ministering to him or her. How then will you serve them?

Discover the "signs of the times" in your parishioners lives. Ask yourself, What do these people have in common? Are they around the same age? Do they share a common educational background? Are they of the same ethnicity? Are they all newcomers to the parish? Are they Catholics who have been away from the church and are returning to it? Or are they all seeking initiation through the *RCIA?* Or are they all college youth or retired couples? The first principle is: Know your people and what they share in common.

Look at What Other Churches Do.[25] There are, in several of our major cities, downtown churches that offer a variety of services based on the signs of the times of workers in their area. The following stories are both mythical and true.

In the New York financial district people who work on Wall Street are invited to gather once a week for conversation about their faith. Their conversation includes reference to their work or the values and meaning attached to their work. The parish does not advertise the meeting as a catechesis for stockbrokers. It describes it as "A Conversation about Finance and Faith for Wall Street Workers." The catechist is familiar with high finance and is, in fact, a Wall Street worker who has been trained as a catechist. She tries to bridge the gap between finance and faith.

In Chicago people from the department stores and offices in the Loop come to Mass in a downtown church and afterward meet for lunch, followed by a fifteen-minute presentation on a topic and conversation about their lives and their faith. The catechesis begins with a focus on an aspect of their lives, perhaps their work, which is for them a sign of the times. The people discuss in small groups how their lives are affected by their work and whether or how their faith does or does not support them in the workplace. Questions about the values of their workplaces often become part of their discussions.

In San Francisco people gather to discuss a book or an article they have all read. Because the church is close to the San Francisco Museum of Modern Art, they consider some of the art works or shows at the museum. After an honest consideration of insights or questions from the book or about the art, the participants may question how their faith relates to their experience with the book or with the paintings. This is not a discussion about the morality of the book or the painting but about insights that arise out of the book or art show and how they relate to faith and life.

Through catechesis the people in these parishes share the world of downtown with its hectic pace and demanding traffic and human interaction. They ask, How is faith related to our lives and work and how are our work and our lives related to our faith? Those from Wall Street share financial knowledge and the energy that comes from their work, but they also share their questions about faith and life. Sometimes they wonder what making or investing money has to do with Christian faith. Catechists in the Chicago parish reach out to workers who have a common experience but emerge from varied backgrounds, diverse ethnic and racial communities, and differing economic conditions. The San Francisco parish found that reading books of interest to the people gave them a common vocabulary and an ability to talk with one another. In all three parishes, small groups of people gather once a week for an hour or so and their faith comes alive. People support one another and even bond with one another through the weekly critique of their signs of the times.

On the other hand, in a suburban parish the catechist will find that the signs of the times differ. In a parish made up primarily of senior citizens, the people may be concerned about volunteer activities or use of leisure time or maintaining self-confidence when no longer working. Often retired citizens live on a fixed income and sometimes this means concern about meeting expenses or affording medical necessities. Some are not well. Others are looking for ways to share their talent through tutoring or teaching classes occasionally. More seniors than other age groups vote and participate in parish activities. What does this tell us about them? Know your people. The catechist needs to know what the signs of the times are in peoples' lives, and then bring people into small groups in which reflection, critical inquiry about life, faith, prayer, and action for justice can flourish.

In the technological world of the twenty-first century the signs of the times seem to include not only computers and the Internet but a renewed search for a spirituality to guide the daily lives of the technocrats. In this "postmodern" world organized institutions of religion are often rejected, and, conversely, the spirituality of the individual apart from society has primary value. T. Howland Sanks notes that postmodernism emphasizes "pluralism, difference and otherness, regional and local," and could lead to a church that "allows and encourages greater autonomy and authority in the particular, regional, and local churches."[26] What are the signs of the times in this postmodern society? These signs could be the focus of parish catechesis and a service to people who wish to critique their lives and culture in the light of their faith.

Observe Present Signs of the Times. As I write this, the countries of NATO, led by the United States, are bombing Yugoslavia, and through television and the Internet, people around the world are watching hundreds of thousands of refugees from Kosovo flee into Albania, Montenegro, and Macedonia. They are also hearing horrific stories about the refugees being given fifteen minutes to leave their homes, then watching their homes burn, and being separated from the men in their families who are of military age. Most of the refugees are Muslim. Most of the Serbs are Christians. This event is an obvious "sign of our time," and if the church does not address it, critique it, consider it through homilies, through catechesis, through providing aid, it shows a separation from the world that is unhealthy.

Another present "sign of the times" is the growing economic disparity among our people. The saying that "the rich get richer" implies that "the poor get poorer." If the gap between the very wealthy and the very poor is growing within our society so that the wealthiest people are getting even wealthier, and the poor are becoming even poorer, then we as church need to critique the economic system that breeds such disparity. We need to critique this cultural phenomenon on the level of parish communities, particularly within well-to-do parishes.

All the people in a parish are at different places on their journey of faith. Some may be beginning their faith journey, while others who have been with the church for a lifetime may be enthusiastic and committed to finding joy and support in their faith. Some people may be questioning whether faith means anything to them anymore. They have come searching for meaning, to see if their faith makes any sense in the light of their experience. The questions the catechists need to ask are: What do these people have in common? What are the signs of the times in their lives? How can I draw them into a conversation that will lead them to recognize the relationship of life and faith?

What many parishioners have in common is a desire to meet with others who share some elements of their lives and who will try with them to bring their lives and their faith together. People will not achieve this goal in one or two or perhaps even ten weeks. But each week as they meet and reflect, pray and do justice, the trust among them may grow and one hopes that they may begin to find both meaning and grace in their lives.

There are many ways of learning about the signs of the times, the interests and concerns of the people in your parish. Read the newspapers. Watch and listen to television news. Walk around the parish and talk with your people. You can learn about your people from observation, conversations, walking around, from interviews, checklists, surveys, and research in the city library. The San Jose Diocese in California gathered information for its parishes about the ethnic, racial, economic, and educational characteristics of the people in its parishes from a census in county records.

Gather Data about the "Signs of the Times." The most common way of collecting data about the signs of the times in peoples' lives seems to be through a survey, often handed out before or after Sunday Mass and collected at the end of Mass or on the following Sunday. But these data reflect the interests and concerns of only a minority of people in the parish. When collecting data it is very important to consider whom you want to survey. A survey conducted at Mass involves Sunday Mass parishioners. Statistics tell us that on the average only 30 percent of our people now attend Mass every Sunday. In some parishes the average may be higher, but the question remains: How will catechists reach the parishioners who are not present at Mass on the particular Sunday of the survey? And do catechists want to know what people from other churches who live within the parish boundaries are thinking? How can they be included in a survey? Whom do you want to survey? Whom do you want to reach through the ministry of catechesis?

Catechesis as a Critique of Culture

Discovering the signs of the times means being attentive to the culture of the people being served. The culture of the people in the inner city is not the same as the culture of the suburban wealthy. The culture of African Americans is not the same as the culture of Euro-Americans. In the United States we live in a multicultural world (racially, ethnically, and economically), and we have subcultures such as the youth culture, the drug culture, student culture. What is culture? How does it develop? What do we mean when we say, for example, that Protestants have a culture of hard work? Is there such a thing as a Catholic culture? Do we want the church to embrace a "Catholic" culture or to maintain many cultures? How does our culture affect our faith?

Theologian Aylward Shorter describes culture as "a transmitted pattern of meanings embodied in symbols, a pattern capable of development and change, and it belongs to the concept of humanness itself.[27] Michael Warren, who writes about culture and religion, describes culture as "the *signifying system* through which a social order is communicated, reproduced, experienced and explored."[28] By "signifying system" he is referring to symbols that express and constitute the life of the community. Thomas Groome states that "culture refers to everything that human beings create (as distinct from what is produced by nature) in order to express themselves and to make the world a more habitable and hospitable 'place.'"[29] Catechists cannot respect the signs of the times in people's lives and not respect their culture. The signs of the times are intimately related to the culture of a people. Both need to be critiqued.

Joseph P. Fitzpatrick wrote about culture from the point of view of a priest sociologist who worked with Puerto Rican immigrants. Fitzpatrick said: "Culture, very simply, is the way of life of a people."[30] Culture is not the same as race; it is not nature. It is learned in a process of socialization. Fitzpatrick gives the following example:

> If a boy were to be born of Irish parents in Dublin and given at the time of his birth to Chinese people in Peking to be brought up, by the time the boy was 21 he would be completely Chinese. He would not be Irish. His features and appearance would be Irish, but everything else—his speech, his way of thinking about things, his way of doing things, his emotional reactions to situations—all of these aspects of his life would be Chinese, not Irish....What has happened? In growing up he had assimilated a culture, the culture of Chinese people.[31]

Culture is like "the air we breathe. Air completely surrounds us as well as filling every cell of our body. We are totally dependent upon it, yet, most of the time we are totally unconscious of it. So it is with culture."[32]

A culture embodies a way of life. The Irish and Italian immigrant cultures (a set of meanings and value informing a common way of life) collided in the first half of the twentieth century. As the end of the twentieth century the Asian and African American cultures quarreled in the 1992 riots in Los Angeles. The values, traditions, understandings, worldview, and symbolizing system of the two cultures clashed. Sometimes Hispanic[33] and Vietnamese cultures do not readily harmonize. How then can one catechize on the signs of the times and respect different cultures and hand on a Catholic way of life or culture?

The Second Vatican Council and Inculturation

With the Second Vatican Council, which was the first truly international gathering of the Catholic hierarchy, the bishops recognized that they themselves came from many different cultures and heritages.[34] While through their faith they shared much in common, to communicate well they needed to respect and understand the cultures from which other bishops came.

The *Pastoral Constitution on the Church in the Modern World* (1965) noted that the church itself is not tied to any culture,[35] and although it has contributed to the progress of many cultures, "it is a fact of experience that there have been difficulties in the way of harmonizing culture with Christian thought."[36] The constitution urges that "the faithful ought to work closely with their contemporaries and ought to try to understand their ways of thinking and feeling, as these find expression in current culture."[37]

In writing about catechesis and culture Pope John Paul II pointed out that catechesis "is called to bring the power of the Gospel into the very heart of culture and cultures." In emphasizing the importance of culture he goes on to state that, "catechesis will seek to know these cultures and their essential components; it will learn their most significant expressions; it will respect their particular values and riches."[38] Catechists need to be aware not only of the signs of the times in peoples' lives but also of the culture of the people whom they are serving and how their culture affects their response to the signs of the times.

Since the Second Vatican Council papal and church documents have encouraged a missionary process of "inculturation." In 1971 the *General Catechetical Directory* noted that "the Christian faith requires explanations and new forms of expression so that it may take root in all successive cultures."[39] This process became known as "inculturation." For missionaries and catechists, inculturation is "the intimate transformation of authentic cultural values through their integration in Christianity and the insertion of Christianity in the various human cultures."[40] *Inculturation* means that the church "takes from every culture all that it encounters of positive value."[41] It does not impose itself on the culture nor is it a simple external adaptation of the culture to the church. *Inculturation* is more commonly known "as the principle of catholicity, or accommodation, or adaptation, or indigenization or contextualization; more radically, the principle of incarnation."[42]

The word *inculturation* is significant for catechists and missionaries today because the church is in an age of mission that is tremendously challenging to it and because global awareness has made us very conscious of cultural diversity. In the midst of this diversity the church is in the process of bringing faith and culture together in a new way. It is a process of the *incarnation* of faith in a new cultural form. When a religious faith has been inculturated, the culture shapes and expresses the faith tradition and the faith tradition shapes and expresses the culture. Pope John Paul II wrote: "Faith which does not become culture is faith which is not received fully, not assimilated entirely, not lived faithfully."[43] Inculturation differs from an imposition of culture. In the past missionaries may have brought with them from their homelands not only the communication of the gospel but the communication of their own national way of life. Today what missionaries in foreign countries do is *inculturation*, that is, unite the faith with the best elements of the new society. What catechists are called to do is inculturation, unite the faith with the culture of their people, and this culture includes the signs of the times in peoples' lives and how they respond as a culture to these signs.

When the *General Directory for Catechesis* (1997) describes catechesis as an inculturation or incarnational process it states:

> The Word of God became man, a concrete man, in space and time and rooted in a specific culture: "Christ by his incarnation committed himself to the particular social and cultural circumstances of the men among whom he lived."[44] This is the original "inculturation" of the word of God and is the model of all evangelization by the Church, "called to

bring the power of the Gospel into the very heart of culture and cultures."[45]

Catechesis as a moment of evangelization is a process of inculturation. It is a process of incarnating the gospel in the culture. The *General Directory for Catechesis* points out that inculturation of the faith in catechesis has different tasks:

> First, the catechist who "possesses a living social conscience and is well rooted" in his cultural environment needs to recognize that the church itself is the principal factor of inculturation.
>
> Second, "local catechisms which respond to the demands of different cultures [cf. *CCC* 24] and which present the Gospel in relation to the hopes, questions and problems which these cultures present" need to be drawn up.
>
> Third, the catechumenate (and catechetical community) should be "'centers of inculturation,' incorporating, with discernment, the language, symbols, and values of the cultures in which the catechumens and those to be catechized live."
>
> Lastly the Christian message needs to be presented "in such a way as to prepare those who are to proclaim the Gospel to be capable 'of giving reasons for their hope' [1 Pt 3:15] in cultures often pagan or post-Christian: effective apologetics to assist the faith-culture dialogue is indispensable today."[46]

These passages certainly recognize the value of peoples' cultures and their experiences. If catechesis is to strengthen faith and call the community to conversion, it must first recognize the good in the culture, draw on it, and unite it with the gospel.

A culture is handed on through a signifying system, through its adherents, through the life of the community, through its teaching, its values, and the way in which it relates with other cultures. Pastorally a Catholic culture is handed on through the church's ministries and through family tradition. The signifying system or meanings and values of the church are its sacred scriptures and tradition as living in the present church. The question is, How can the Catholic community hand on its meanings and values and vision of life in the modern world?

Pastoral Planning for a Catechesis of Life and Culture

There are alternate ways of planning and bringing to fruition a catechetical program. Planning for any program presumes that the parish has developed a mission or vision statement and that the planning will build on the principles of that statement. The following recommendations offer an abbreviated approach to designing a catechetical program through four steps: planning, preparing, promoting, and processing.

Planning

Proximate planning begins approximately two months before a catechesis begins. (Long-term planning would begin much earlier.)[47] In the planning stage the director of religious education and her staff, relying on the data collected throughout the parish, choose the life experience or "sign of the time" to be probed. After this has been done, the director of religious education and the catechist select two or three parishioners to work with them as a team for a particular life experience. These parishioners would be people who share the common experience or "sign of the time" that will be interpreted through catechesis. They become members of the catechetical team that will plan, prepare, promote, and process the catechesis.

Planning for the year will include many catechetical programs. Several different forms of catechesis for adults can go on at the same time. A parish might decide, for example, to follow an annual schedule similar to the following one.

Parish Catechetical Calendar (Sample)

July	Vacation
August	Parish planning and goal setting; teams form for adult programs of October and November and choose "signs of the times" (examples, single parents, care givers, leisure time of seniors)
September	Children and youth programs begin; planning continues
October	Four-week catechesis for single parents (Tues. night, Sat. A.M.) Four-week catechesis for care givers (Wed. afternoons)
November	Four-week catechesis for seniors (Tues. and Thurs. 10:30 A.M.) Four-week catechesis for new parishioners (Sunday after Mass)
December	Parish planning
January	Proximate planning for Lent
February–March	Five-week Lenten catechesis offered three times each week (Sunday afternoon, Tuesday and Thursday evenings) Three-week catechesis for couples in their fifties Three-week catechesis for recently married couples (first three years)
April	Three-week catechesis for teachers/professors Three-week catechesis for parish ministers to the sick
May	Three-week catechesis for people who are divorced Dinner for all who participated in catechesis during the year
June	Time for retreat and vacation

165

The suggested schedule is ambitious in that it plans for catechesis for ten different adult concerns or issues in a particular year. It presumes that there are at least three teams of two professional prepared catechists who will lead the catechetical programs and that the three teams have additional parishioners to work with the catechists. It also presumes that other forms of adult catechesis such as the catechumenate, preparation of liturgical ministers, and children and youth programs will also be going on.

Preparing

In order to catechize well the catechist or team needs to prepare well for the catechesis. Once the catechist has chosen an issue and created a team, then she can begin to prepare for the catechesis. The catechetical team will then brainstorm the questions, concerns, problems, and opportunities that arise out of the life sign. Together the expanded team decides on what they think the questions of people may be and how many times they think this particular catechetical community should gather, when they will gather, and where they will gather. The preparing process is fluid, each question relating to the others.

Together the team gathers resources in the form of people, pamphlets, articles, books, and videos that might address the questions or concerns of a community of, for example, people who are divorced. Some of these resources may become part of the catechesis. Each time the team meets, the catechist will have prepared a ritual prayer to be celebrated by the team. Prayer is as essential to the team as it is to the parish catechetical community.

The catechist(s), because she is professionally prepared to do so, is the person primarily responsible for choosing the faith symbols that will assist people who are divorced to interpret their life experience. This is a major way in which catechists are a resource for the community. The catechist may turn to the Scriptures, to the teaching of the church, to liturgical rituals as a way of responding to concerns. Though the real questions of people need to surface and be faced, there are seldom easy answers that respond to people's concerns. And neither the catechist nor her team can readily foresee what questions may arise from the catechetical community. Once the catechist has chosen a biblical passage or a teaching of the church, she may present it to her team, and together they would consider how the biblical passage or the teaching speaks to the concerns of the people in the catechetical community.

Catechists turn to their own resources and to references such as the *Catechism of the Catholic Church* to help them interpret or respond to the concern. For people who are divorced, the correlating of their experience with a faith symbol may be a saying of Jesus, a reflection on his life as a single person, a consideration of how the church as a community can and ought to support those who live without an adult partner, an invitation to participate in ministry to others. After reviewing possible correlation topics with the team, the catechist will usually know which topic will best respond to the questions of the community.

The catechist and her team also need to consider how those who are divorced can turn from themselves, beyond their own concerns and problems, to the concerns of others. The doing of justice is a requirement for Christians, and the team needs to prepare a few options from which the community can choose to be of service to others. The catechetical community should also be consulted to discover if there is some way associated with their immediate concern that opens itself to action for justice. The catechist should be ready with several suggestions from which the community can choose.

The ritual prayer needs to be carefully prepared with attention to detail. The ministries in the ritual prayer may be shared by members of the team. What hymns can this group sing? Should we support them with a tape recording? Are there some psalms that reflect the needs of this group? Who can best read the Gospel passage? Who will give the homily? Can we plan it together? What general intercessions will we pray? What ritual action will speak most positively to this group? How and when shall we use it? With what message shall we send them forth?

Preparing for the catechesis means developing a minute-by-minute plan such as:

8:00–8:05	Gather, introductions, opening prayer
8:05–8:45	Discuss what it feels like to be divorced. What are difficulties and opportunities? How has divorce changed your life?
8:45–9:05	Correlate topic with faith symbol. Dialogue
9:05–9:20	Plan a way to reach out to others
9:15–9:30	Ritual prayer and sending forth

This is an overall schedule which can change but which will set up parameters for conversation, reflection, community planning for justice, and prayer.

Each one of the four movements of the catechesis will need to be carefully prepared. The catechist and team will develop questions that will invite the community members to participate. They will remind one another that if someone is shy and does not speak they can invite that person to speak so that the conversation will be inclusive. Not everyone has the same response to divorce. For some it may be a life-saving and freeing experience. For others it leads to loneliness and a kind of poverty they had not experienced before. Each person will have his or her own response, and some responses may be in conflict with the experience of others. The point is to be present as a loving supportive Christian community offering solace, encouragement, faith, and whatever else is needed by members of the divorced community.

I have used divorce as an example of an issue or sign of the time. Other signs could be single parenthood, being an unwed mother, caring for the sick or disabled, being retired or unemployed, living in a nursing home, speaking English as a second language, being a recent immigrant. These are all signs of the times in people's lives. There is no human condition that we cannot address in catechesis.

Preparing means getting ready once the pre-planning has been done. It means paying attention to detail. This includes knowing the names of those who participate as soon as possible, greeting them by name. It means seeing that a pleasant adult environment welcomes them. Preparing includes planning many questions though you may ask only two. It means being ready to respond to the community's concern with a faith symbol and providing them with a way to look toward others in need. It means being a good leader of prayer, knowing how the prayer will develop, preparing the ministers, and perhaps writing a short two- or three-sentence homily. It means being at home and comfortable with yourself, with what you are doing, and with the community.

This may seem like much work for a few people. It is a good deal of work when the parish begins such a program. But once the pattern takes hold, others become involved, the catechetical teams grow, new people are seen and heard, solace is given, faith is strengthened, grace is apparent.

Symbolic catechesis on the signs of the times becomes easier the second time with a new group, and the third time the process almost moves itself. An average parish could have three or four different meetings with two or three different issues meeting in one week, possibly two meetings for those who are divorced and three for young adults who are questioning their faith. The next month the catechist can plan and prepare for unmarried mothers with children, or new immigrants, or whatever concern is on the parish agenda. One catechist could lead two or three different groups during the first year, and perhaps three or four groups in the second year. Because the catechist is working with a team whose members take on parts of the catechetical process, the ministry becomes less demanding and gives the catechist more time for reflection and study.

Promoting

Parish personnel do well in planning and preparing but do not usually do well in promoting programs. In a world of computers and Kinko's there is no excuse for less than a professional way of inviting parishioners to participate in our programs. Just as a survey given at Mass ordinarily reaches fewer than half of the people, so the announcement of a meeting in a parish bulletin reaches only those people who are attending Sunday Mass. People who attend

Mass are important components of the parish and will probably be members of the planning team, but we need to invite those who may be estranged from the church, or those who have only a tenuous relationship. We need to invite people who live within our parish and have no religious affiliation at all. Letters of announcement are expensive. Bulk mailings with a calendar of significant meetings to be held during the year can reach more parishioners. But there are many other ways of promoting our programs.

Promotion by e-mail can be developed. Do you have a listing of the e-mail addresses of people in your parish? E-mail goes directly into the home, can go out as close to the date as you want it, and is inexpensive. E-mail addresses can easily be divided into many different interest groups. Computer software has made it possible to design attractive invitations or announcements. Presently computers are in fewer than half of our homes, but they soon will be in most homes. The parish church needs to take advantage of this form of communication, which can bring the whole parish together according to interests.

When composing invitations or announcements, be sure to use inclusive and inviting language. I suggest the word "catechesis" not be used. It is too technical and is sometimes threatening. A bit of humor always helps. Sample announcements:

> *Come, join other adults who share your experience of divorce for a conversation about both the positive and negative aspects of being divorced. Meet some new friends and parishioners and relax in an accepting environment. (Bring the children, if you wish. We have babysitters. Meeting will last only 90 minutes.)*

Or, *Seniors! Join us for a discussion of the challenges and opportunities you face. Meet other seniors.*

Or, *Newly married? Come and tell us what you think the parish can do for you. Meet other newly married members of the parish.*

Promotion takes creativity and sensitivity. How can you attract your people to your parish? Be positive. Be warm and inviting.

Make sure that it does not seem like an invitation to dinner or to fun and games, but don't make it too heavy.

The most important thing in promotion is one-to-one contact. If your program is for new immigrants, find two or three people who have been immigrants to plan and prepare it with you and then ask each of them to personally call and invite at least two new immigrants. They will know how to speak to others and invite them to participate, especially if they have been involved in the planning and preparing.

When promoting a program, let people know about transportation possibilities for those who don't have cars, don't drive, or prefer not to drive at night. Announce babysitting for parents, or provide a substitute for care givers. If you schedule your meeting on Monday night in the fall, you'll probably miss many men who will want to watch the football game on TV. Be realistic. Check other parish and community calendars. Put the same program on at more than one time during the week.

Processing

The process is the catechesis itself and the evaluation of the catechesis. The process works best when the participants are unaware of it as a carefully planned process. When the four catechetical movements are so smoothly integrated that the community is unaware of the movements, then the process has achieved its purpose. The catechist will have a clear outline in her head or on index cards of the sequence of events, but she needs to be so well prepared that her attention can focus on the people and the interaction that is taking place among them. The catechist is like a host or hostess. This is not a dinner party, but it is a time when people are welcomed into a parish community where their needs and primary interests are embraced and critiqued by faith. It is an invitation to conversion.

People are accustomed to coming to church for religious answers to questions they may not have asked. In this catechesis they come to consider their own questions. A catechist may design a catechesis for parents of adolescents. They will be invited to come to four sessions on four successive Wednesday nights. Specific concerns of parents will be considered. If you want to know what those concerns are, ask three parents of different backgrounds to come and discuss the concerns they have about their adolescent youngsters with you. Develop a catechesis out of that discussion.

Experience is interpreted in catechesis. God is with us in our daily lives. God is with us even as we worry and love and fret about and don't know what to do with our adolescent children. The experience of being a parent of an adolescent may be a revelatory experience. Examining that experience in the context of prayer and faith can help parents be more secure in dealing with their youngsters. Through this catechesis they may become confident parents who are supported by others and who know how to turn to prayer in their time of need.

Catechesis is a ministry that reminds the gathered church that we are brothers and sisters in Christ, that we are *for* one another and that God is *for* us. In the few times parents meet, they may experience what it means to be church and have their faith strengthened. In your prayer, anoint parents for their parenting, bless them for the love they give their children, lead them to recognize that to be an authority is "to author life."

Some parents will be called to a major conversion by the insights they gain from other parents, from the catechists, and from their prayer. Catechesis aims at conversion and strengthening of faith, but conversion happens over time and is not instantaneous. It takes place in a context of prayer and justice and mutual love or acceptance. We cannot plan for it to happen. Certainly we cannot program conversion. If or when it happens, it happens because of God's grace.

In every catechetical session on an experience there is a point at which the catechist will change the topic from the concern of the community to the concerns of those who are less fortunate or who are in need. A wealthy and generous friend once asked why the church had a "preference for the poor." It should not, she said, prefer anyone. Pope John Paul II explained that the church has a preference for the poor just as a mother has a preference for the child who is ill. Her preference does not mean that she does not love the other children. It is just that she realizes this child is in most need now.

172

Catechesis aims at conversion, and conversion is supported by the four acts that make up catechesis: the building of community, the sharing of our stories and beliefs, reaching out in justice to others, and ritual prayer. The process is itself the content of catechesis, for the process immerses the community in living Christian life.

Evaluation follows every catechesis. An evaluative process is a way of judging what has been done in order to see how we can do it better the next time. It is a kind of education for the catechetical team. What is evaluated is the *catechesis*, not the *catechist*. Ask: How well did we do each of the following acts?

Objective	Excellent	Very Good	Fair	Poor
1. Strengthen relationships among members of the community				
2. Interpret their experience by reference to a particular faith symbol				
3. Reach out in justice to others				
4. Pray together in ritual				
5. Comments:				

_____

_____

After the meeting is over the team can ask how well those four objectives were fulfilled. Four possible judgments may be made: excellent, very good, fair, or poor. Do not have five possible judgments because ordinarily the team will choose the third of five options simply because it is the middle one.

It will be helpful to create a profile of the people who gather for catechesis. Each time the catechetical community meets, the catechist can add new information to the profile so that as the weeks go by she records more knowledge about the community, knowledge that will help her serve them more fully. The more you know about your parishioners, the better you will be able to plan your catechesis to serve them.

In Summary

In symbolic catechesis the community gathers to examine the "signs of the times" which affect their lives and which concern or preoccupy them. Symbolic catechesis is a catechesis on life, its joys and anxieties, its hopes and fears. It is a catechesis for people who see life as a gift, though sometimes a painful one, and for those who can see only the pain. It is for seekers and searchers for meaning, for the desperate and the hopeful, the poor and the wealthy, the blue-collar worker and the millionaire.

Symbolic catechesis is for believers of all levels, the holy and those who are hanging on to their faith in fear and doubt. It is for sinners and the redeemed, for those who have been forgiven and for those who have not even sought forgiveness. It is a ministry of the gospel, the good news. It is open to every ethnic and racial group, and it respects all cultures. In symbolic catechesis the gospel is being incarnated in the lives of the marginalized as well as in the lives of the favored.

Symbolic catechesis addresses the concerns of the people, and it always respects their culture and cultural expressions. Culture is a way of life brought about through the sharing of significant symbols. What the church does in catechesis is an *inculturation* process. Inculturation is a process of incarnating the gospel in the culture of the people.

Finally, in symbolic catechesis the catechist and her team go through the four steps of planning, preparing, promoting, and processing. These four simple steps will assist the catechist in preparing for her ministry. All four steps are of little avail if the catechist and her team do not pray regularly to the Holy Spirit, asking the Spirit to lift up the hearts of the people and give them insight and wisdom and grace.

Catechesis is the exploration as well as the communication of a way of life. It takes place within a community searching for the meaning of ordinary daily life through Christian faith. It fulfills the challenge of the Second Vatican Council, which urged us to "answer the ever recurring questions that people ask about the meaning of this present life and the life to come and how one is related to the other."[48]

FURTHER READINGS

Congregation for the Clergy. *General Directory for Catechesis.* Washington, D.C.: United States Catholic Conference, 1997.

Fitzpatrick, Joseph P. *One Church Many Cultures: The Challenge of Diversity.* Kansas City, Mo.: Sheed & Ward, 1987.

Groome, Thomas H. *Sharing Faith: A Comprehensive Approach to Religious Education & Pastoral Ministry.* San Francisco: Harper, 1991.

Pineda, Ana María, and Robert Schreiter, eds. *Dialogue Rejoined: Theology and Ministry in the United States Hispanic Reality.* Collegeville: Minn.: Liturgical Press, 1995.

Schineller, Peter. *A Handbook of Inculturation.* New York: Paulist Press, 1990.

Schreiter, Robert. J. "Faith and Cultures: Challenges to a World Church." *Theological Studies* 50 (1989): 744–60.

Shorter, Aylward. *Toward a Theology of Inculturation.* Maryknoll, N.Y.: Orbis Books, 1988.

Vogel, Linda. *Teaching and Learning in Communities of Faith: Empowering Adults Through Religious Education.* San Francisco: Jossey-Bass Publishers, 1991.

Warren, Michael. *Communications and Cultural Analysis: A Religious View.* Westport, Conn.: Bergin & Garvey, 1992.

————. *Faith, Culture, and the Worshiping Community: Shaping the Practice of the Local Church.* Rev. ed. Washington, D.C.: Pastoral Press, 1993.

CHAPTER 7

The Bible as a Symbol of Faith

"The Bible," says Karl Rahner, "is the Church's Book."[1] It is no more possible to think of the church without Scriptures than it is to think of the Scriptures without the church.[2] The Jewish Scriptures were inherited by the church and its Christian Scriptures emerged from the experience of the apostolic community. The early Christian communities believed that God inspired these books and that they were normative for Christian faith. Two millennia later the bishops of the Second Vatican Council affirmed the significance of the Bible in the life of the church when they wrote, "The Church has always venerated the divine Scriptures just as she venerates the body of the Lord."[3] The Bible is a preeminent symbol of the Catholic Church. It is the word of God. And "the study of the sacred page should be the very soul of sacred theology."[4]

The Bible is both a fascinating book and a mystery to most Catholics. Many Catholics, particularly older Catholics, would find it difficult to recognize that the church venerates the Scriptures just as it venerates the body of the Lord. They seldom had a strong biblical component in their childhood or adolescent catechesis, though they had a strong sacramental catechesis. Because of this most of the catechists of today's children and adolescents were not very familiar with the Bible until they were adults. This was not unusual, for since the sixteenth century as Reformers focused on the Bible as an expression of their doctrinal foundation, Catholics turned to the church's doctrinal teaching, not the Bible, as the source for their understanding of faith.

Those of us who lived before the Second Vatican Council did hear a Gospel passage read each Sunday at Mass, which meant we probably heard the same one-fourth of the four Gospels repeated year after year. We were unfamiliar with many Gospel passages and with the Old Testament. Many Catholic homes had a large family Bible in which they recorded their genealogy and special days such as the first communion, confirmation, and marriages of the children. But the Bible was not read very often.

Thirty-five years after the council, Catholics are more biblically literate. Those who attend Mass hear over a three-year period many more biblical passages from both the Old and the New Testaments. Homilies are more biblically oriented. Bible study is growing as a parish activity, but we still have a long way to go before the people venerate the Bible just as they venerate the body of the Lord.[5] In 1984, almost twenty years after the closing of the Vatican Council, only about 6 percent of core Catholics were involved in Bible study groups.[6] In 1986 a study conducted by the Gallup Organization demonstrated that 32 percent of Catholics had "read the Bible" within the past thirty days. Among younger Catholics, those between the ages of eighteen and twenty-nine, 32 percent said they read the Bible.[7]

The Bible is so important in the life of the Catholic Church that in recent directives an understanding of Sacred Scripture is seen as essential for the catechist. The United States Catholic Conference Commission on Certification and Accreditation of "persons in ministry" prepared in 1990 requires that candidates for ministry "understand and have working knowledge of current Roman Catholic theology including:....scripture."[8] The National Federation for Catholic Youth Ministry requires in its "Competence-Based Standards" that youth ministers have "an understanding of revelation, inspiration, historical development, and literary criticism," and "an understanding of literary forms found in Old and New Testaments." Competencies needed include the "ability to design a learning experience to assist youth in understanding Scripture in light of church teaching that illuminates an understanding of their experience."[9] Clearly, church authorities expect that catechists on all levels be familiar with and able to introduce the Sacred Scriptures to the people to whom they minister. The question is, How are the catechists to get the education needed in order to fulfill these standards?

This chapter will examine what we mean when we say the Bible is a preeminent faith symbol within the church. It will also consider, through the lens of a significant church document—*The Interpretation of the Bible in the Church*, prepared by the Pontifical Biblical Commission—principles for interpreting the Bible in the church today. Because fundamentalism raises questions about interpretation of the Bible and has created confusion about biblical interpretation among some Catholics and catechists, a brief analysis of fundamentalist positions will be presented. This analysis will be based on the Biblical Commission's commentary on the methodology of fundamentalism.

Questions about biblical interpretation have also been raised by scriptural scholars who resist the exclusive or "sexist" language of biblical translations and texts in the worship of the church. The work of many men and women scholars has brought renewed energy to recognizing the influence, the significance, and role of women in the apostolic church. The feminist approach to interpretation will be considered, and questions about this methodology and approach to biblical interpretation will also be reviewed, based on the Biblical Commission's study. This review is important because it contributes to a more authentic interpretation of Scripture and thereby enriches the church.

A brief study of the purpose and composition of the *Lectionary* as the book of scriptural readings for sacramental celebration will contextualize the Bible in the church's worship. Finally I will propose a response to the questions, How do we do a biblical or a lectionary catechesis? And, Is a biblical catechesis different from a study of the Bible?

The Bible as a Symbol of the Church

A symbol, as noted in chapter 4, is *that through which* a reality is present to the world. It is through their symbols that realities are encountered. Symbols address peoples' imaginations and memories, and they challenge those whom they engage. The words of great thinkers or writers are symbols that generations of people preserve not only because they express the speaker but because they affect the lives of those who read or hear them. The actions and especially the oratory of Adolf Hitler led many of the German people to envision themselves as a special and superior race of people. On the other hand, the oratorical skills of Martin Luther King, Jr. made him an agent of pride among African Americans. Through his words he greatly influenced civil rights legislation in the United States, which brought a measure of freedom and safety to many of his people.

The words and actions of Jesus of Nazareth led people to change their lives, to willingly and freely accept martyrdom. Jesus symbolized himself in his words, as in the Sermon on the Mount, and in his actions of healing and welcoming, of teaching and loving, of being poor and compassionate. The union of his words and actions as he blessed, broke, and gave the bread and the wine to his disciples, telling them to eat and drink it are profound symbols of his love. Through these symbolic actions and words Jesus expressed himself and evoked a response which the apostolic community symbolized in its life and in its writings, particularly New Testament writings.

Jesus, whom Christians recognize as the Incarnate Word of God, saw and named God as his "father." The closeness of their relationship may be expressed by saying that Jesus is the symbol of the Father.[10] Their relationship is intimate, as noted by Jesus' using the word Father to describe their closeness. Jesus expresses and makes present the one whom he calls Father. He is not the same as the Father, but is one with him. This is a unique symbolic relationship, as no other relationship is so intimate that the two individual persons are truly one. The Father and the Son are one with the Spirit, a trinitarian God.

Jesus also symbolized himself in the community of disciples he formed. This community, the church, makes Christ present in the world. The church is not the same as the risen Lord, but it represents him on earth as his symbol. It is intimately related to him. It is an expression of his living presence. He brought it into being. He speaks to it and through it to the world. The church is so closely related to Christ Jesus that, with St. Paul, Christians name the church "the body of Christ."

This church symbolizes or makes itself present through both word and action. It is a church that has expressed itself verbally, particularly through the Bible. The Bible is the church's book, "the book in which the church of the beginning always remains tangible as a norm for us in the concrete."[11] In the Bible the church symbolizes through word its experience of God and of Christ Jesus through the Spirit. The Bible is, therefore, the word of God addressed to the present and future community from the community of the past. In writing about the timeliness of the Scriptures, Cardinal Joseph Ratzinger said, "The biblical word comes from a real past. It comes not only from the past, however, but at the same time from the eternity of God, and it leads us into God's eternity, but again along the way through time, to which the past, the present, and the future belong."[12]

The Bible is a preeminent and normative symbol of faith. It is a symbol of the covenant that exists between God and humankind. It is a narrative symbol in which the authors describe the religious experiences of our ancestors in faith. The Bible is primarily a love story, and in song and poetry, lament and history, through myth and teaching, through the lives of individuals and the faith community, through the history of the Jewish people and the early Christian community, through letters and apocalyptic this love story is proclaimed. It is our most treasured text.

Yet the Bible is not always easy to read. Most people do not know its original languages. It is difficult in a technological culture to understand the agrarian culture out of which it emerged. We are not familiar with much of the Old Testament, so we do not understand the relationships and cross-references that abound within the books and with which the people of the time when it was written would be familiar. We are not accustomed to reading some of its literary forms such as laments, and we read some forms that are meant to be sung, for example the Psalms. When we read the daily newspaper we shift our minds according to its literary forms from news reporting, to obituaries, to horoscopes, to the comics, to want ads, to editorials, always conscious of the literary form we are reading. Only this shifting of the mind makes the different forms intelligible. But many of us are unable to do this when we read the literary forms of the Bible.

Also, when reading or listening to the Bible many of us forget that originally it was meant to be heard, not read. The Gospels, for example, are dramatic narratives. As dramatic narratives the Gospels were meant to be proclaimed and heard. They are not simply sources of information, but, like all good drama, experiences in which the listener is drawn into the narrative, becomes part of it, and is transformed in some way by it.

Joseph Grassi points out that "dramatic narratives" are like a good play, an opera, or movie. He writes, "People today would quickly abandon crowded movie halls if they knew they had to attend classes or lectures to find out the meaning of what they have seen and heard, and worse still if they needed to take notes during performances or take an exam afterward!"[13] We will be able to relate to the Bible and understand it when we hear it proclaimed well, when we listen attentively, when we learn to trust ourselves, and finally, when we turn to one or two good commentaries for help.

Because the Bible is the church's book, the church interprets the meaning of the Bible for us. But even the teaching office of the church is subject to the word of God. As the constitution *On Divine Revelation* states in its very first words, "Hearing the word of God reverently and proclaiming it confidently, this holy synod makes its own the words of St. John." As Cardinal Ratzinger commented, "this is certainly one of the happiest formulations in the text: the dominance of the word of God, its sovereign supremacy above all human eloquence and activity of the Church is given due prominence. The Church itself is depicted in its double role of listening and proclaiming."[14] The church is not above the Scriptures but recognizes them as the word of God. It is to the Scriptures that the church turns for guidance as it lives out its commitment in faith.

Interpreting the Bible, the Word of God

How then are we to read this word of God? We call it "the church's book," but it is "the word of God," not "the word of the church." In the Bible God speaks to us through human words.[15] They are human words through which the authors of the Bible, inspired by the Holy Spirit, described the individual's or community's experience of God. The authors interpreted the experience, and the faith community, Jewish or Christian, accepted that interpretation as inspired by God, who is in this sense "the author of Sacred Scripture."[16] The presence of God experienced by the individual or the community is represented in the words which interpret and express that experience. When the Bible is proclaimed, God speaks to us in human words *because that is the only way we can hear and understand* what God wishes to say to us.

The Formation of the "Canon"

The books or writings that make up the Bible were canonized by the Council of Trent (1545–1563). Trent confirmed the Council of Florence's earlier decision (1438–1445) about which writings were to be included in the Bible. Florence was itself affirming the decisions of other local Christian communities. The criteria for authenticity or inclusion in the canon of sacred books were (1) apostolic origin, (2) orthodoxy, and (3) liturgical use.[17] Apostolic origin means that the books of the New Testament were thought to belong to the time of the foundational revelation of Jesus and were the activity of his apostolic and founding community The books of the Old Testament were the inherited Hebrew Scriptures which the community accepted with the writings of the apostles or one of their associates.[18] The second criteria, orthodoxy, means theological conformity to the essential message, "the purity of the gospel." Third, constant use, particularly in the liturgy secured the inclusion of the writing in the canon of inspired books.[19] The fulfillment of these three criteria means that these books were "canonized." The church named and accepted them as the Word of God. The canon of the Bible includes seventy-two books, twenty-seven Christian Scriptures in the New Testament and forty-five Hebrew Scriptures in the Old Testament.

The Interpretation of the Bible

In 1993 the Pontifical Biblical Commission published a document entitled *The Interpretation of the Bible in the Church*.[20] The document begins thus:

> The problem of the interpretation of the Bible is hardly a modern phenomenon, even if at times that is what some would have us believe. The Bible itself bears witness that its interpretation can be a difficult matter. Alongside texts that are perfectly clear, it contains passages of some obscurity. When reading certain prophecies of Jeremiah, Daniel pondered at length over their meaning (see Dn 9:2). According to the Acts of the Apostles, an Ethiopian of the first century found himself in the same situation with respect to a passage from the Book of Isaiah (see Is 53:7–8) and recognized that he had need of an interpreter (see Acts 8:30–35). The Second Letter of Peter insists that "no prophecy of Scripture is a matter of private interpretation" (2 Pt 1:20), and it also observes that the letters of the apostle Paul contain "some difficult passages, the meaning of which the ignorant and untrained distort, as they do also in the case of the other Scriptures, to their own ruin." (2 Pt 3:16)

How then are we to interpret the Bible or help the community to do so?

The fourth chapter of *The Interpretation of the Bible in the Church* addresses that very question and suggests certain principles, methods, and limits that will help us to interpret the Bible. It also acknowledges the importance of our own culture in helping us to interpret, and it suggests what catechists, preachers, and other pastoral ministers might do when examining the Bible or biblical texts.[21]

The Interpretation of the Bible in the Church points out that biblical scholars or exegetes have as their primary task "to determine as accurately as possible the meaning of biblical texts in their own proper context,...in their particular literary and historical context and then in the context of the wider canon of Scripture.[22] In contrast, as catechists or other pastoral ministers work with communities, they draw on the work of exegetes and try to "actualize" the biblical text, that is, to read the text in the light of new circumstances and apply it to contemporary situations of today's church. The "actualization" of the text is possible because the meaning of the biblical text gives it a value for all time and all cultures.

The Interpretation of the Bible in the Church notes that "actualization is necessary" because the biblical passages were composed in cultures of the past and in a language with its own particular and unique expressions. It is therefore necessary through actualization to apply the message "to contemporary circumstances and to express it in language adapted to the present time."[23] This means the community needs to go beneath the historical expressions and discover the true meaning of the biblical passage.

How do we find that meaning? "Actualization," or finding the meaning, "is not a matter of projecting novel opinions or ideologies upon the biblical writings, but of sincerely seeking to discover what the text has to say at the present time" from the point of view of the faith we hold in common.[24] The Bible expresses our faith, and our faith expressions are shaped by the Bible. What we hold in common as the teaching and practice of the church we bring to our interpretation of the Scriptures from which these teaching and practices come.

What methods can we use, then, to actualize the biblical passage? First of all, we as pastoral ministers need excellent and fairly recent translation(s) of the Bible.[25] Second, *The Interpretation of the Bible in the Church* recommends that catechists turn to good introductions[26] and commentaries on Scripture, which will ensure that the catechists are proceeding in the right directions. There are many good commentaries or study guides to the Bible that parishes should have in their pastoral ministry library.[27] Third, in reading the Old Testament, we need to remember that Scripture itself interprets Scripture. Some later passages of the Old Testament interpret earlier passages, and Old Testament texts have also been interpreted in the New Testament. Fourth, Christians read the Bible from the point of view of being Christian; that is, the community reads the texts in relation to the mystery of Christ and of the church. In this way the faith community interprets the text from within the church. As an example of this *The Interpretation of the Bible in the Church* points out that proposing *only* Old Testament events and figures as models of a struggle for liberation is inadequate. The whole of Jesus' life is a struggle for liberation from all forms of oppression.

The Interpretation of the Bible in the Church suggests that interpretation in pastoral ministry includes three steps: (1) hearing the word of God from within our own cultural situation; (2) identifying the present situation that is highlighted by the biblical text; (3) drawing from the biblical text the meaning that clarifies our present situation in a way that enables us to live according to "the saving will of God in Christ." By using this methodology the catechist and/or the community can shed light on various current issues or concerns, such as the preferential option for the poor, or the place of women in society and the church. This method can also lead the community to recognize values of our own culture that were not always acknowledged in biblical times, such as the rights of the human person, the need to preserve and protect the environment, and the longing for world peace.

The Interpretation of the Bible in the Church points out that the process of actualization must operate within certain limits. First, "care should be taken to avoid tendentious interpretations, that is readings that instead of being docile to the text, make use of it only for their own narrow purposes."[28] Some Christian sects do this in order to make the text fit their own purposes. Second, every interpretation that is contrary to justice and charity ought to be rejected. We need to be especially careful of this in reading New Testament texts that refer to "the Jews" or "the Jewish people."

There are many other methodologies for interpreting the meaning of the Bible. Two that raise serious pastoral questions today are the fundamentalist methodology and feminist interpretation. Let us take a look at those methodologies.

185

Fundamentalist Interpretation

One form of interpretation that needs to be avoided is fundamentalism. *The Interpretation of the Bible in the Church* states:

> fundamentalist interpretation starts from the principle that the Bible, being the word of God, inspired and free from error, should be read and interpreted literally in all its details. But by "literal interpretation" it understands a naively literalist interpretation, one...which excludes every effort at understanding the Bible that takes account of its historical origins and development.[29]

Fundamentalism refuses to recognize the historical character of biblical revelation and so is incapable of accepting the full truth of the Incarnation. The writings inspired by the Holy Spirit came from the inheritance and the experiences of the apostolic church, were used in the church's worship, expressed the church's truth, and were canonized by the church fifteen centuries after the New Testament writings were composed. And it is the church, the faith community, that responsibly interprets the text.

The Bible challenges the church and calls it continually to conversion and repentance. The church recognizes that the Scriptures proclaim truths that are normative for the faith community. These truths need to be articulated, preached, taught, and lived by the church. In its interpretation fundamentalism does not follow guidelines of the church because it does not consider the church to be the authoritative body from which the Bible emerged, was approved, and was handed on. Fundamentalism is often anti-church and pays little or no attention to doctrine, creeds, and the liturgical tradition. *The Interpretation of the Bible in the Church* describes fundamentalism as dangerous, for "it invites people to a kind of intellectual suicide."[30]

Sandra Schneiders, a biblical scholar, describes fundamentalism as an extreme position that involves three faulty presuppositions. First, it rests on the false theological position that the authors were verbally inspired by God, a kind of verbal dictation by God to the writer in which the individuality and writing characteristics of the author are subsumed. Second, fundamentalism believes there is such a thing as the "face value" of a text, that is, that one can read a text without interpreting it and that this is the best way to read it. Third, fundamentalism projects a kind of "magic," which implies that God "responds to a disordered human need for absolute certitude."[31]

Fundamentalists ignore the historical roots of the biblical text and its evolution through history. If the text says that God created the world in seven days, fundamentalists accept seven twenty-four hours days as the literal description of creation. They pay no attention to literary forms, even when different biblical texts contradict one another's literal "truth." Sometimes fundamentalism is attractive to people who are seeking absolute certitude, but in giving absolute certitude it denies the questioning character of human life and the possibility of the text being at the same time both rich in meaning and ambiguous.

Feminist Biblical Interpretation

The development of feminist scholarship in the disciplines of theology and biblical studies in the past thirty years has resulted in the recognition that in patriarchal literature such as the Bible the domination of men is not only oppressive for women but is the paradigm for all social oppression. When a society operates under "father rule," the male owns all persons and properties. He has absolute power by reason of being the *paterfamilias*, or head of the household. All who live under his rule are "minors," even sons who are not yet heads of their own households. But a son may some day be a *paterfamilias*, whereas a daughter will never assume such rule. Patriarchal societies exercise control and power over women, who cannot control or rule unless specifically given such power by a male. This system of oppression must, according to feminists, be annihilated.[32] Why, then, do feminist biblical scholars who consider patriarchy oppressive remain members of the Roman Catholic Church, which is one of the most patriarchal social organizations in the world? And since these scholars are united with us in faith, what can we learn from them, particularly about the Bible?

Elisabeth Schüssler Fiorenza, a feminist biblical scholar, proposes that we interpret the Bible from a point of view of "suspicion."[33] Schüssler Fiorenza describes a feminist Christian stance as presuming "that we can trust our lives to the 'word of God' in the Bible and that we should submit to its authority and liberating power." However, this means "that a *hermeneutics of suspicion* should…be applied to the history of exegesis and contemporary interpretations."[34]

Schüssler Fiorenza points out that "the Bible is a male book." "Not only is scripture interpreted by a long line of men and proclaimed in patriarchal churches, it is also authored by men, written in androcentric language, reflective of religious male experience, selected and transmitted by male religious leadership."[35] It is for this reason that she advocates the hermeneutics of suspicion, "the first and never-ending task" of which is

> to elaborate as much as possible the patriarchal, destructive aspects and oppressive elements in the Bible. Such an interpretation must uncover not only sexist biblical language but also the oppressive language of racism, anti-Judaism, exploitation, colonialism, and militarism. An interpretation of suspicion must name the language of hate by its true name and not mystify it or explain it away.[36]

Phyllis Trible, another feminist biblical scholar, describes some of these oppressive elements or problematic texts as "texts of terror."[37] They present women as naturally inferior and subordinate to men. But it is too simple to say that the texts have been misinterpreted, for some biblical texts truly are androcentric, patriarchal, and sexist. What, then, is the church to do about this?

Sandra Schneiders, also a feminist biblical scholar, points out that there are three ways in which women have responded to problematic texts. First, some women have accepted and interiorized their status as subordinate. Second, other women "concluded that the biblical text is so totally and irredeemably oppressive of women, so destructive of female personhood, that it cannot function as word of God for self-respecting women." And finally, writes Schneiders, there are some women who recognize the problem but are so "profoundly christocentric" with "the roots of their identity and personal history" deep in the soil of Christianity that they have "continued to struggle with the question, both theological and exegetical, of the Bible and its role in Christian faith."[38]

How, then, do catechists who are feminists face the biblical text? First of all, they need to understand what we mean when we say the Bible is *the word of God.* The words of the Bible are like all language, symbolic. Symbol is, as described earlier in this chapter and in chapter 4, *that through which* a reality is present. The apostolic faith community symbolized its experience with Jesus in the words of the New Testament. These words of the New Testament are *that through which* the reality of the experience is present to us. They are rich in meaning and at the same time ambiguous. The scriptural words both conceal and reveal. They are intimately related to the reality (the experience of Jesus) they make present, but they are not the fullness of that reality. The words of the Scriptures reveal the Divine Mystery to us. They are not the fullness of revelation, for only Jesus as the Incarnate Word symbolizes the fullness of the Divine Mystery. But God is present to us through the Scriptures. As symbols, the Scriptures are truly the word of God.

But this biblical word, like all symbols, is not always easy to interpret, for it is present to us not as divine speech but through human speech, and it participates in all the limitations of human speech. As human speech it is multivalent, very rich in meaning. As human speech it is also limited. It participates in the culture, characteristics, and faith of the writer. If the writer is a misogynist, androcentric attitudes will undoubtedly be present in his writing.

The human words of the Scriptures are interpretations of the experience of God written by human authors and accepted by the community They are *interpretations* that truly reflect the experiences, but no interpretation can ever match the experience in its fullness. The human words, accepted by the church, attempt to describe the faith community's indescribable experience of the Divine Mystery, and it is impossible to do so fully. The Bible bears witness to the faith of the authors and the community. It also bears witness to the culture and society out of which it emerged.

How then are we to interpret the Bible? While several approaches may be offered, I have selected one as representative of those feminists who remain committed Christians and do not want to excise all offending statements from the text. This methodology also has the advantage of being not simply a feminist methodology but a method acceptable by most exegetes who are biblical centrists. This approach is described much more fully in the writings of Sandra Schneiders.[39]

Reading the biblical text or hearing it proclaimed is not simply a searching for the facts. It is an encounter between the reader and the revelatory experience symbolized through the text. The reader or listener becomes engaged with the text and through this participation arrives at an understanding of the meaning of the text. What happens between the reader and the text is not simply *exegesis* (a process by which one extracts the meaning the author intended from the text) but *interpretation.*

It is possible for every reader to interpret the same text differently, since we all bring our own experiences, education, and prejudices to a text. So it is necessary, states Schneiders, for the community "to develop criteria of validity and to submit diverse interpretations to these criteria applied both by the community of scholars and by the community of believers."[40]

The first criteria of interpretation is to acknowledge that it is the community, inspired by the Spirit that inspired the authors of the Scriptures, which authentically interprets the text. We rely on the community through its teaching, life, and worship to guide us in our interpretation. Second, because exegesis is necessary in the process of interpretation, we turn to reliable commentaries of centrist exegetes for assistance. Third, if the readers or listeners become engaged with the text, they will begin to live in the world of the text while at the same time inhabiting their own world. This will lead the listening or reading community to draw on its own experience as disciples of Jesus in interpreting the biblical text. The surplus of meaning in the original text may emerge as the meaning for this community here and now.[41]

This does not mean that a text can be given any meaning. As Schneiders states, "the competent reader of the classical or normative texts of any community is not first and foremost the individual community member but the community itself."[42] We turn to the community for interpretation, and we find that the community lives not by Scripture alone, though it is a privileged norm, but also by Tradition, by the teaching, life, and worship of the church, and Tradition helps us to interpret the Scriptures.[43]

Both Tradition and Scripture go together in the hermeneutical or interpretive task. Just as through the centuries the church came to understand that the slavery approved of in Paul's letters is not in harmony with Christian discipleship, and that the suggestions of anti-Semitism in John and Matthew are not compatible with the Christian vision, so an interpretation that brings the world of today in conversation with the biblical world can transform our understanding of the place of women in the world. Listeners to or readers of the Bible need to recognize that the faith and the culture of the writers influenced their biblical writings just as our own faith and culture influence our understanding of the biblical text. As the two cultures challenge each other, the unity of faith enables us to arrive at new and transforming insights. The Spirit who inspired the writers is still with the community, inspiring it as it reads and hears the biblical word. Women's experience affects their faith and vision and their insight often enables us to read the Scriptures with a fresh perspective.

The Interpretation of the Bible in the Church addresses the question of feminist interpretation of the Bible as one distinctive approach among others. It mentions that feminist interpretation follows the historical-critical method of exegesis and it adds two criteria to its investigation of the biblical text:

> Feminist exegesis has brought many benefits. Women...have succeeded, often better than men, in detecting the presence, the significance, and the role of women in the Bible, in Christian origins, and in the Church. The world view of today,

because of its greater attention to the dignity of women and to their role in society and in the Church, ensures that new questions are put to the biblical text, which in turn occasions new discoveries. Feminist sensitivity helps to unmask and correct certain commonly accepted interpretations that were tendentious and sought to justify the male domination of women.[44]

Feminist scripture scholars such as Sandra Schneiders, Elisabeth Schüssler Fiorenza, Pheme Perkins, and others are bringing the richness of women's experience and insights to their work and those of us who are pastoral ministers need to recognize their work, which is now available to assist us in our ministries.

The Lectionary for Mass

The *Lectionary for Mass* is a book that includes the selection of biblical readings to be proclaimed during Mass throughout the liturgical year. At the request of Vatican Council II the lectionary for the Roman Catholic Church was revised so that "the treasures of the Bible [may] be opened up more lavishly so that a richer fare may be provided for the faithful at the table of God's word. In this way the more significant part of the sacred Scriptures will be read to the people over a fixed number of years."[45] This richer fare includes three readings at each Sunday Eucharist: one from the Old Testament, the second from the New Testament apart from the Gospels, and the third from one of the Gospels.

In a three-year cycle of readings, the Gospel of Matthew is proclaimed the first year, Mark the second, and Luke the third year. The Gospel of John appears on special feasts during each of the three years. Selections from the Old Testament include texts that relate to the Gospel passage and/or foreshadow the deeds and actions of Jesus.[46]

Daily readings for Mass are arranged on a two-year cycle, with the first readings changing each year while the Gospel passages remain the same. The lectionary also includes readings for Masses on special occasions. The Roman lectionary or ones similar to it are used in other Christian churches, including the Episcopal Church, the United Presbyterians, the United Church of Christ, the United Disciples of Christ.

The first edition of the revised lectionary was published in 1970. A second edition, in three volumes, was published for all the dioceses of the United States in 1999.⁴⁷ The "Introduction" to the second edition is important reading for all directors of catechetical ministry and members of parish staffs, particularly anyone who is doing lectionary catechesis.

The lectionary is a liturgical book. It is the Bible contextualized in the life of the faith community. It is the word of God addressed to the people as a community. As a biblical word, it a living and active word, as sharp as a "two-edged sword penetrating even between soul and spirit, joints and marrow, and able to discern reflections and thoughts of the heart" (Heb 4:13). Those who "proclaim" the lessons or readings are proclaiming the word of God to the community assembled for worship. As the word of God, the biblical reading challenges the community to conversion and transformation.

Gerard Sloyan comments that the "Introduction" to the *Lectionary* (1970 edition) gives the impression "that no one should be allowed to read publicly or preach but those who know the Bible."⁴⁸ This is also true of catechists: only those who know the Bible should catechize from it. As suggested: catechists can develop an "intimate knowledge of the Bible," beginning with the Gospels, by prayerful study and using recommended commentaries.⁴⁹

The church has always considered the word of God as a treasure comparable to the Eucharist. It cannot be carelessly or inadequately proclaimed. As the proclaimed word of God, the lessons must be read well, clearly and distinctly with rhythm and interpretation, without drawing attention to the reader. As a catechetical word they must also be read and interpreted well. Both the lector and the catechist need to be friends with the Bible, reading it regularly as a form of prayer. Lectoring and catechizing are ministries for which the gifts of the Spirit are needed. Not everyone has the right to be a minister, but only those who have been gifted for the ministry. Those who prepare readers or catechists for their ministry must be able to recognize the gift of the Spirit within them for these ministries.

An important aspect of the reading or hearing of the lections at Mass or the proclamation of the word in lectionary catechesis is that we recall that in the proclamation and the catechesis Christ is always present. The word is like the Eucharist, itself a manifestation of Christ's presence with his community. It is for this reason that the "Introduction" to the lectionary notes: "The word of God constantly proclaimed in the Liturgy is always, then, a living and effective word through the power of the Holy Spirit,"[50] so it expresses God's love that never fails in its effectiveness toward us.

In some parishes people gather with the homilist and reflect on the Sunday readings in preparation for a homily, and a team gathers with the catechist to explore a biblical passage. Sloyan points out that in gatherings for lectoring (or catechizing) groups tend to ask the question, What does this passage mean to me? much too early. Reflection on the scriptural passage is not just a search for meaning for me but an entry into the life of the community and a search for what it means for *us* as a community. In lectionary catechesis the catechist leads the community to recognize and read the Bible as its own story, the story of its past as a clue to its present story.

Most homilists and most catechists seem to focus on the Gospels when they preach or catechize. As a result the people seldom discover the riches of the Old Testament. Sloyan accurately describes the lack of regular Bible reading from the Jewish Scriptures as causing a "hellish cycle of poverty" for all of us.[51] This is also true in catechesis. Catechists need to do a basic introduction to the Old Testament for most adult groups. This catechesis is not meant to be an instruction, though a parish may offer a class on how to read the Bible. In catechesis we need to share the stories of the Hebrew/Jewish Scriptures and their relationship to the Gospels. Frequently it is only when we know the story of the Hebrew Scriptures that we can understand the stories of the New Testament, and knowing the New Testament helps us understand the Hebrew Scriptures.

The lectionary organizes biblical readings for the community. This can be a real help for catechists who need help in organizing their reading. But the selection of readings in the lectionary is both a gift and a problem for the church. It is a gift in that it offers what those who compiled it thought were important stories from the Gospels and the whole Bible. It is a problem in that the compilers approached the Bible as all of us do with a certain bias in support of some passages and perhaps a cultural bias that prevented other readings from being included. Many women have, for example, found the biblical readings from the lectionary ambiguous. The community does not hear the stories of women, nor are most women presented in the readings as other than subservient or inferior to the men. For example, a significant Gospel story, the healing of the "bent-over woman" who stood up and praised God in defiance of the religious leaders is not included (Lk 13:10–17). This is only one example of many.[52] While the Bible itself incorporates a cultural bias (How could it do otherwise?), a cultural bias is still present twenty centuries later as is evident in the choosing or non-choosing of the readings. Both catechists and homilists need to be aware of this and their own cultural bias.

In the past decade many parishes have introduced a form of catechesis called "lectionary catechesis," which is offered primarily for children. This form of biblical catechesis is often welcomed by adults. In many dioceses the Renew program has as its core reflection on the biblical readings from the lectionary. Lectionary catechesis, like all biblical catechesis, focuses on the significance of the Bible in the life of the Christian community.

Befriending the Bible

The Bible is a love story—not a story about a wonderful love of the past but a story about God's love for all of us and each one of us now. If the past is prelude to the present, surely the wondrous story of the love of the Mystery for our ancestors is a prelude that describes the extraordinary love which the Mystery offers us now. In biblical catechesis the community looks at its concerns and questions and then turns to the Bible and seeks to discover what it says to us about our current concern or question. The Bible is not an answer sheet but a symbolic word, rich in meaning and at the same time ambiguous. It both reveals and conceals at the same time. As a community seeks insights from the Bible that will enable it to understand its life concerns and issues, it cannot expect specific answers for every question. The community needs to pray patiently, reflecting on and studying the meaning of the biblical passage or story. The Bible is not a "magic" word that gives immediate assurances about all exigencies. It is a loving word that, once we engage it, enlightens us, informs us, challenges us, and embraces us. It calls us to a conversion of heart and mind and action.

Every catechist needs to befriend the Bible. As catechists we need to ask the Holy Spirit to give us wisdom, knowledge, and truth. We need to turn to the Scriptures in quiet and listen as God's word speaks to us. As we reflect we remember that the Bible is a love story, a love story that involves us. It is the story of our past, but it is also our present story, a story through which God is speaking to us. Catechists cannot turn to the Bible in catechesis for a word of comfort or a word of challenge unless they have internalized through prayer and reflection the nature of the story the Bible tells. An oil painting teacher once told me that if I wished to paint well I needed to "caress the canvas" with my brush. Catechists need "to caress the Bible" with eyes and ears, with minds and hearts, if they are going to lead the community in a biblical or lectionary catechesis.

Catechists and ministers of the gospel need to listen to the biblical readings attentively, with faith. It is only then that they can lead their communities or small groups to listen reverently and respectfully. Such listening will sometimes challenge the community or members within it to change their favorite habits, to do what they really don't want to do, to become what they are afraid to become. When Jesus spoke of leaving mother and father and letting the dead bury the dead he was calling his listeners to conversion and transformation. The gospel does this all the time. It challenges people to a commitment to gospel living. It calls them to transformation in life. It says "take up your cross," and who among us wants to do that? It does what a loving God does—call us to be our best selves.

People befriend the gospel by living with it, by meditating on it, by turning to it for their vision of reality. Catechists cannot catechize with the Bible if they are not friends with the Bible. They cannot decide what Bible stories or teaching will help a community if they are not familiar with the biblical stories and teachings. Daily reading of the Bible with an accompanying commentary prepares catechists for their ministry. Befriending the Bible means seeking the presence of God's word as you would seek the presence of a friend, listening to the Bible as you listen to a friend, speaking with the Bible as you speak with a friend, loving the Bible as you love a friend.

When we as catechists turn to the Bible in catechesis we turn to it as a holy book which is calling the community to transformation or conversion. Whether questions about the Bible are what bring the community together, as in a Renew Program or Bible study group, or whether we turn to the Bible to help us interpret a particular human experience such as a divorce or a fatal illness, we turn to it with reverence and as a faithful community of pray-ers and believers. For the believing person and community the Bible is a symbol of our belief and of the belief of the community which has befriended and revered it for twenty centuries.

Befriend the Bible and teach your catechists to be friends with the Bible. If a catechist visits the office of the director of catechetical ministry and sees an artistic and worthy edition of the Bible enthroned in a special place, and if the director occasionally reads the Bible with the catechists in prayer, the catechist will learn to turn to the Bible for sustenance and life.

Catechizing with the Bible

Symbolic catechesis on the Bible recognizes that the Sacred Scriptures are the preeminent writings in the church. The New Testament writings, particularly the Gospels, come from the apostolic community, and consequently they have a special place in the life of Christians and in catechesis. Biblical catechesis follows the same pattern as other forms of occasional catechesis. It begins with the gathering, which is followed by (1) reflecting on a common experience; (2) correlating the experience with a faith symbol (e.g., the Bible); (3) moving outward in acts of justice together; (4) praying together; and finally, the sending forth or *coda*. In biblical catechesis the Bible becomes central in the second of the four catechetical movements. After considering in movement 1 a common experience such as the death of a loved one or a serious illness, the community turns in movement 2 to a biblical passage or teaching for deeper meaning. The community listens as a particular passage is read, for example, the death of Lazarus and Jesus' crying at the loss of his friend, or the story of the resurrection of Jesus, and then together the community seeks to relate the biblical passage to its own experience and insight. The community may turn to the First Epistle to the Corinthians, in which Paul writes of the resurrection and sings:

> Listen, I will tell you a mystery! We will not all die, but we will all be changed, in a moment, in the twinkling of an eye, at the last trumpet. For the trumpet will sound, and the dead will be raised imperishable, and we will be changed. (1 Cor 15:51–52)

The richness of the biblical story and the variety of experiences that each of the participants brings to the correlation may lead the community to some new insight about its own experience. At the same time its own experience can lead to a richer appreciation for the biblical story.

Or if a catechetical community comes together because it is interested in a specific book such as the Gospel of Matthew, it may, during the first movement, examine how Matthew's Gospel came into being, for whom it was written, and what it means in the life of the church. In the second movement the community could read a number of chapters aloud and then together reflect on what Matthew was saying to his listeners and what the Gospel is saying to us today. At a second or third meeting the community may in movement 1 reflect on the previous week's reading and discussion and how it relates to their lives. In movement 2 they would read another section of Matthew's Gospel aloud, for example the Sermon on the Mount, and then reflect on the sermon. The community will seek to discover how this sermon relates to its life today.

In both examples, beginning with a previous experience and with an interest in the Gospel of Matthew, the community follows the same process of interaction and participation. In the third movement the community turns to the question of how this Gospel moves it as a community to do justice. And finally, in the fourth movement whatever biblical passage was the focus of movement 2 will be the biblical passage from which a few verses will be read during the ritual prayer.

Joseph A. Grassi, a biblical scholar with extraordinary pastoral insights, recommends that Christians need to both *discover* and *rediscover* the Jesus story in the Gospels. Grassi notes that the word "discover" means "to remove some kind of impeding 'cover.'"[53] The "cover" to which Grassi refers is twofold: first, our cultural inadequacy in that we do not have the knowledge and familiarity with the Hebrew/Jewish Scriptures possessed by ancient audiences, and second, a lack of appreciation for the Gospels as "dramatic narratives." In regard to the recovery of the Gospels as dramatic narratives, Grassi writes:

> This recovery is essential; over the centuries, the inner drama of the gospels has become cluttered by intensive use of these stories as sources of information, fact-finding and sometimes even dogmas about Jesus. This has resulted in some scholars even setting themselves up as possessing a privileged monopoly on the understanding of the gospels.
>
> The expression "dramatic narrative" is not just another phrase of scholarly lingo. A similar example today would be a good play, opera or movie. People today would quickly abandon crowded movie halls if they knew they had to attend classes or lectures to find out the meaning of what they have seen and heard, and worse still if they needed to take notes during performances or take an exam afterward![54]

The question is, How can the director of catechesis or the parish staff prepare catechists to read the Bible as God's word addressed to them, as a love story?[55]

One way to learn to appreciate the Gospels as dramatic narrative is to read a Gospel aloud. Grassi recommends that before starting to study the Gospels one should "read (aloud if possible) the entire gospel...in one or two sittings. As dramatic narrative, each story has meaning in light of the whole story of Jesus. Not to do this would be like returning to a movie for ten-minute sections each week!"[56] Catechizing through the Bible means reading the Bible aloud with the community, helping them to become familiar with its parts and themes so they can comfortably read and pray with it when alone or with family or friends. Every member of the catechetical community needs to have his or her own Bible. When the Bible is being proclaimed in prayer, it is preferable to encourage the community to listen attentively rather than to read it while it is being read to them.

Since the catechists or catechetical team will know the human experience the community will consider, they can prepare for the catechesis by choosing which biblical passage relates to the experience. It is important that the catechist know the literary form and historical situation in which the passage was written. Commentaries by centrist exegetes will help the catechist understand the biblical passages. As noted earlier, *The New Jerome Biblical Commentary* (Englewood Cliffs, N.J.: Prentice-Hall, 1990), the *Sacra Pagina* series, or *Zacchaeus Studies* of the Liturgical Press are reliable references. Every parish ought to have at least one copy of the *New Jerome Biblical Commentary* available, and catechists can purchase for their own personal use copies of *Zacchaeus Studies* or *Sacra Pagina*. Some catechists will want to have a copy of Raymond E. Brown's *An Introduction to the New Testament* and/or Walter Brueggemann's *The Bible Makes Sense*. *The New Jerome Biblical Handbook* is another valuable and inexpensive commentary that can be of major assistance to the catechist.[57] A parish library with recent biblical references will make the catechesis more interesting and representative of the church as a community.

Since many Catholics, particularly adult Catholics, have not had much biblical education, it is important to give them whatever basic information about the Bible they might need.[58] This includes the names of the divisions into the Old and the New Testaments (now often referred to as the First and Second Testaments), the relationship that exists between the First and Second Testaments, the recognition of the Gospels as preeminent Christian books,[59] the kinds of literary forms found in the Bible, and what the church means when it says the Bible is an inspired book. Commentaries by centrist exegetes may be shared with them or recommended to them.

The Interpretation of the Bible in the Church describes the Sacred Scriptures as "the starting point, foundation, and norm of catechetical teaching." When the community turns to a symbol of faith to shed light on the meaning of its own experiences or questions, it turns first to the Bible, the foundation of church teaching and the norm of Christian living. The catechist will initiate both individuals and the community into "a correct understanding and fruitful reading of the Bible."[60] Catechists can also employ the interpretation methodologies recommended earlier and use several commentaries in introducing the community to the Bible.

While catechesis cannot introduce the whole Bible, it should make use of "stories, both those of the New Testament and those of the Old. It will also single out the Decalogue," and introduce prophetic oracles, the wisdom teaching, and the sermons of Jesus in the New Testament.[61] In all ministries "the presentation should be done in such a way as to elicit an encounter with Christ, who provides the key to the whole biblical revelation and communicates the call of God that summons each one to respond."[62]

Lectionary catechesis follows the same approach as biblical catechesis, an approach that follows the four movements of catechesis. In lectionary catechesis, however, the readings for the Sunday Eucharist are the experience to be considered (movement 1), and the correlation of the lections with life will be movement 2. In the correlation movement the catechist and community may draw on any one of the three lections.

Catechists might also consider that the preparation or training of men and women to be lectors is a catechetical moment. Being a good lector involves much more than being a good reader. It means that the reader can interpret the text because he or she is familiar with and reverences the Bible as the word of God. Good mechanics are not enough to make a good reader. Even the best of voices cannot invite the community to conversion if the meaning of the text is not clear to the reader.

In catechetical preparation for lectors, movement 1 could be an examination of why one would want to be a lector, or the relationship of the lector to the community and to the Bible. Other topics that might be considered are: Why is the Bible called the word of God? Why is the word proclaimed whenever the community assembles for public worship? Why do we turn to the church for the meaning of the word we proclaim? What is it that the lector is really doing? How can a lector proclaim the word of God and the meaning of that word and not intrude on it by our own mannerisms or idiosyncrasies?

The second movement of correlation could be a reflection on Hebrews 4:13: "Indeed the word of God is living and active, sharper than any two-edged sword, piercing until it divides soul from spirit, joint from marrow; it is able to judge the thoughts and intentions of the heart." Or the catechist might turn to a concordance and see what other biblical passages on "the word of God" are listed. We move from the Bible to its commentaries and concordances and back to the Bible, and as we do that we consider our own insights and experiences and the insights and experiences of the church itself. Discerning which passages may be used with particular communities takes time and prayer. The process cannot be rushed.

The *Christian Community Bible* prepared for the people of the Philippines has been used in biblical catechesis for quite a number of years and offers within the text, as footnotes, some of the comments of ordinary people who have read and interpreted the Bible in a catechetical situation. These comments remind us that to understand the Bible one must listen prayerfully and attentively, knowing that it is the story of God's love for all the people. An illustration of the kind of profound insights ordinary people have to offer may be found in the following short commentary on Exodus 2.

Exodus 2 begins with the story of Pharaoh's command to his people that "every boy that is born to the Hebrews you shall throw into the Nile, but you shall let every girl live" (Ex 1:22). The chapter goes on to tell the story of a Levite woman who has a son, hides him for three months, then makes a basket in which to hide him among the reeds on the bank of the river. His sister keeps protective watch over him. The daughter of Pharaoh discovers the child, recognizes that he is probably a Hebrew, protects him, and is led by his sister to give the child into the care of his Hebrew mother. He, Moses, grows up to become the great leader of the Hebrew people.

This biblical story was told to a small community of people in the third world and from that community came the following commentary on or interpretation of the story:

> The liberation of the Hebrew people begins with a simple, solitary act—that of a mother risking her life to save her son.
>   Her action is the manifestation of a mother's love. It is the rebellion of a conscience that refuses to obey an inhuman law. It is the act of faith of a mother who anticipates the wonderful future that God opens to a newly-born life, knowing also that children are the future of her people.[63]

This unique interpretation may be the story as seen from the point of view of a mother. It is the interpretation of a faithful person, in community, who recognizes the significance of the mother's act. It interprets the story from a particular viewpoint and out of the interpreter's culture. It is a catechetical reflection.

Many catechetical communities with whom this approach has been tried have expressed great joy and appreciation for the process. It relates the Bible to life. It relates life to the biblical word. The Bible is the word of God, a symbol of faith and a symbol of catechesis. It is living and active as symbols are, and it calls the reader or the hearer(s) to conversion. This is how the Bible elicits a response. And this is how catechists present it in catechesis. It reaches into the innermost thoughts and hearts of people.

FURTHER READINGS

Brown, Raymond E. *An Introduction to the New Testament*. Anchor Bible Reference Library. New York: Doubleday, 1997.

Brueggemann, Walter. *The Bible Makes Sense*. Revised edition. Winona, Minn.: St. Mary's Press, 1997.

Gallagher, Maureen. *The Art of Catechesis: What You Need to Be, Know, and Do*. With a Foreword by Archbishop Rembert G. Weakland. New York: Paulist Press, 1998.

Grassi, Joseph. *Rediscovering the Jesus Story: A Participatory Guide*. New York: Paulist Press, 1995.

The Pontifical Biblical Commission. *The Interpretation of the Bible in the Church*. Vatican City: Libreria Editrice Vaticana, 1993.

Schneiders, Sandra. *Beyond Patching: Faith and Feminism in the Catholic Church*. New York: Paulist Press, 1991.

———. *The Revelatory Text: Interpreting the New Testament as Sacred Scripture*. San Francisco: Harper, 1991.

Schüssler Fiorenza, Elisabeth. *Bread Not Stone: The Challenge of Feminist Biblical Interpretation*. Boston: Beacon Press, 1984.

———. *In Memory of Her: A Feminist Theological Reconstruction of Christian Origins*. New York: Crossroad, 1992.

CHAPTER 8

The Church Symbols:
Doctrine and Saints

The young girls and boys who graduate from elementary school today have a rudimentary knowledge of mathematics. That knowledge will not carry them very far into the work world of the twenty-first century. Even if they complete their secondary education and have several more courses in mathematics, they will not be ready for work in the technological world. In fact, technology companies are so concerned about the education of their future workers that in several cities they have entered into alliances with local school districts. They pay some of their employees to teach in the local public high schools or community colleges. But even after two years of community college students are often lacking in the basic tools of technology. They must continue to be taught after they enter the workplace. Surely an elementary or even a secondary education will not prepare one for adult work in a technological world that is constantly changing.

But strange as it may seem, many Catholics think an elementary school education in a Catholic school gives them enough understanding to prepare them to live a faithful life in a world that often sees their faith as an anachronism. Or if they have gone to a Catholic secondary school they do not realize that they are still novices in understanding what the Catholic Church professes as truth. Of course regular participation in Sunday Eucharist with good homilies does challenge and support some growth in faith, but it is the equivalent of learning how to be a gourmet cook by occasionally attending lectures by chefs of various competencies. When people are facing a crisis or are simply bored with life, their limited understanding of the teachings of the church does not always support them. Too many Catholic adults live with what amounts to a child's understanding of the church's teachings. A child's understanding won't sustain them in an adult world.

This chapter will consider from an adult point of view why doctrine is not only important to the church, but is a gift to us as the people of God. It will describe some forms of doctrinal language. It will not examine particular doctrines but rather the place of doctrine in the life of the church.

Language about God

The *General Directory for Catechesis* notes that theology is the "systematic treatment and the scientific investigation of the truths of faith." It also describes theology as an enterprise that "seeks to develop understanding of the faith." It points out that "theology, in order to fulfill this function, needs to confront philosophical forms of thought, various forms of humanism and the human sciences, and dialogue with them."[1]

Gerald O'Collins described theology as "any scientific or methodical attempt to understand and interpret divine revelation mediated through the data of Scripture and tradition."[2] Theologians bring the resources of reason in union with faith to describe the Mystery of God in itself and in relation to the world. Theology preserves the thought and teaching of the past even as it describes our present understanding. Theologians are constantly reinterpreting reality; not constantly changing but constantly seeking meaning within the parameters of present life and culture and the church's life. Theologians do theology for other theologians, for the magisterium, and for the whole church, that the church may understand, clarify, and teach about the Mystery, *God for us.*

In the eleventh century St. Anselm of Canterbury defined theology as "faith seeking understanding." Today theologians expand on Anselm's basic definition. Elizabeth Johnson states that theology is "a discipline of speaking which moves back and forth, spiraling around life and faith within the cultural context of a given time and place." Dermot Lane describes theology as "the critical unpacking of the revelation of God that takes place in human experience through faith." Gregory Baum presents the task of the theologian as "to interpret the faith-experience of the Church." Anne Carr reminds us that theology "should include serious reflection on the experience of the female half of the human community, which has long been excluded from theological discussion."[3]

Very few theologians in the history of the Christian church have attempted to study all areas of theology. Most of them confine themselves to a particular speciality, for example, moral theology, fundamental theology, liturgical theology, Christology, or ecclesiology. The whole of Christian faith is too broad and deep an area of study for most theologians. People such as Thomas Aquinas and Bonaventure, or in our own time Catholic theologians such as Karl Rahner and Edward Schillebeeckx are unusual in their ability to synthesize and integrate multiple theological specialties.

There are and have been from the beginning multiple theologies. Peter and Paul had differing views about the initiation of Jews into the community. Paul's view became the church's teaching. Some of St. Thomas Aquinas's teachings were condemned after his death, but his theology has since been formally endorsed by various popes and has acquired a quasi-official status in the church. When theologians disagree and when it is important to do so, the magisterium speaks and interprets for the whole church the experience which the theologians debate.

The *magisterium,* or teaching office of the church, is the final arbiter of theological discourse. Generally the Latin word *magisterium* refers to the teaching role of bishops. It sometimes refers to papal infallibility, that is, those times when the pope definitively declares a teaching on faith or morals. "Supreme magisterium" refers to the bishops gathered with the Roman pontiff in an ecumenical council.[4] The bishops and pope together exercise what is called the "ordinary magisterium" when they pronounce in a definitive but not infallible manner a teaching "that leads to better understanding of Revelation in matters of faith and morals."[5]

Catechesis and theology are closely related, but catechesis is not simply a delivery system for theology. It is not the popularization of theology nor a mere repeating of the teaching of the church. *Sharing the Light of Faith* states that "catechesis draws on theology, and theology draws in turn on the richness of the Church's catechetical experience. Both must be at the service of the Church. Though intimately related, they are distinguishable by their goals, methods, and criteria."[6]

Some theorists have proposed that catechesis, or so-called religious education, is a kind of "practical theology," an education guided by theology and focusing on ethics or "practical living."[7] This resembles in some ways the thinking of those who believe catechesis is no more than a simplified teaching of the truths of the church for children or uneducated adults. While the advocates of practical theology are not in any way recommending a watered-down theology, their theory promotes another form of theology rather than a catechesis. The primary goal of catechesis is the conversion of the community. That is not the primary goal of theology.

Catechesis reflects theology in that it is a ministry in which the community seeks understanding, but unlike theology it does not require knowledge of the languages of research, nor is it a scientific treatment of the truths of the faith. Catechesis uses the language of the people—image and metaphor and story—and the experience of the people in correlation with the church's faith symbols in order to describe the profound and extraordinary character of our relationship to the Mystery and to one another.

The Language of Mystery

John Shea is a great storyteller and promoter of storytelling as a way of speaking about God and religious faith. He is a master in the use of language. This is because his imagination leads him to tell us old stories in such a new way that we don't realize they are old stories.[8] His imagination is alive, energetic, and dynamic, while many of us have let our imaginations wither. Imaginations don't exactly die, but they can become dull.

Shea tells us that there are different ways of describing God.[9] He calls them "The Ways of God Language." What are these languages? They are the language of awe, of image, of story, of doctrine, and of dogma. Each form describes God in a different way, and each has its own time and place for use. Let us examine them.

The Language of Awe

According to Shea, the first way we speak about God is through a word of awe. When people have an unusual or extraordinary experience, they respond with a gasp of passion or a single word of surprise. The birth of your own child is an example of an awe-inspiring experience. The mother and father take the child into their arms and are so overwhelmed that often they cannot speak. Tears or a smile express the meaning that words cannot say. Or perhaps they say softly, "O God. O God."

When we have an awe-inspiring experience, we cannot speak. What has happened to us is more than we can utter. There is a mystery about it that precludes our use of language. I remember driving with a friend one summer from Illinois to California. One evening as the sun started to set we completed a curve in the road and came upon Grand Tetons National Park. It was a glorious sight. I don't know if it was the time of the day and the placement of the sun's rays, or if the mountains would have seemed so extraordinary at any time of the day, but we were so moved by the beauty of this unexpected sight that we pulled the car over to the side of the road, got out of the car and stood and looked. We did not say a word. Indeed, we could only gasp. Finally we exclaimed simply, "O God, how beautiful!" and we knew we had said a prayer.

The phrase "O God!" is not simply a word of exclamation but an actual calling on the Mystery. The awe expresses us. It is a word of wonder, a prayer. Shea says this is "vocative" language; it calls on the Mystery. The experience of the Divine in our lives evokes from us a response to that Mystery. Abraham Heschel wrote that "the beginning of awe is wonder, and the beginning of wisdom is awe."[10] The language of awe is relational language describing our self-involvement with the Mystery, whom we can only inadequately name no matter how much or often we try.

The Language of Image

The language of awe is satisfying, but unsatisfactory for communicating the reality of the experience of God. So people struggle to name the Mystery through *images*, which are a second form of God-language. We proclaim our amazement, and then we say that God is creator, artist, father, mother. No one image satisfies; each image is inadequate, so, according to Shea, we pile image upon image and continually struggle for new images to name God. The traditional images of the past still carry meaning, and some are special in the Tradition because they were introduced to us by Jesus. But in our metropolitan, technological, and intergalactic world of the twenty-first century, shepherd and scribe are images that often do not affect us. So we search for new images that fit our time and culture: friend, counselor, mentor, lover, liberator, artist, comforter, sophia-wisdom.

The Language of Story

But images alone are not a strong enough form of God-language for most people, and so we turn to a third way of speaking about God, the language of *story*, or narrative. Jesus not only imaged God as "father," but he told the story of a father prodigal with his love so that we would know what kind of father God is. So that we might know what a true neighbor is, Jesus told the story of a Samaritan who befriended a Jew. In describing God's forgiveness Jesus told the story of a woman who lost a coin and went searching for it. In God-language we move from wonder to image to story—all evocative forms of language, ways of language that stir the heart and call for the response of love.

The Language of Doctrine

But God-language cannot end with story, for people extract meaning from stories. While stories are powerful carriers of meaning, they are, as symbols, ambiguous as well. The constant search for meaning leads to the distilling of the core of the story into the fourth and fifth forms of God-language, the language of doctrine and dogma. We move from the image and story of God as father (or mother) to the statement that God is a loving father or mother. That is a *meaning* that may be distilled from the story of the prodigal son. In formulating doctrine we move from the concrete to the abstract, from the story of a loving parent, to God is loving. The abstract language of the catechism—God is all powerful, all knowing, infinitely perfect—while it might be less effective catechetically, emerged from the concrete language of the images and stories of the Bible. It is less ambiguous, and it expresses the meaning of the stories and images.

Meaning gives life purpose and makes it comprehensible. Meaning can free people and bring new insights. Our minds move rapidly from one insight to another, and from those insights we develop an understanding of our world. We develop convictions about reality. We make decisions based on those convictions. Those convictions become constitutive of our personhood and identity. We become ourselves because of our convictions. Meaning enables us to envision the world and our relationship to it. People need meaning; they seek meaning; they desire meaning; they search for meaning.

All language forms communicate meaning, and narrative may be the most expressive form, particularly for God-language, but theologians and philosophers tend to abstract meaning from its story context in order to clarify a concept. The concept is doctrine. Different doctrines or meanings relate or unite and new insights emerge. And these new insights are constantly being restated in language that speaks to different cultures in different times. Doctrines are a way of responding to the human search for meaning.

Doctrines are meant to be life-giving. If they have not always been so, it may be because not all of those who formulated doctrine recognized the relationship of doctrine to other forms of language, to the human community, or to human experience. This is what Josef Jungmann decried when he spoke about "arid intellectualism" in the catechisms. But "aridity" is not a characteristic of doctrine. It describes an inadequate expression of truth, though expressions of truth about God are never completely adequate.

The Language of Dogma

Doctrines are distilled into a form of language which we call "dogma," or which Shea calls the "non-negotiable" doctrines. Dogmas describe our most precious and significant meanings. For Christians there is no question about the acceptance of dogmas; they are the essentials of the faith. These "dogmas" will never change, though the way in which the church expresses them may change. For example, the teaching that God is trinitarian is "non-negotiable." It is a dogma. The catechism describes it as "the central mystery of Christian faith and life."[11] The Trinity distinguishes Christianity from all other religious traditions. It formulates the church's understanding about God, an understanding not dogmatically stated by Jesus but evident through his words and actions. Speaking of God as Trinity expresses the church's understanding about the Mystery to which all Christians commit themselves. There is no option about accepting this or other dogmas, though the dogma may be articulated or described in many different ways.

That Jesus, the Christ, is truly human and truly divine is another central dogma. The mystery of the incarnation which that dogma describes is a foundational truth for Christians. That the Holy Spirit is always with us as comforter and spirit of light and truth, is another non-negotiable doctrine. That the church with all its failings and inadequacies is the symbol of the risen Lord is a dogma. We as church proclaim these dogmas in the creeds, both the Apostles' Creed and the Nicene Creed.

The Nicene Creed as an example of dogma is full of images, none adequate, each one trying to outdo the other in speaking its truth, most of them poetic. It describes Jesus as "God from God, Light from light." It images the Holy Spirit as "the Lord, the giver of life,…who has spoken through the prophets." It is a proclamation of faith, that is, a declaration of commitment to the Trinity, the Triune Mystery. The Nicene Creed which the church proclaims at Sunday Eucharist is a translation from Greek into Latin and then into English. It is prayed in a language that preserves the church's meaning but may for cultural reasons be inadequate for evoking faith from men and women of the twenty-first century. That is one reason why Pope Paul VI pronounced the "Credo of the People of God," in St. Peter's Basilica in June 1968. Pope Paul's Credo was a reaffirmation of the fundamental truths of Christian faith, an affirmation written in language designed to appeal to and evoke a response from people of Pope Paul's time.

The Nicene Creed is a prayer that proclaims non-negotiable doctrines. It is a declaration of commitment to the Trinity, to the Mystery of salvation through Jesus, to the gift of the Spirit, to the place of the church in this Mystery of our liberation and freedom (salvation) from evil. It is a proclamation of the life-death-resurrection of the Lord. Dogmas like those in the Nicene or Apostles' creeds are proclaimed in a form of God-language used to communicate, express, and make understandable the Mystery that is beyond all comprehension. Unfortunately its language, which is itself a translation of the original language, is not always adequate for people who proclaim it sixteen centuries after it was composed.

From its beginning the apostolic community tried to understand what meanings were evident in the life and teaching of Jesus. This was not simply an intellectual game but a necessary step in determining how to live out its faith commitment. Sometimes the meaning was not as obvious as at other times, and so the community debated within itself and tried to discern within an environment of community prayer and trust in the Spirit the meaning of Jesus. An obvious example of this is the discernment described in the Acts of the Apostles about whether Gentile Christians needed to keep the Jewish observances (chapter 15). Luke tells us that Paul and Barnabas "had no small dissension and debate" with those who taught that without circumcision you cannot be saved (Acts 15:2). So they went to Jerusalem and considered the matter with the apostles and elders. "After there had been much debate (Acts 15:7)," a decision was made. The church examined the life and teaching of the Lord to decide what the truth was. And from that debate came forth, in this case, an understanding about what practices were essential in Christian life. The debate brought forth a decision that affected peoples' lives. Formulations of both doctrine and dogma can do that. Understanding them can transform our lives.

Doctrine and Dogma as Symbolic Expressions of Faith

Doctrinal statements are symbolic expressions that express and constitute our relations with God. They are powerful symbols, for they call us to transformation of life. They call us to re-creation. They influence our lives in a powerful way. They are ambiguous and at the same time rich in meaning. They continually manifest new meaning, meaning that was once hidden in them.

The Language of Doctrine Challenges

Christian doctrine is dangerous, for it reveals that the God who loves all people unconditionally, dynamically, and eternally is calling us to this same kind of unconditional love. It is evocative. Doctrine challenges us to respond to the Mystery it reveals. Through doctrine God is daring us to treat all people with reverence and respect. The truth that God loves us and calls us to love our neighbor unsettles us. It evokes change in the way we live. We must care for those who are marginalized or dispossessed, those who are poor and in need. We must care for them not only by providing temporary assistance but by changing the systems that keep them oppressed. Doctrine calls us to conversion. It is dangerous for it makes ultimate sense, and by making sense it gives us meaning and power and vision—it can transform us.

Accepting Christian truth is not just the acceptance of a statement about truth, but the acceptance of the profound meaning that it re-presents. Accepting Christian truth challenges us to recognize and accept the divinity within ourselves and not act as if we were not holy. If the act of baptizing by immersing or plunging the cate-chumen into the water symbolizes entrance into the body of Christ and freedom from all sin, then the doctrine of baptism tells us that this is a sacrament through which we are re-created. We are made new. It challenges us to recognize that we actually share in the life of Christ; we are members of a pilgrim community that dares to name itself the people of God.

The Language of Doctrine Praises

The words of Christian doctrine are the church's way of giving praise to God for all the gifts God has given it. "Orthodoxy" means that the doctrine praises rightly, or is "full of praise." It is some-times translated as "thinking straight thoughts" or "right opinion." Expressing the truth revealed to us is a *doxa*, an act of praise. But today many Christians seem to have lost their understanding of the beauty and wonder of religious truth. Only too often we see doc-trine as a burden put upon us, compelling us to be what we do not freely wish to be. But that cannot be so. Religious truth is our her-itage from a thinking and believing community and is the commu-nity's expression of ultimate meaning. It is the faith community's way of expressing those meanings without which it could not exist.

Whether the church communicates its meaning adequately is another question. Too often, it does not. Gregory Baum says that the problem with inadequate and unworthy expression of doctrine arose because we had

> been content to look upon religious truth statements as we do
> upon truth-statements having to do with ordinary life situa-
> tions. A statement is true if it corresponds to the reality before
> us; it is false if it does not thus correspond. We tended to look
> upon religious statements as propositions of clearly definable
> content, representing a supernatural or sacred reality.[12]

Baum goes on to say:

> The great theologians,...never adopted such a naive corre-
> spondence theory of truth in regard to religious statements.

215

They always understood, each in his own way, that the divine pervaded all being and in particular was operative in the very act of knowledge by which people recognize the divine in their lives. Since God is the source of human life and the ground of significant wisdom and action, these theologians never considered God a divine reality existing apart from humankind as the supreme object of his mind, and hence never applied a simple correspondence-theory of truth to religious statements.[13]

Theologians who tried to express religious truth as a one-to-one correspondence with the reality it represented did not treat doctrine as symbolic or analogic. They seemed to think that they might encapsulate the Divine Mystery itself in the language of doctrine. But God is above and beyond all theological discourse. Through our God-language we give praise and thanksgiving for the insights which speak truthfully of the Mystery.

The Language of Doctrine Is Analogical

St. Thomas Aquinas taught that everything we say about God must first of all be denied. He said that God is so different from us and all that we know that we cannot speak truthfully about the Divine Mystery.[14] We can only speak through analogy, knowing that every analogy is inadequate. This does not mean that we ought not speak about God as truthfully as we can. It simply means that God is within and beyond and that everything we try to say about God is imperfectly said. Symbolic speech is the best we can do.

Theology is symbolic speech or discourse about God. The truths that the church teaches are discourse that is true and at the same time inadequate. It is truth or doctrine which can be expressed in a variety of ways and which, because of its very nature as truth about God, elevates, inspires, lifts up, restrains, and praises. How can we have gone so astray that we have forgotten the most important truth about doctrine? It is truthful praise, and when shared it is good news for all of us.

The Language of Doctrine Is Full of Power

Symbols are full of power. They appeal to the imagination and awaken us to the ultimate depths of reality. Symbolic statements about God are not just poetic speech. They are powerful statements that unite believers to the divine already present in our lives. They change us and the world in which we live. They reveal the presence of divine love in our lives. They open up the world as both the home and the creature of the Divine, who abides with us always. They appeal to the deepest dimension of human life. They challenge, confront, provoke and summon us. They do not let us rest satisfied with ourselves, but they continually call us to conversion. Doctrines and dogmas are symbolic statements that are essential to life because they give it meaning and purpose. They relate us to God, to one another, and to the universe in which we live. They have the power to transform us and all our relationships. They must be worthy of that of which they speak.

The Language of Doctrine Reveals a Hierarchy of Truths

All dogmas are doctrines, but not all doctrines are dogmas. There is a hierarchy among the doctrines of the church.[15] Creeds are, of course, dogma and are uppermost in that hierarchy of truth. Other proclaimed dogmas such as those on Mary precede some doctrinal statements in their significance. Doctrinal statements have a hierarchy among themselves. This hierarchy has never been carefully delineated, nor does it need to be, though the catechism describes the mystery of the Most Holy Trinity as "the central mystery of Christian faith and life," and "the most fundamental and essential teaching in the 'hierarchy of the truths of the faith.'"[16]

Doctrines also develop. *The Catechism of the Catholic Church* notes: "Thanks to the assistance of the Holy Spirit, the understanding of both the realities and the words of the heritage of faith is able to grow in the life of the Church." This growth takes place:

217

— "through the contemplation and study of believers who ponder these things in their hearts";[17] it is in particular "theological research [which] deepens knowledge of revealed truth."[18]

— "from the intimate sense of spiritual realities which [believers] experience,"[19] the sacred Scriptures "grow with the one who reads them."[20]

— "from the preaching of those who have received, along with their right of succession in the episcopate, the sure charism of truth."

Doctrines develop, and we continually try to state them in a more adequate way, but we can never exhaust or express the fullness of our knowledge about the Mystery of God, who is incomprehensible. So we do our best, and the church finds the most adequate statement about God and hands it on to us, all the time telling us that we cannot confuse our statements about the truth with the Truth itself. They are symbolic statements which participate in the reality they represent, but they are not the fullness of that reality.

The Symbolic Language of Doctrine Is Androcentric

Of course doctrinal language is androcentric, or male-centered. How could it be otherwise? Church teaching and church doctrines were written by men who were the accepted leaders. The established teaching of the synagogue and church has throughout the centuries been written in a patriarchal culture by men and primarily for men. The church's teaching is available through conciliar documents, all of which were debated and written by men, and since the sixteenth century presented in the *Catechism of the Council of Trent*, a document written by men and translated into English by men.

Until the last third of the twentieth century the church had few women theologians on whom it could call, because women were ordinarily not permitted or were at best discouraged from the study of the languages, history, and theological sources necessary to prepare them to be theologians. The few women doctors of the

218

church, St. Catherine of Siena, St. Teresa of Avila, and St. Thérèse of Lisieux, are the exception to the rule. This is not a uniquely church problem. It demonstrates a deficiency within society which only in recent times admitted women to professional studies for law or medicine or advanced studies in the humanities. It was not until the last half of the twentieth century that women were admitted in any numbers for doctoral degrees in accredited universities and seminaries in order to study theology or related disciplines. Before this time women did not have the opportunity to directly influence theological writings or the language of the church in its official catechisms. Even at the beginning of the twenty-first century it is still commonplace for the authors of children's catechisms to be both a male and a female. The common presumption seems to be that the man (preferably a priest) provides the theology and the woman the methodology for teaching. Catechetical works written by women alone are still the exception to the rule.

Women's theological writings make available new insights and new questions that emerge from women's experience of the Divine Mystery. Am I saying that the Divine Mystery responds differently to men than to women? No, I am saying that men and women each bring their own experiences, insights, values, and desires to their study, and because their experiences and subsequent insights are obviously different, they may describe and present the Divine Mystery to us in different ways. Neither theology done by men nor that done by women is necessarily a better expression of truth, but either one without the insights of the other is a less adequate and more limited expression of truth.

Women are now accepted into accredited universities and some seminaries for advanced theological studies. At this time many of the first generation of women who have earned their degrees are recognized as accomplished and leading scholars in every area of Christian studies, including biblical studies, the theology of God, Christology, ecclesiology, ethics, church history, liturgical studies, catechetics, and spirituality. Catechists will find new insights when they read the works of women theologians. We have been formed theologically by the writings of male teachers, so the writings of women theologians cannot help but open us to new and fuller understandings of the church's teachings. While it is risky to recommend any group of women theologians simply because some are thereby excluded, I do include a number of women theologians in the brief bibliography at the end of this chapter.

Today most publishers require inclusive language, and many readers expect it.[21] At the most fundamental level inclusive language is simply using words that include both genders and all races. The National Conference of Catholic Bishops of the United States in its "Criteria for the Use of Inclusive Language Translations of Scriptural Texts for Liturgical Use," describes exclusive language as "language which seems to exclude the equality and dignity of each person regardless of race, gender, creed, age or ability."[22] It is important to note that many male authors use inclusive language.

The original translation of *Catechism of the Catholic Church* into English using inclusive language was done by Fr. Douglas Clark of Richmond Hill, Georgia. Cardinal Bernard Law of Boston praised Clark's translation, saying that Clark "has rendered a magnificent service to the church in putting into English the *Catechism of the Catholic Church*." Law then went on to say that "there was a time when *man* would generally be understood in the light of the context of a sentence as meaning all human beings. This is not always the case today, given the cultural shifts concerning inclusivity."[23] Unfortunately, Fr. Clark's translation with inclusive language was resisted by some and as a result of a Vatican ruling the sexist language was reinserted into the catechism.

The use of inclusive language in liturgy will be addressed in chapter 9. Principles of inclusive language should be part of every catechetical endeavor and every's catechist's speech.

Catechism of the Catholic Church: A Resource for Parish Directors of Catechesis

The teachings of the Catholic Church are presented in *Catechism of the Catholic Church*. In the introduction to the catechism Pope John Paul II refers to these teachings as "the deposit of faith" and "the deposit of Christian doctrine." He notes that the church and the pope are "to guard and present better the precious deposit of Christian doctrine in order to make it more accessible to the Christian faithful and to all people of good will."[24] This is catechists' work also. As we invite and lead our catechetical communities toward conversion and faith, we share with them the teaching of the church. It is not our own teaching that we share but the teaching of the church.

The *Catechism of the Catholic Church* is a reference book for directors of catechetical ministry. It is a source book, a kind of encyclopedia of the truths of the faith. After prayerfully studying it, directors can share the truths it proclaims with communities of catechists *in language that makes it meaningful to the catechetical community.* Sometimes we can use language from the catechism itself, but we must always take into consideration the level of education, the culture, the age, and the maturity of the people with whom we are working and adapt the language to them.

Cardinal Joseph Ratzinger, who chaired the commission responsible for writing the catechism, wrote:

> We therefore agreed that the book should be aimed above all at the persons who have responsibility for holding together the whole overall catechetical structure—the bishops. It was to be first and foremost a tool for them and for their helpers, a means of assisting them in the task of consolidating the work of catechesis in the various local churches.[25]

The catechism presupposes a certain theological sophistication in its readers, as we would expect from a book written specifically for the bishops. The language itself is often theologically technical and advanced, presupposing a theological background in the readers. Not everyone has such a background. For this reason, the catechism is ordinarily not the book for use with catechumens or many adults in catechetical programs. It should be available for directors of catechetical ministry who have had education in theological programs and for those with enough background to read and understand it. Directors will find a number of shorter catechisms that are based on the official catechism, such as *The Peoples' Catechism: Catholic Faith for Adults*, helpful in parish programs.[26]

Many catechists study the doctrines of the church in programs directed by either their parish director or by the diocese. Others follow degree study in universities. Some professional groups like the National Conference of Catechetical Leadership are publishing booklets on doctrinal topics which are based on the Second Vatican Council and the catechism and written especially for parish catechists. These and other books and articles based on the council and the catechism need to be available for every catechist.

Catechetical Language

Apart from the use of inclusive language the question is, What form of language should catechists use with their people? The language of awe, of image, of story, of doctrine, of dogma? As ministers of the word we can use all of these forms of language. The question is, What form best communicates the Mystery and calls the community to conversion? We cannot limit ourselves to any one or two forms. We cannot use only the language of doctrine, or only the language of image, or only the language of story. We need to use all the forms of language we can, the language of wonder and image and story and doctrine and dogma. And we can use those language forms in drama, in poetry, in pantomime, in art, in writing, in dance, in speech, in gestures, and in actions.

There are many forms of language we can use to name the Mystery. But the real question still remains: What form or forms of language are most likely to evoke the experience of the Mystery in this new century to the people of this time and of a particular place? What forms shall we use for the poor and the wealthy, the uneducated and the educated, the gardener and the computer scientist? Are the same forms significant in the different cultures of India, Egypt, Kenya, Israel, Italy? In rural, suburban, and inner city neighborhoods? Are the same forms evocative for women as for men, or for children?

Is there one form of language that is suitable for all people in all places? Is there a classic way of expressing the faith, a way that has universal appeal to the Catholic community on all continents, in all countries, for people of all levels of education and intelligence? And if so, does this classic form of language fit all epochs and all ethnic groups? I suggest that the Sacred Scriptures, and for Christians particularly the Gospels are the preeminent source of faith and a "classic" form of Christian language, a form that should permeate catechesis. The language of the Bible includes poetry and song, story and image, teaching and exhortation. It is moral and evocative, rich in meaning and at times ambiguous. For centuries it has transformed its hearers. It appeals to people of every age and every nation. It is centered on Jesus as Lord, human and divine, sent by God to free us from the power of evil. It is full of truth, but it is not the only form of catechetical language.

Official catechetical directories tell us that in catechesis the ministers are inviting the adult community, the family community, the youth community, the children's community to conversion. If we seek *conversion*, or its corollary for children, *initiation into the community of faith*, then our language for each cultural and age group will differ. A form of language suited to the particular group will need to be used with that group. And if we believe different language, idioms, images, stories, and gestures are needed if we are to serve the pluralistic multicultural communities within the church, then we will find ways to incorporate a variety of languages and literary forms in our catechism and catechesis.

The Lives of the Saints

Dogma and doctrine are not the only church symbols of faith. The witness of the lives of the church's holy people, the saints, both express and create faith. The saints are all who share in the holiness of God. Holy people and holy things share in this divine energy, and in sharing they give glory *(doxa)* to God.

The holy ones symbolized their faith through their lives and through their deaths. They are *that through which* faith is present and effective. The saints lived out their commitment, and often they died for this commitment and their beliefs. The church remembers these people with whom it is joined in a living faith, and it hands on that memory in liturgy and in catechesis.

From its beginning the church was a community of memory. It did not forget its past. It memorialized or remembered its holy ones, and it tells the story of these holy ones over and over again to every generation. The primary memory of the church is what Johann Baptist Metz calls "the dangerous memory of Jesus Christ."[27] The Gospels are, above all else the story of the life-death-resurrection-glorification of Jesus and the sending of his Spirit. They are the memorialization of Jesus in a language through which it can be shared with others. The earliest oral form of the Synoptic Gospels was the story of the passion-death-resurrection of Jesus to which were later added the teachings and works of the Lord. The Gospels honor, venerate, and celebrate the good news of Jesus, the holiest of all that is holy.

In Luke's narrative, the Acts of the Apostles, the church preserves the memory of the early Christian community of the first century. Acts tells the stories of many of Christian women and men who were the "holy ones" of the apostolic church. The church was a communion of saints made up of women and men who, because of the gift of the Holy Spirit poured out upon them, shared in the holiness of God. It was a holy community reflecting the holiness of God.

The lives of men and women of faith have been a source of energy and life to the Christian community for two millennia. We profess this in the Apostles' Creed when we proclaim that we believe in the "communion of saints," which means both those saints who have died, and the saints among the living.[28] In the beginning the church venerated and kept alive the stories of its martyrs as friends of Christ. After the age of persecution it honored the lives of other men and women—confessors, leaders, wise teachers, and workers of mercy like Benedict, Scholastica, Augustine, and Monica.

It is not necessary to look back twenty centuries to discover a communion of saints. Such communities still live and give witness, and communities still honor and venerate the martyrs. The four United States women missionaries in El Salvador, Ita Ford, Maura Clark, Dorothy Kazel, and Jean Donovan personify these martyrs.

They were middle- and upper-middle-class Americans, educated women of faith who left their faith communities in North America to join in the struggle for human dignity among the saints of Central America. Twenty years after their deaths the faith communities they left still venerate and honor them. These women taught families in Central America how to care for the sick, eat nutritionally, and plant economically. They preached the gospel through word and through example. They were martyred because of their ministry. Not the martyrdom alone but the ministry made them holy. It was their ministry that led to their martyrdom. It is their holiness and their relationship with the Christian community which the church honors when it celebrates their lives and their faith.

Other examples of holiness are Archbishop Oscar Romero, the Jesuits of the University of Central America in El Salvador and the women who served them, the hundreds of lay catechists, both men and women, who were martyred because of their ministry in Guatemala[29] and El Salvador.[30] In Africa, in Asia, in Central America, the number of martyrs has increased during this past century. What Christians need to remember is that saints do not become holy because they were martyred, but they were martyred because they were holy. When the church celebrates their lives it celebrates living in a communion of friendship with them even now. As Elizabeth Johnson notes, "One does not leave the church by dying."[31]

Today we do not hear much about the saints. Books are seldom written about them. Films do not tell their stories. We seem to believe that their stories may be good for children, but with few exceptions their lives bear little weight in the world of most adults. Johnson writes that we live in a world of "silence about the saints," almost as if we were afraid that others would hear us talk about them.[32] Lawrence Cunningham speaks of our "alienation from the tradition of the saints."[33] Most surveys of parish life and catechetical ministry do not even mention the saints.[34] And of those that do, it is only a passing reference. The *National Certification Standards for Professional Parish Directors of Religious Education* sets "personal," "theological," and "professional" standards for catechists. There are twenty-one theological standards, the last of which is that parish directors of religious education should have an understanding of "Marian theology and the lives of the saints." According to the text this means that the directors should have the ability to "explain the place of Mary and the saints in the life of the church,"[35] a solid but hardly energetic recommendation about the lives of saints.

One of the reasons why saints seem to have little effect on our lives is that most of them are not like us. Though they are holy and inspirational, they do not live a life remotely resembling most of ours. Johnson reports that between the years 500 and 1200, "the average percentage of women recognized as saints was less that 15 percent of the total."[36] When the formal process of canonization came into effect in the tenth century, the statistics did not change much. Johnson points out:

> Between the tenth and nineteenth centuries, 87 percent of those whom Rome recognizes as saints were men, while only 13 percent were women; in the first eight decades of the twentieth century, the proportion was 75 percent men and 25 percent women, a small gain but far from equality.

If women were not acknowledged in the official process, neither were married men.

> Similarly, those recognized as saints from the tenth to the nineteenth centuries were 82 percent clergy and 18 percent laity, as compared with the twentieth century's 79 percent clerical and 21 percent lay saints, hardly a change at all. The vast majority of those on the list are Europeans, although that balance is slowly shifting as John Paul II has canonized groups of lay martyrs from developing nations.[37]

Perhaps when ranks of canonized saints mirror the overwhelming preponderance of laity in the church and reflect lay lives in the modern world, devotion to the saints will reawaken. What catechists can do is recall the lives of holy ones within the community and begin to acknowledge that the church itself is a community of holiness, for the Holy Spirit dwells within it.

The *Catechism of the Catholic Church* has fourteen paragraphs on the communion of saints, noting that "the term 'communion of saints,'...has two closely linked meanings: communion 'in holy things *(sancta)*' and 'among holy persons *(sancti)*.'"[38] Most of us know what "holy persons" are although we may forget that this category includes the living as well as the dead, but what are these "holy things" about which the church speaks? They are primarily "the elements of the eucharist."[39] Vatican Council II's *Dogmatic Constitution on the Church* notes that "in the sacrament of the Eucharistic bread, the unity of believers, who form one body in Christ (see 1 Cor 10:17), is both expressed and achieved."[40] Our union with one another and with Christ the Lord comes from our participation in the Eucharist, the body of Christ. And the profound relationship and union we share with those who eat at the table of the Lord brings us into communion not only with one another but with the whole of creation. Johnson writes that "holy things" are, by extension, "sharing in the sacred community of life that is creation itself."[41]

In this vision of reality, ecological sensitivity is not an option. The relationship that exists among all of us because of our union with God is a communion that is lessened whenever any part of creation is destroyed. In an extraordinary book entitled *The Body of God: An Ecological Theology*, Sallie McFague looks at our world as "God's body."[42] This metaphor emphasizes the intimacy of all of creation with the immanently transcendent God. God is with us always and everywhere. According to McFague, "God is...closer to us than we are to ourselves."[43] All creatures share in the one life of God. Together we are the embodiment of God. This metaphor of the earth as God's body helps us to see the vital and interdependent relationship that exists between nature and the human family and between all of creation and God. Creation is the "holy thing" and whatever creatures exist in this universe are "the holy things" with which we are one in communion.

Catechesis on the Church Symbols of Faith

Most of what the church knows about God it learned from Jesus. In story and parable, through action and prayer Jesus taught his disciples and the crowds who followed him. He taught profound

truths through imagery, story, and proverb. He taught about the
qualities of God not through analytic classification but by relating
God's qualities to human life.

> And why do you worry about clothing? Consider the lilies of
> the field, how they grow; they neither toil nor spin, yet I tell
> you, even Solomon in all his glory was not clothed like one of
> these. But if God so clothes the grass of the field, which is alive
> today and tomorrow is thrown into the oven, will he not much
> more clothe you—you of little faith? (Mt 5:29–30)

Or he used simple, homespun, direct language:

> Ask, and it will be given you; search, and you will find; knock,
> and the door will be opened for you. For everyone who asks
> receives, and everyone who searches finds, and for everyone
> who knocks, the door will be opened. (Mt 7:7–8)

Those who heard Jesus preach would long remember what he said
because what he said affected them cognitively, affectively, and ethically. The images and stories he used stayed in the minds and
hearts of his listeners. The parables surprised them; the proverbs or
adages were unexpected. And the people listened because he spoke
to them with respect and with clarity.

The church has spent much time and energy thinking about
and trying to plumb the meaning of Jesus' words and actions. For
two millennia the church through its preachers, theologians, and
the magisterium have carried on discourse about the words and the
meaning of Jesus' life-death-resurrection. In teaching about the
humanity of Jesus, the Second Vatican Council wrote:

> He who is the "image of the invisible God" (Col 1:15), is him-
> self the perfect man who has restored in the children of Adam
> that likeness to God which had been disfigured ever since the
> first sin. Human nature, by the very fact that it was assumed,
> not absorbed, in him, has been raised in us also to a dignity
> beyond compare. For, by his incarnation, he, the Son of God,
> has in a certain way united himself with each individual. He
> worked with human hands, he thought with a human mind. He

acted with a human will, and with a human heart he loved. Born of the Virgin Mary, he has truly been made one of us, like to us in all things except sin.[44]

The mystery of the incarnation, God becoming human, is incomprehensible. It is a source of wonder and awe. How does one hand on such a truth and other doctrines like it in its catechesis? The catechist follows the lead of the church and teaches as the church does.

But how do catechists teach? First, they do as the church does. The church hands on its understandings in its prayer. It "teaches" about God as Trinity every time it prays the sign of the cross, the doxology of the eucharistic prayer, the giving of blessings, the trinitarian formulae with which it ends its "collects." The church prays to the Father and to the Son and to the Spirit. It teaches Trinity through its prayer.

The law of prayer is the law of belief. *Lex orandi, lex credendi.* The confession of sinfulness at each Eucharist is an acknowledgment of the individual and communal sins of the members of the community. It is a recognition that evil exists in the world and that the church bears some responsibility for that evil. In asking for forgiveness the church is teaching that God is a merciful and just judge who forgives and graces the people. The missioning prayer through which the presider sends the community forth, "Go forth to love and serve your neighbor," is a teaching on justice. In other liturgical celebrations the church teaches through its actions and words. The prayer which blesses the rings at matrimony, "May the Lord bless these rings which you give to each other as the sign of your love and fidelity," teaches that married life is expected to be a life of loving fidelity. In baptism as the baptizer immerses the person in the baptismal water he teaches all who are present that in baptism we enter into the death and new life of Jesus the Lord. The church teaches through the words and actions of prayer.

The catechist also hands on doctrine and dogma through relating the stories of the lives of the saints. For catechumens the catechist may say, "this is what Christians believe." Or they may tell the stories of the martyrs and note: "This is how Christians act because of their beliefs." Or they may teach about justice by telling the stories of Christians who have worked for justice and who lived according to the Judeo-Christian ethical norm that "justice is not an option; justice *is* religion."[45] The history of the church or the story of its leaders, its heroes and heroines is a significant way of handing on the church's teaching. Through history, through biography, through proverb, prayer, and action catechists hand on the truth.

A catechist also hands on the doctrine, dogma, and tradition of the church by teaching. Teaching is a dialogical act in which the learner is set free, liberated, opened toward the future. It is an art, not a science. Through teaching, one lifts the learner out of darkness and touches the very soul of another. Teaching is a relational act; it gives life and hope to another. When teaching happens, lives are changed, not just the lives of the teacher and the learner but the lives of those who are close to both the teacher and the learner. Teaching is an exhilarating activity, for the teacher attempts to share not just facts but wonder, insights, and curiosity with learners. Sometimes teaching means giving people a skill that will affect them forever. When I was a teacher of first grade I taught children to read. The day a child looked at a word and recognized that word by name was a "miracle" day. The life of the child was changed forever.

Teaching is also an expression of power. Most of the time it is adults who teach and children who are taught. But that is changing. Parish catechetical programs for adults are growing in both size and effectiveness. When a catechist is teaching, she knows that adults learn best through participatory learning. Adults learn through dialogue with other adults. They learn by being treated as adults. Because education is an act of empowering, people often distrust and fear it, for it can have either marvelous or disastrous effects on a person's life. Teaching should be an empowering relationship.

Not all teaching or all learning takes place in a school. Parents are a child's first teachers. They teach a child the most difficult concept of all: they teach the child to speak, to use language, one of the most abstract concepts human beings will ever learn. How do parents know how to teach a language to their children? What parents teach, primarily, is the most important lesson of all, how to live.

Parents hand on to their children their values and their attitudes about life and about people. If a parent is not prejudiced or biased against people, it will be very unusual for the child to be prejudiced or biased. If parents are happy with one another, it is more than likely that their children will seek happiness. Children may outgrow what their parents have handed on, but it will take effort, experience, and reeducation to do so. Parents are the first and most important of a child's teachers, not only when a child is young but throughout the children's lives.

Good teachers have intellectual curiosity and want to teach others how to discover things for themselves. They communicate joy in learning and appreciate whatever effort the learner makes. A teacher is a person who knows she doesn't have all the answers, is comfortable with ambiguity, has a lot of questions, and is patient. Teachers are patient because they respect and reverence those whom they teach. All of us are teachers, though not all of us are professional schoolteachers.

Teaching is part of the catechetical enterprise. Sometimes catechists teach. In each of the four movements of catechesis, both teaching and learning may be going on. This does not mean that the catechist will *explain* what the doctrines mean. To reduce teaching to explaining is to belittle the act of teaching. Gabriel Moran points this out when he writes:

> To reduce teaching to explanation is to be blind to the full context of human life in which teaching is embedded. There is nothing in itself wrong with explaining; it is just that explaining is nowhere near wide enough to be the ground for "to teach."[46]

Teaching and learning go on when the catechist or preferably the catechetical team shows the catechetical community how to live and die as Christians.

Jesus never taught in a school, though he did teach in a synagogue, only infrequently as far as we know, yet the title "teacher" is applied to him in the Gospels more than any other title. He taught through his sermons, but he also taught through his actions. He taught, silently and unobtrusively, when he ate with sinners and had dinner with the "undesirables." He taught by the way he related to and treated women. But he taught only when he related to people who wanted to learn.

Some of Jesus' teachings he repeated again and again through word and through action: care for those who are in need, the widow, the orphan, the neighbor, the prostitute, the sinner, the leper, the blind man, the woman with a hemorrhage, the children, those who were marginalized by society. If the people who heard his words or watched his actions were not open to learn from Jesus, then neither teaching nor learning took place. Learning happens only when there is a mutual relationship of openness and desire to know between the teacher and the learner.

Teaching is one characteristic act of catechesis. It is not the only action, nor is it the most important one. It is part of all four component actions of catechesis: examining life experiences, reflecting on them in relationship to a faith symbol, acting for justice, and praying in community. The actions themselves are teaching actions, for they are all showing the community how to live and die as Christians. No one of these actions is more significant than the other in catechesis. The synthesis of all these actions is the catechetical act. But all kinds of teaching—through story, discourse, dialogue, action, relationship—are integral to each of the four movements in catechesis.

In the twentieth century some scholars in the Western world began to consider how adults learn. They realized, finally, that "pedagogy," the way in which we teach children, did not work well with adults. Over the decades a new science of learning developed, a science called "andragogy," the teaching of adults. Among other things educators learned that adults learn best in small groups and that the more they participate in the learning process the more likely they will learn. They learned that learning is a lifelong process and that adults bring a great deal to the learning process from their life experience. Educators also learned that adults are highly motivated to learn when it makes sense to them and relates to their lives.

The interesting thing about all these discoveries is that the more we learn about how adults learn, the more applicable the same ideas seem to be for children. The new andragogy is related to a renewed pedagogy. Perhaps there is neither pedagogy nor andragogy but only education, and education happens wherever human beings are free to participate, to ask questions, and to discover for themselves.

The ability to listen is one of the most important qualities a catechist can bring to her ministry of teaching. Listen to adults as they speak. Listen to their words, to their voices, and to their body language. Listen to the words they use to describe themselves and those who are closest to them. Listen to how they speak and listen to one another. Listen to them week after week and you will come to know them. Only when you know them can you really teach them.

Every catechist is a resource, a leader, a listener, a teacher within the catechetical community. Everyone in the catechetical community is a resource, a leader, a listener, a teacher. Catechesis takes place in a learning and teaching community. While everyone in the community is a resource for others, the catechist is the prime resource by reason of her call to catechize by her study and preparation of the catechetical session.

The catechist influences the teaching and learning that takes place by the way she speaks of and participates in the symbols of the faith. If the catechist thinks that doctrine is a freeing symbol that enables the Christian community to move intelligently and with spirit through life, she will present it in that way and the community will accept doctrine with the same spirit as she presents it. If the catechist thinks that doctrine is a burden or that it has nothing to do with life, then the community may follow her lead and think the same way. The catechist is the one to whom the catechetical community looks for insights about the faith. Often what the catechist does is help the members of the community to recognize the value of their own insights.

As a director of catechesis or a catechist, you need to draw on your own faith commitment and then study. As a director it is important that you include an hour for study in your daily calendar. Encourage your catechists to put aside a half hour a day for reading books and articles on catechesis, on doctrine, the Bible, or liturgy either at the beginning or end of the day. This will help you and your catechists to become better prepared for each meeting with the community. Catechesis is a ministry, a service that you offer to others, and that service cannot be offered out of an empty heart or head.

In Summary

The Second Vatican Council described the church as "a sacrament—a sign and instrument, that is, of communion with God and of the unity of the entire human race."[47] The church is a communion of love which symbolizes the Mystery of God in its life, in its teaching, in its worship. Catechists hand on the life of the church as they hand on its teaching, stories of its holy ones, and the doctrines that express the church's understanding and beliefs. Catechists hands on these doctrines through community prayer, through reaching out to others in justice, through dialogue and discourse, through stories and images. The symbols of the church can lift up and free the community, stretch and expand its understanding of itself as the body of Christ on earth, move it to reflection, to deeper understanding, to action.

As the church or the catechetical community feeds the hungry and clothes the naked, as it provides homes for the homeless and looks out for the rights of people who are underprivileged and poor, it symbolizes powerfully and often without words the presence of Christ in our midst. As it recognizes its interdependence and intimate relationship with all of creation, it shows forth more clearly than ever its communion with the Divine Mystery. As it reflects and as it acts, every small church in union with the whole church learns. In catechesis, the catechist calls on the *ecclesial* symbols to respond to the questions and concerns, the interests and issues that the catechetical community raises. Catechesis introduces or reintroduces church symbols to the community. Through all four movements of catechesis the Tradition of the church is handed on in a teaching and learning community of faith.

FURTHER READINGS

Carr, Anne E. *Transforming Grace: Christian Tradition and Women's Experience*. San Francisco: Harper, 1988.

Catechism of the Catholic Church. Washington, D.C.: United States Catholic Conference, 1994.

Collins, Mary. *Worship: Renewal to Practice*. Washington, D.C.: Pastoral Press, 1987.

Cunningham, Lawrence, ed. *The Catholic Faith: A Reader*. New York: Paulist Press, 1988.

Gallagher, Maureen. *The Art of Catechesis: What You Need to Be, Know, and Do*. With a Foreword by Archbishop Rembert G. Weakland. New York: Paulist Press, 1998.

Hilkert, Mary Catherine, O.P. "Experience and Tradition: Can the Center Hold." In *Freeing Theology: The Essentials of Theology in Feminist Perspective*, ed. Catherine Mowry LaCugna, 59–83. San Francisco, Harper, 1993.

———. *Naming Grace: Preaching and the Sacramental Imagination*. New York: Continuum, 1997.

Johnson, Elizabeth A. *Consider Jesus: Waves of Renewal in Christology*. New York: Crossroad, 1991.

———. *Friends of God and Prophets: A Feminist Theological Reading of the Communion of Saints*. New York: Continuum, 1998.

———. *She Who Is: The Mystery of God in Feminist Theological Discourse*. New York: Crossroad, 1993.

La Cugna, Catherine Mowry. *Freeing Theology: The Essentials of Theology in Feminist Perspective*. San Francisco: Harper, 1993.

———. *God for Us: The Trinity and Christian Life*. San Francisco: Harper, 1993.

Lucker, Raymond A., Patrick J. Brennan, and Michael Leach, eds. *The People's Catechism: Catholic Faith for Adults*. New York: Crossroad, 1995.

McFague, Sallie. *The Body of God: An Ecological Theology*. Minneapolis: Fortress Press, 1993.

Marthaler, Berard L. *The Creed: The Apostolic Faith in Contemporary Theology*. Revised edition. Mystic, Conn.: Twenty-third Publications, 1993.

Moran, Gabriel. *Showing How: The Act of Teaching*. Valley Forge, Pa.: Trinity Press International, 1997.

Schüssler Fiorenza, Elisabeth. *Discipleship of Equals: A Critical Feminist Ekklesia-logy of Liberation*. New York: Crossroad, 1993.

———. *In Memory of Her: A Feminist Theological Reconstruction of Christian Origins*. New York: Crossroad, 1992.

Sobrino, Jon. *Companions of Jesus: The Jesuit Martyrs of El Salvador*. New York: Orbis Books, 1990.

———. *Jesus in Latin America*. New York: Orbis Books, 1987.

Vogel, Linda J. *Teaching and Learning in Communities of Faith: Empowering Adults Through Religious Education*. San Francisco: Jossey-Bass, 1991.

CHAPTER 9

Liturgical Symbols of Faith

When I was a very young child, a preschooler in fact, I walked with my grandmother Anne Devitt O'Connor to Mass at Resurrection Church in Chicago every morning. She took me by the hand and shortened her step as we walked through neighbor's yards taking the shortest way possible to the church. At that time Resurrection Parish had five Masses scheduled each morning beginning at 6:00 A.M., and continuing every half hour until the pastor "said" his Mass at 8:00 A.M. Each Mass was a "Mass for the Dead," and even though I did not understand a word of Latin it didn't make any difference because nothing was said loud enough for me to hear, though I did especially like the singing of the *Dies Irae,* a lament for the dead. My grandmother taught me to say the rosary during the Mass. As I look back I recognize that daily Mass with my grandmother was for me, as a child, a memorable experience.

Anne Devitt came to the United States in 1908 from the west coast of County Clare, Ireland. She brought with her a fierce devotion to the Mass. I say fierce because her devotion to the Eucharist was intense. She would no more miss Mass on a weekday than she would miss eating and drinking. Irish devotion to the Mass seemed to grow as they were deprived of it by their Protestant rulers. This deprivation seemed to heighten their realization of the importance of the Eucharist in their lives. For them the Mass was the basic expression of their faith and a source of their identity.[1]

Today as I look ahead into a new century I see our Catholic people in rural towns and in some cities again being deprived of the

Mass, and I wonder what our response to this will be.[2] Will we become as devoted to the Eucharist as many of our ancestors were? Or will we have to sustain our faith, as did the people of Latin America, through devotions, primarily to Mary and the saints? Will we both long for the Eucharist and turn to devotions? Will we turn away from the church altogether when we are no longer able to celebrate regularly what the Second Vatican Council called "the source and summit of the Christian life?"[3]

How can we get along without the Eucharist, which is the way in which Jesus asked us to memorialize his life-death-resurrection? And what will this mean for celebrations of the other sacraments? Will it make any difference if in times of serious illness or declining health we cannot join ourselves with Christ and the whole church and sacramentalize our prayer for recovery or happy death? Will we as the church give up the sacrament of reconciliation altogether as priests become less and less available? And how will we celebrate initiation at our Easter vigils in another decade or two when so many parishes will have combined to form a new and larger community? What does our liturgical future look like? Is the United States to become a "missionary" country importing priests from other cultures to lead us in worship? Can we maintain a vigorous Christian life without weekly Eucharist?

I cannot answer those questions about the future, but I can say that liturgy is so important in the life of the church that the first document that the Second Vatican Council approved was the *Pastoral Constitution on the Sacred Liturgy*, which was promulgated on Wednesday, December 4, 1963, by Pope Paul VI. The fathers of the council approved the constitution by a vote of 2,147 in favor to 4 against. The purpose of the council itself is clearly stated in the first paragraph:

> The sacred council has set out to impart an ever increasing vigor to the Christian lives of the faithful; to adapt more closely to the needs of our age those institutions which are subject to change; to encourage whatever can promote the union of all who believe in Christ; to strengthen whatever serves to call all of humanity into the Church's fold.[4]

238

These extraordinary goals are followed by the words, "Accordingly it sees particularly cogent reasons for undertaking the reform and promotion of the liturgy."[5] Did the council fathers really believe that liturgical reform could help (1) to impart an ever increasing vigor to the Christian lives of the faithful; (2) to adapt...to the needs of our age those institutions which are subject to change; (3) to encourage...the union of all who believe in Christ; and (4) to strengthen...the call to all of humanity into the church? Their votes say they did, and they give evidence of profound insights about the nature of liturgy and its transforming effects upon the community.

Almost forty years have passed since the constitution was approved. Since that time the church has renewed and/or reformed all its liturgical rites and books including all the sacramental rites: the *Rite of Christian Initiation of Adults* (1972, 1985), *Rite of Baptism for Children* (1969), *Rite of Confirmation* (1971), *General Instruction of the Roman Missal* (the Eucharist, 1975), *Rite of Penance* (1973), *Rite of Marriage* (1969), *Rites of Ordination* (1968), and the *Rites for the Pastoral Care of the Sick: Rites of Anointing and Viaticum* (1972, 1983), and other rites such as the *Order of Christian Funerals* (1969, 1985). This is no small achievement, but it is only the beginning of liturgical renewal. As Mary Collins noted, "the reform of the structures of worship is neither co-extensive with nor the equivalent of the renewal of worship."[6] We still have much to do on the parish level if we are to renew our worship.

This chapter examines liturgical questions insofar as they relate to catechesis. At present about 80 percent of catechetical ministry is related to some liturgical experience. For adults it is catechesis for initiation with the rhythmic movement from catechesis to liturgical rites to catechesis. It is catechesis after initiation, which we call "mystagogical catechesis." It is catechesis or preparation for the sacrament of matrimony. It is catechesis for parents before the baptism, first reconciliation, and the first communion of their children. We catechize liturgical ministers and those who will bring the sacrament of the sick to our members who are ill. And even as families prepare for the funerals of their loved ones, we catechize them as we involve them in preparation for the funeral. Our liturgical rites and celebrations as well as their catechetical preparations are embedded in our lives.

This chapter will examine, briefly, (1) the nature of liturgy, (2) the language of liturgy: gesture, word, music and song, (3) the relationship of catechesis and liturgy, and (4) some forms of liturgical catechesis including lectionary catechesis. Each of these topics is itself worthy of a book and can be treated here only in an abbreviated way.

The Nature of Liturgy

A study of the nature of liturgy can be either exhilarating or frustrating or both exhilarating and frustrating, for when we study liturgy we are ordinarily examining it apart from the actual practice of a local church. An idealized liturgy sometimes contradicts the experience of the people and it can create what Regis Duffy calls "a credibility gap."[7] Duffy states that "there is…an implicit warning here not to offer idealized images of the Church which will only frustrate our hearers."[8] However, the following few paragraphs do describe an idealized liturgy. If your experience does not relate to this description, that may be a sign that your parish liturgy has not been renewed liturgically, and more catechesis is needed in your parish community and/or local church. Change, reform, and renewal in the way we worship come slowly, for the church is a flawed community. We have not reached our ideal.

In the liturgy we declare and celebrate our commitment to God as Trinity. In liturgy we confess the wonderful works of God the Creator, particularly the giving of the Son as the one who graces us and frees us from the power of evil, and the outpouring of the Holy Spirit-Sophia whom the Son sends to energize, console, and strengthen us in this time. It is the Holy Trinity whom the church confesses in liturgy. Our sacramental life is founded in the work of the Blessed Trinity. We are a trinitarian people. Our liturgy is our blessing (adoration and surrender) of the Trinity,[9] a form of public prayer in which life and time and space are all offered back to their divine Source.[10] Liturgy is public worship of the whole church joined with Christ in his act of worship of the Father and his act of liberating us from the power of evil.[11]

In Christian liturgy the whole church proclaims and celebrates the mystery of Christ, the mystery of the life, death, resurrection, and glorification of the Lord, which we call the Paschal Mystery. Liturgy is profoundly christological. It is Christ's prayer in which we share. In our liturgies we unite ourselves with the action of Christ as he offers worship. We celebrate the Paschal Mystery, in which Jesus by "dying destroyed our death, and rising, restored our life." We proclaim the Paschal Mystery so that we "may live from it and bear witness to it in the world."[12] But we can never fully proclaim the Paschal Mystery, for it is like a prism, multifaceted, reflecting different forms and different light, never revealing itself wholly. The liturgical year is the celebration of the Paschal Mystery in time so that the church can experience and savor the mystery of the life, death, resurrection, glorification, and sending of the spirit in its many-faceted dimensions.

As the assembly praises, blesses, and gives thanks, it acts in union with the risen Christ, who, as the *Constitution on the Sacred Liturgy* states, is present

> in the sacrifice of the Mass both in the person of his minister,...
> and most of all in the eucharistic species. By his power he is present in the sacraments so that when anybody baptizes it is really Christ himself who baptizes. He is present in his word since it is he himself who speaks when the holy scriptures are read in church. Lastly, he is present when the church prays and sings, for he has promised "where two or three are gathered together in my name there am I in the midst of them" (Mt 18:20).[13]

It is not ourselves that we celebrate in liturgy.[14] It is the life-death-resurrection of Christ and our participation in it.

The Holy Spirit prepares us to celebrate before we ever begin to worship. The Spirit awakens the response of faith in our hearts and draws us together as one in faith and one in the Lord. Liturgy is our response in faith to the overwhelming graciousness of God. It is a song of praise erupting from the community through the power of the Spirit within us, that Spirit who "is the Church's living memory."[15] The Spirit constantly and continually calls us to conversion and therefore to faith and worship. It is this oneness in the Spirit that enables us to come together in worship. The *Catechism of the Catholic Church* points out the mission of the Holy Spirit when it states that

> the mission of the Holy Spirit in the liturgy of the Church is to prepare the assembly to encounter Christ; to recall and manifest Christ to the faith of the assembly; to make the saving works of Christ present and active by his transforming power; and to make the gift of communion bear fruit in the Church.[16]

It is the Spirit indwelling that gives the church breath and speech for worship.

Every liturgy is an expression of the faith of the church in which we share and by which we live. Our faith commitment brings us together to celebrate, and every time we come together to worship, our faith is renewed. The *Constitution on the Sacred Liturgy* states that "before people can come to the liturgy they must be called to faith and to conversion." "How," wrote St. Paul, "are they to believe in one of whom they have never heard?" (Rom 10:14). Faith is a response to God's self-communication. It is the giving of ourselves to God who reveals.[17] Christian faith is an existential act of commitment and acceptance of Jesus as Lord. In liturgy we express that faith commitment, and as we confess it our faith is renewed.

Liturgy is an action of the church, the whole church, the church united with Christ, the church which is the body of Christ. Sacraments are rooted in the church, which is itself the sacrament "of communion with God and of the unity of the entire human race."[18] When the church celebrates sacraments, it is the church interceding through Christ, its source and head and mediator. In liturgy the church acts and "the liturgy daily builds up those who are in the church, making of them a holy temple of the Lord, a dwelling-place for God in the Spirit…to the full measure of the fullness of

Christ.[19] The sacraments are both from the church and for the church. The church is itself the great sacrament, and all sacraments spring from it. The church (meaning the whole people of God) constantly reconstitutes itself as church when it celebrates liturgically. Through its liturgical celebrations the church continues to be disciples of the Lord, a community of believers, a pilgrim people. Without liturgical celebrations, the life of the church withers.

Liturgy is a ritual. Like all rituals, it is a repeated pattern of behavior that expresses meaning. In Christian liturgy the pattern includes a liturgy of the word and a liturgy of the action of the sacrament. The liturgy of the word is preceded by a gathering ritual and the liturgy of the sacrament is followed by a commissioning or sending. The liturgy of the word includes a number of readings from the Bible (always one from the Gospel) with responses to each reading by the assembly. The rituals of liturgy have the power to transform us, for they relate our lives to the memory of Jesus Christ, to his presence among us through the Spirit, and to our communion with one another.

The primary symbol of the church in liturgy is the assembly. In liturgy people who share the same faith and whose lives are directed by that faith gather to express their faith. These people share a common memory, a common experience, and a common purpose in coming together.[20] They are the assembly, and the assembly offers a kaleidoscopic view of the church. In the assembly we have a variety of gifts, male and female, some young, some not so young, people of every color and every ethnic background, and while we are one we do not erase our differences.[21] The literate and the illiterate gather together to offer praise and thanksgiving, to bless and to worship in solidarity of faith. As they gather for Eucharist they share in the body and blood of Christ. When else, we may ask, do all these diverse people gather at one table, eat the one food, become one body in Christ?

Every sacramental rite is an act of the total assembly. John Baldovin writes:

When we understand the nature of sacramentality as arising out of the faith experience of Christian people, the eucharist is no longer a sacred rite performed by some (the ordained) on behalf of others who are powerless. Rather, it is the self-expression of the Body of Christ, head and members, made visible in a ritual manner.[22]

It is the people who act *in persona Christi* at the Eucharist.[23]

In sacramental liturgies our salvation is effected. Through his life-death-resurrection Christ freed us from the domination of evil. He is our liberator. In the sacraments it is Christ who acts to share God's grace with us and saves us. It is he who baptizes, forgives, and frees us from the chains of evil. In older theological language we say that the sacraments effect what they signify. As Christ acts in the sacraments and as we participate with Christ in them, the sacraments grace us; that is, they have the power to change, transform, sanctify, deify us. This happens not because of our own merits but because of Christ who acts through the sacraments.

In liturgy the assembly experiences a foretaste of life after death. As one with our brother and sister believers, with the poor and the wealthy, the infirm and the healthy, the educated and the ignorant, with the newborn and the dying, with presidents and paupers, the assembly blesses, praises, and give thanks. It experiences the reign of God present and the reign of God that is to come. Liturgical celebrations give the assembly "a foretaste of that heavenly liturgy which is celebrated in the holy city of Jerusalem toward which we journey as pilgrims, where Christ is sitting at the right hand of God, minister of the sanctuary and of the true tabernacle."[24]

Liturgical celebrations can transform and change our lives. Without the constant growth in faith which sacramental celebrations engender, faith can weaken and whither. Through participation in liturgy, the assembly is "deified," because through these celebrations we are ever more intimately united with Christ. Liturgical celebrations grace us, make us new. They remind us who we are and that all creation is holy. In liturgy we pray together as one with bread and wine and perfumed oil, and we see and taste and hear and touch the symbols of our salvation. We perform sacred actions through the power of the Spirit. It is perhaps this insight that led Annie Dillard to write:

> On the whole, I do not find Christians, outside of the catacombs, sufficiently sensible of conditions. Does anyone have the foggiest idea of what sort of power we so blithely invoke? Or, as I suspect, does no one believe a word of it? The churches are children playing on the floor with their chemistry sets, mixing up a batch of TNT to kill a Sunday morning. It is madness to wear ladies' straw hats and velvet hats to church; we should all be wearing crash helmets. Ushers should issue life preservers and signal flares; they should lash us to our pews. For the sleeping god may wake someday and take offense, or the waking god may draw us out to where we can never return.[25]

Such action can be transformative not only for the individual but for the whole assembly.

The primary goal of renewal of the liturgy is full and active participation of the people. The *Constitution on the Sacred Liturgy* states: "In the restoration and development of the sacred liturgy the full and active participation by all the people is the paramount concern, for it is the primary, indeed the indispensable source from which the faithful are to derive the true Christian spirit.[26] As the assembly is the primary symbol of any liturgical event, so the participation of the assembly in the liturgical celebration must be full and active. No one is invited to come and be an interested but passive bystander.

The Language of Liturgy

There are many languages in liturgy: the language of space and time, the language of the visual and performing arts, the language of music, verbal language, the language of gesture. These languages come together in a unique constellation in each of the church's liturgical rites. The book of rites, called the *Sacramentary*, is the church's script, the basic book for all liturgical celebration. This book contains the prayer texts, prescribed gestures, and symbolic actions for the celebration. Its companion book, the *Lectionary*, contains the scriptural readings that accompany the rites.

A *rite* is the script for the celebration of the sacrament. It is meant to be performed, not to be read. A liturgical celebration is like grand opera, but unlike grand opera it has no audience. Everyone present is one of the participants. Everyone needs to know the script. Those members of the assembly who have performed many times or those with special ministries will be at home with the script even though it may be modified at every celebration. New members of the community will need guidance in enacting it. When there are new members in the assembly, friends or other members of the assembly help them to participate.

Originally Christian rites emerged out of the life of the apostolic and early Christian communities. The original sacramental rites were an expression of the religious community's awareness of its identity as a "living, contemporary realization of its faith-tradition."[27] They expressed this identity in the idiom of their own historical epoch. Aidan Kavanagh points out that "no ritual can ever come alive as a community act unless it first possesses the confidence of the real people for whom it may be designed. Their participation in it makes it live. Nothing else does."[28]

Without modifications through time a rite is in danger of ossifying and like salt losing its savor. Kavanagh states:

> In the some seventeen generations since the sixteenth century western civilization in all its aspects—industrial, technological, urban, political, religious, and cultural—has been repeatedly wrenched by a succession of social and cultural revolutions that took place while liturgical evolution, which should have responded to them vigorously, stood still.[29]

The idioms of historical epochs change, and if the rites do not continue to reflect and express the church in a given epoch they lose some of their strength. The reform of the church's worship was a major agenda of the Protestant Reformers of the sixteenth century.

They called for radical changes in the manner of liturgical celebration in order to correct abuses, bring it into harmony with the Scriptures, and express the worshiping congregation. In response to the Reformers, the Council of Trent initiated some changes but postponed serious reforms until an unspecified future time, which Kavanagh notes, "is our own era." The Second Vatican Council took up the call of the Council of Trent and demanded reform of the church's liturgical rites. It said:

> With the passage of time,…certain features have crept into the rites of the sacraments and sacramentals which have made their nature and purpose less clear to the people of today. Hence some changes are necessary to adapt them to present-day needs.[30]

This brought about the reform of the rites of all sacramental celebrations, particularly the sacraments of initiation in the *Rite of Christian Initiation of Adults.*

Each sacrament has its own rite, which relates the symbolic actions, prayer texts, and scriptural readings. The written rite is like a script for a play or a libretto for the opera except that it did not emerge from the imagination of a playwright. It came from the faith and imagination of a graced people. People can read the script of a play to understand what the play is about, but the play is only in the imagination of the reader until it is enacted before an audience. Then it comes to life. The liturgical rite is the work of the people, and sometimes our work is not worthy of the rite because we become so involved with parts and with trivialities like banners and missalettes and microphones that we miss the whole. Liturgy is God's act. It is "more of God than about God."[31] The rite is a sacred act in which a faithful people enter into communion with the Divine Mystery.

As catechists we need to be aware of the many languages of the rite, verbal, and nonverbal, and how they affect the community. Each symbol and symbolic action expresses the faith of the assembly. In the following section we shall consider the symbolic languages of gesture and word, for they are major languages not only in liturgy but also in liturgical catechesis.

The Language of Gesture

Human gestures communicate. The arms opened wide to embrace another or the closed fist raised in defiance speak without words. The tender hand of a nurse soothing a forehead or wiping tears speaks to every patient. The mother or father who holds the hand of a sick child is speaking to that child though they may not voice a word. Our gestures communicate, and often they communicate more fully than our words. The young people who stood silently with their backs to the political speaker "shouted" their politics. The thousands of people who stood silently in line to pay respect to police officers killed at the nation's capitol spoke without words. Sometimes we speak by bringing flowers to a place of glory or tragedy. Human beings are always communicating by their actions.

Luke tells us that at the supper on the night before the Lord's death, Jesus

> took a loaf of bread, and when he had given thanks to God, he broke it and gave it to them, saying, "This is my body which is given for you. Do this in remembrance of me." And he did the same with the cup after supper, saying, "This cup that is poured out for you is the new covenant in my blood." (Lk 22:19)

He *took* the bread, *gave* thanks, *broke* the bread, and *gave* it to them. He did the same with the cup. In this account some of the actions were accompanied by words. Others were not. But every action was a form of communication. Jesus spoke through his actions. His gestures carried thought and meaning with them.

Today in our liturgies we continue to speak through actions. Liturgies are bodily prayer. In liturgies we stand and sit, process and dance, eat the sacred bread and drink from the cup of salvation. We immerse new members in water. We light fires, anoint the senses, lay on hands, and incense one another. We listen, kneel, strike our breasts, and sign ourselves with a cross. We stand in reverence and walk in procession. We lift high the cross or crucifix. We bow our heads and sometimes we prostrate our bodies. Our gestures speak. They speak for us and they speak to us. They symbolize us. Seldom do they need interpretation.[32]

No one sits down and arbitrarily decides when the assembly will express itself through gesture and when it will speak verbally. Our sacramental speech, both words and actions, evolves out of what it is that we as a community are doing when we worship. The actions evolve out of our culture as well as out of our tradition of worship. If standing is a gesture of respect, as it is in the United States culture, then, for example, we stand to offer respect when the Gospel is read. When we stand and speak through song as for the *Alleluia* or the great *Amen* we give added emphasis to our response. If standing was a sign of disrespect in a culture, then surely we would not stand at the proclamation of the Gospel.

By using the language of gesture, action, and movement, the assembly expresses its faith commitment and unites itself with all who have done these same actions through the centuries. Movement and gesture are powerful human forms of communication. When they are joined to word, they are an eloquent, effective form of communication.

The Language of Word

Word in liturgy takes different forms. We have the word of Scripture, the word of song, the word of prayers. We have gathering words and missioning words. We have words that give us directions, "Let us proclaim the mystery of faith," and we have words of commitment, "Amen." The church at worship expresses itself in every human way possible, for it is expressing full commitment and a full heart.

Whenever the church gathers for public prayer at the celebration of a sacrament, it proclaims the Scriptures. The liturgy of the word focuses on the proclamation of the Scriptures, particularly the Gospel, but also readings from the Old Testament and other New Testament books. As noted earlier, Christ "is present in his word since it is he himself who speaks when the holy scriptures are read in the church."[33] Reverence for this word is a characteristic of the assembly. The "General Instruction of the Roman Missal" states:

> The readings must therefore be listened to by all with reverence; they make up a principal element of the liturgy. In the biblical readings God's word addresses all people of every era and is understandable to them, but a living commentary on the word, that is, the homily, as an integral part of the liturgy increases the word's effectiveness.[34]

There is a rhythm of proclamation and response in the liturgy of the word. The readings are followed by the Psalms, alleluia chants, the homily, and the profession of faith, and general intercessions or prayers of the faithful,[35] all of which are responses to the readings.

As the Bible is the church's book, so the liturgy is the church's work. Part of that work is the proclamation of the gospel. During the church's two-thousand-year tradition of worship it has always proclaimed the Scriptures. The church proclaims the gospel to remember and re-present God's great love for humankind expressed particularly in Jesus. At every liturgical celebration a Gospel passage is read. The Gospel is God's word, which calls us to conversion of life. It continually summons us to justice, to worship, to love. It presents us with a norm for our living in all situations.

The church necessarily uses verbal language in its public prayers. These include the opening prayer or collect, the dialogical exchanges between the priest and the people, the prayer over the gifts, the eucharistic prayer, and the prayer after communion. These are spoken by the priest and are called "the presidential prayers." The priest prays in the name of the whole community. The eucharistic prayer, "a prayer of thanksgiving and sanctification," is preeminent among all presidential prayers.

The Language of Music and Song

Hymns, Psalms, and acclamations are sung forms of prayer. Music is not an optional but an integral part of liturgy. The church musicians and liturgical scholars at the Milwaukee Symposia for Church Composers in 1992 describe music as "a language of faith." The composers also state that:

Ritual music draws us from our habitual ways of seeing the world and one another to a way of receiving and intending the world as the arena of God's glory. The aesthetic is prophetic. Ritual music draws us out of presumptive and self-preoccupied ways of being. It questions our human arrangements of power and domination. It renders a genuine, new possibility for facing God, the world, neighbors and ourselves.[36]

Church composers tell us that "music making is a profoundly human experience."[37] The "General Instruction of the Roman Missal" describes choral music in another way. It states, "Song is the sign of the heart's joy. Thus St. Augustine says rightly, 'To sing belongs to lovers.'" There is also the ancient proverb: "One who sings prays twice."[38] Song and music are integral elements in liturgy, and they enhance and support the prayer of the community.[39] Ritual music takes different styles: folk music, classical music, chant; but whatever style it takes, the music should promote unity and integrity within the rite.

Music is a powerful language in every area of life. It is prophetic. It moves us to tears, raises our spirits, expresses our grief. It is a language worthy to express the community's faith. As an expression of faith the quality of the words and the music ought to be worthy of worship.

The Use of Inclusive Language in Worship

The language we use, whether it is the scriptural word, the presidential prayers, the dialogues between the presider and the assembly, or the musical word, not only expresses who we are but it shapes us; it, in effect, constitutes us. Our language creates and recreates us. We become what we speak. Aidan Kavanagh describes the power of language in an analysis of its social consequences:

What happens in an act of language is not only a transfer of data from speaker to hearer, but a social transaction with reality whose ramifications escape over the horizon of the present and beyond the act of speech itself. *The act changes the society in which it occurs.* The society then adjusts to that

251

change, becoming different from what it was before the act happened. This adjustment means that no subsequent act of language can ever touch the society in exactly the same way as the previous act did.[40]

Liturgy is a language that both constitutes and is constituted by the church. It creates and expresses the church even as it is created by the church.

All of us are born into a world of language that shapes us and our reality, but even as it shapes us, language is a dynamic reality that is itself continually changing. As individuals and institutions change, their values, attitudes, behavior, and language change. Through language society and communities articulate a world vision, a vision of reality for both themselves and others. There is a reciprocal relationship between language and culture, language and individuals, language and thought, language and experience. Our language shapes the world in which we live, and then the world which we have shaped by our language in return influences our language and shapes us.

For the past forty years there has been in the United States and in many nations throughout the world an effort to shape our language so that it becomes gender inclusive. This effort has expanded so that inclusive language, which once referred to gender alone, now refers to the inclusion of every person regardless of ethnicity, class, race, status, or gender. The change in language grows out of the realization that language is not gender or ethnically or racially neutral and that language is an instrument of power. Our language emerged from a patriarchal and paternal society. The language we use is not neutral. Society now expects that we use a language that includes all people.

These expectations carry over into the church, which is a patriarchal and paternalistic society. Particularly through its liturgical language, the church, through action and word, tells us that women are inferior, no matter how much the leaders say we are "complementary." This creates a huge problem for women who seek recognition of their dignity, their value, and their equality with men within the church. Should worship language that subordinates them be tolerated? Where shall they worship? What shall they do? Or what shall the hierarchical church do? To maintain the unity of the community, not simply for the sake of unity but for the sake of the gospel, those who recognize the necessity of inclusive language as well as those who resist inclusivity in language need to acknowledge the problem and work together to resolve it.

Being inclusive in our "horizontal" language (language referring to the human community) is a first step, which our bishops took in their statement *Criteria for the Evaluation of Inclusive Language Translations of Scriptural Texts Proposed for Liturgical Use.*[41] In this statement the bishops proposed two general principles for judging translations of the Bible: (1) "the principle of fidelity to the Word of God" and (2) "the principle of respect for the nature of the liturgical assembly."[42] While the bishops have not accepted inclusive language when referring to God (vertical language), the use of both feminine and masculine images taken from the Bible or Tradition is not only desirable but imperative. A third needed step is discernment in the choice of texts to be read, so that women are represented, and so that the representations do not reflect patriarchy.

In 1997 Bishop Donald Trautman of Erie, distinguished the use of inclusive language from endorsement of a feminist agenda or women's ordination. He stated that "there is an urgent need for a scripturally sound Lectionary with the use of horizontal inclusive language," and he noted: "Inclusive language is simply a recognition of contemporary culture and the changes in the English language. It is clearly a response to the *Constitution on the Sacred Liturgy* that there be full participation in the liturgy."[43]

The language of worship can be particularly divisive because the act of worship reaches into the very heart and soul of our people. Each one of us wants to worship with integrity, and we want to worship as part of a larger reality, the community. The tension emerges as the integrity of the individual and the language of the community conflict.

The Relationship of Catechesis and Liturgy

The relationship between catechesis and liturgy is most readily seen in the *Rite of Christian Initiation of Adults*, where the community moves from catechesis to a liturgical rite (acceptance) to catechesis to another liturgical rite (election), to a catechesis which culminates with initiation into the church. But even the initiation celebration is not the end, for the community quickly moves from initiation into a post-initiation catechesis, called mystagogical catechesis, which then alternates with regular celebration of the Eucharist. Catechesis moves into liturgy, which then moves to catechesis. There is no sharp division between catechesis and liturgy in the *RCIA* in the sense that each catechesis and each liturgical celebration is seen as both the beginning of one and the culmination of the other. This process is not unlike that in the early catechumenate. Catherine Dooley notes that in "the early catechumenate there was almost no distinction between liturgy and catechesis. The classic catechumenate set out an integrated vision of coming to faith that wove together the biblical, liturgical and ecclesial signs within the human situation."[44]

Pope John Paul II described the relationship of catechesis and liturgy in *On Catechesis in Our Time*: "On the one hand, the catechesis that prepares for the sacraments is an eminent kind, and every form of catechesis necessarily leads to the sacraments of faith. On the other hand, authentic practice of the sacraments is bound to have a catechetical aspect."[45] Good liturgy is itself catechetical.

There is a natural rhythm between catechesis and liturgy. The community celebrates liturgy and seeks catechesis. In catechesis the community reflects on what it has done and what has been done to it in worship and this leads the community to desire to worship together again. Pope John Paul described this relationship by saying that "Catechesis is intrinsically linked with the whole of liturgical and sacramental activity."[46] The church proceeds from liturgy to catechesis to liturgical action to catechesis in a dynamic grace-filled movement.

Sharing the Light of Faith noted that both catechesis and liturgy "are rooted in the Church's faith, and both strengthen faith

and summon Christians to conversion although they do so in different ways." It goes on to point out the differences, saying:

> In the liturgy the Church is at prayer, offering adoration,
> praise, and thanksgiving to God, and seeking and celebrating
> reconciliation: here one finds both an expression of faith and a
> means for deepening it. As for catechesis, it prepares people for
> full and active participation in liturgy (by helping them under-
> stand its nature, rituals, and symbols) and at the same time
> flows from liturgy, inasmuch as, reflecting upon the commu-
> nity's experiences of worship, it seeks to relate them to daily
> life and to growth in faith.[47]

There is an intrinsic unity between the two ministries, and that is
perhaps why liturgical catechesis is a major form of ministry in the
church today.

However, liturgists and catechists have not always had a harmonious relationship. Charles Gusmer, a liturgical scholar,
describes the relationship as "feuding."

> For a long time liturgy and catechesis have been feuding like
> two estranged partners whose marriage was on the rocks.
> Angry recriminations have been hurled back and forth. Litur-
> gists accused catechists of not understanding the nature of
> liturgy, or manipulating worship for didactic purposes as if it
> were a kind of catechetical tool. Catechists responded in turn
> that liturgists were too rubrical, too rigid, too unyielding and
> inflexible, not really in touch with reality, sometimes calling
> them "litniks."[48]

The recognition that liturgists and catechists have not always
worked well together is not new.[49] John Westerhoff describes the
relationship as one of indifference rather than alienation. He points
out that catechists and liturgists could not converse because they
did not have "a common vocabulary," or a natural forum for the
exchange of scholarship.[50] Westerhoff sees the separation as a challenge to bring unity to the ministries stating that "the challenge
remains to integrate the theory and practice of catechetics and
liturgics. For too long the fields of catechetics and liturgics have

existed independently of each other; for too long catechists and liturgists have gone their separate ways."[51]

Although catechesis and liturgy were initially unified, they have, particularly since the Reformation of the sixteenth century, become more and more separated until at the beginning of the twentieth century they seemed almost unrelated. During this time there were few relational definitions of catechesis and liturgy. Even today catechists and liturgists frequently have different definitions of each other's ministry.[52]

There were also social or cultural reasons for the separation. Liturgy was the provenance of the priest. Catechesis, on the other hand, which was synonymous with children or CCD, was the work of women, although usually the parish priest was the "manager" of the catechetical programs. Priests were highly educated. Catechists were generally mothers who were not as well educated but who often had knowledge, intuitions, and faith that enabled them to be extraordinary catechists. The equation was unbalanced.

For the past forty years, however, this equation has been changing. Women have earned academic degrees in many disciplines, and it is now commonplace for women to earn graduate degrees in catechetics or in liturgical studies. Also, the Second Vatican Council made the participation of the people in liturgical celebrations the primary principle of renewal. Lay women and men minister to one another and to the community in liturgical celebrations. This does not mean that the priest is unimportant. Indeed the priest is still the leader of the assembly in all sacramental celebrations. But now together with the priest, lay women and men prepare ministers, plan liturgies, and on occasion give homilies.[53] Moreover, priests are recognizing that catechesis is not the same as the religious instruction they may have administered or received in their childhood. The more priests work with adult catechists, the more they are introduced to a renewed catechesis.

Whatever the difficulties of the past, it is incumbent on both liturgists and catechists to work together for the good of their people. In most parishes this is presently being accomplished through the *Rite of Christian Initiation of Adults* and to some extent through the

Christian Initiation of Children Who Have Reached Catechetical Age,[54] both of which are catechetical-liturgical rites.[55] The *Rite of Christian Initiation of Adults*, which is "the model for all catechesis,"[56] has helped many Catholics to recognize the depth of the catechetical renewal.

Both catechists and liturgists need to understand the meaning of "liturgy" and "catechetics" and have mutual respect for the service each offers to the church. Catechists need to be familiar with the rites for the different liturgical celebrations and liturgists need to be aware of the renewal in catechesis which replaces instruction in doctrine with a process leading to conversion as the goal of catechesis.

Liturgical Catechesis

Liturgical catechesis is catechesis that prepares a community to participate in a sacramental celebration for the first time or reflects with a community on a liturgical celebration already experienced. This catechesis takes different forms according to the people being catechized and the liturgical event for which they are being catechized. It may take the form of occasional catechesis on the sacraments for adults, lectionary catechesis, the catechesis of children for confirmation, first Eucharist, and penance and the catechesis of parents when their children are preparing for a new sacramental event.

Liturgical catechesis is one form of catechesis among many, although all forms of catechesis have a liturgical dimension. It promotes "a deeper understanding and experience of the liturgy."[57] It is, like other forms of catechesis, related to human life and is experiential, paschal, ecclesial, biblical, liturgical, and ethical. It calls participants and the community to conversion and transformation of life. As a form of symbolic catechesis it is a reflection on the symbols, scriptural readings, and prayer texts of liturgical experiences, contextualized within the liturgical year, rather than on the Bible or the doctrine and life of the church.

Liturgical catechesis prepares the community to return to the liturgical event with new insights and new desires. Kavanagh describes sacraments as "analogies" which work by repetition and accumulation.[58] He reminds us that sacraments are like "grand opera," or "love poems." He goes on to say:

> Sacraments do not teach; they seduce. Sacraments do not force people into corners at the point of ideological guns; they are keys that open doors and set people free. Sacraments are not exceptional and extraordinary events; they are standard and ordinary—like baths and dinners, kisses and loving touches, hugs and perfume, prayers and celebrations.[59]

Liturgical celebrations of sacraments are community encounters with Christ through the Holy Spirit. They express and create relationships. Entering into liturgical celebration of sacraments precipitates conversion, transformation of life. It is being bathed and fed, embraced and anointed with grace in an environment in which the Spirit flourishes. It is not for the unwary or the self-satisfied. Robert Hovda describes it in this way:

> Good liturgical celebration, like a parable, takes us by the hair of our heads, lifts us momentarily out of the cesspool of injustice we call home, puts us in the promised and challenging reign of God, where we are treated like we have never been treated anywhere else...where we are bowed to and sprinkled and censed and kissed and touched and where we share equally among all a holy food and drink.[60]

In liturgical catechesis we gather to reflect on what we have done and what has been done to us.

Liturgical catechesis gives the community an opportunity to consider why it gathers for liturgical prayer and what it does when it worships. In liturgical catechesis the catechetical community reflects on its own life, on a particular liturgical ritual and its tradition within the church, and, it is hoped, the community recognizes how liturgy connects it with its life and with its faith in accepting Jesus as the Christ. It reflects on God's work in Christ through the Spirit. It considers how the whole world is related to the sacraments and how the world itself is sacramental.

Liturgical catechesis helps the community to recognize that worship is the breath of Christian life. Worship events bring the community together as Christians in the Spirit to proclaim and act out its faith in Christ as the one who inaugurates the reign of God. In this proclaiming and acting out, the community is graced and its own commitment to announce the reign of God is strengthened. Liturgical celebrations generate the fruits of the Holy Spirit, the first of which is justice in the world.

The Process of Liturgical Catechesis

As an "eminent" form of symbolic catechesis,[61] liturgical catechesis follows the same process as all other forms of symbolic catechesis. First, it begins with a reflection on a common experience and the symbols associated with that experience. Second, it interprets that experience by drawing on the liturgical metaphors and symbols. Third, it explores the intimacy between the liturgical experience and justice and finally it gathers the community together to express its faith in ritual prayer.

There is more than one acceptable approach in liturgical catechesis. There are many approaches, each valid in its own way. Symbolic catechesis with its fourfold movement from human experience to faith symbol to doing justice to climaxing in ritual prayer is one of many ways. The following description of liturgical catechesis is based on the process of symbolic catechesis described in chapter 5. It expands on that process inasmuch as it refers specifically to liturgical catechesis. It draws on the process of the *Rite of Christian Initiation of Adults* as a model for all liturgical catechesis.

First, liturgical catechesis is related to human experience. Liturgical catechesis begins with a reflection on a human reality related to the particular liturgical celebration being considered. It considers a concrete human event. Are you going to get married? Then let us examine love relationships, human commitment, sexuality in life, beginning a new family. See what these experiences mean to the couple and their life together. How did each member of the couple experience the marriage of their mother and father? What do they expect their relationship to be like in two years? five years? ten years? The multitude of questions young people ask of themselves about the commitment in marriage need to be asked in a semipublic way in catechesis for the sacrament of matrimony.

Are you ill, or going to undergo serious surgery, or elderly? If someone is going to be anointed for sickness and there is a opportunity for catechesis, the community of people who are ill or elderly may wish to consider what it means to be sick or elderly. What is special about this time of life? What are the strengths of being "senior"? What are the weaknesses? If the catechesis is for Eucharist, first Eucharist, or a renewal of Eucharist, the community would need to consider special family meals or doing sacrifice for others or the use of bread and/or wine in our lives. What happens to a person who is hungry, always hungry? How does food affect life? There are myriad concrete human experiences that can be addressed in liturgical catechesis.

In preparing for or reflecting on the celebration of reconciliation, the community could consider both the experience of giving and the experience of receiving and accepting forgiveness. What does it mean to offend others? to sin? What are the ramifications of evil and good actions? What are signs of repentance in human relationships? What is the place of penance in human life?

In the baptism of infants the predominant human experience that parallels it is entry into a new community. How will the new community affect the life of the child? Will the child effect change in the life of the community? How is new life treated and respected in this community? What is the responsibility of the community for a new life? Catechesis for the baptism of infants is a catechesis for the parents, but it is also a catechesis for the community.

Liturgical catechesis may begin with the question of why people are going to participate in a sacramental celebration. Most of those being catechized for sacraments of initiation are adults or children who are going to participate in those sacraments for the first time. The preparation for celebration becomes the human experience probed in the first movement of liturgical catechesis. In catechesis for the sacraments of initiation the rite itself states that this catechesis is a catechesis of welcome, of inquiring, of acceptance, of enlightenment, of election, of initiation, and finally of continuing life in the community. This is primarily a catechesis of adults for it is adults who are able and prepared to commit themselves to God through Christ and this community. It is also a catechesis of initiation for children who are growing into the community.

Second, in liturgical catechesis the community interprets the liturgical experience through reflection on a faith symbol. To catechize for liturgy, catechists need to know the rite well.[62] One of the most important tasks of the director of catechetical ministry is to introduce the study of the rite for which the community is being prepared to the catechists. Unless the catechist knows the rite well she will miss opportunities for preparing the community for liturgy or leading them to reflect on the celebration already experienced. The most important concept for the catechist to remember is that first of all every public liturgy is a celebration of the life-death-resurrection of Jesus and the relationship of his life to us. It is Jesus we celebrate, and our faith commitment to him.

Second, although the parallel is inadequate, it can be helpful to consider the elements of the ritual and how they are performed. Just as the director of a play studies the play from many angles, so must the catechist study and reflect on the rite. (What is the point of this performance? How do the characters interact? How do they relate to one another?) The catechist needs to know the rite for which she catechizes. (What do these symbols mean in the tradition? Why were these readings chosen? What is the primary symbol? How do the prayer texts, scriptural readings, and other symbols relate?). The parish director can provide opportunity for each catechist to study and to recognize that each celebration is entry into the paschal mystery, is an act of worship, an act of faith.

The relationship and the meaning of the scriptural readings, the symbolic actions, and prayer texts come from the action of God in the lives of the people. The actions, words, and prayers of the liturgy are all interrelated, each one bringing fullness to the totality of the rite. For example, the taking, blessing, giving, and eating of the bread of the Eucharist have multiple meanings because of the multiple meanings bread has in our lives. Bread is a daily food which we call "the staff of life." Is bread a metaphor for all foods?

What is the place of food in our lives? What happens if we hoard food? Or share food? Or are without food? Why do we sometimes use bread as a celebratory food? The catechetical community can relate its knowledge and experience of bread to bread in the Bible: the manna from the desert, the multiplication of the loaves, the actions of Jesus at table on the night before he died, the Easter story of the disciples walking to Emmaus and recognizing the Lord in "the breaking of the bread." The church, as a community, has a millennial history of interactions between itself and the Holy Mystery, and it has saved the memory of many of those events in the Scriptures, which it reads and reenacts whenever it worships. In liturgical rituals the assembly relates its sacred symbols to Christ, to our life as the body of Christ now, and to Christ's promise of future glory.

But symbols can lose or change their meaning because of cultural developments and the new insights such developments bring. Once the crowning of a king by the pope was a significant liturgical (though not sacramental) event. Today the pope no longer crowns governmental leaders. Nor does a religious leader ordinarily effect the change to a new government. From the fifteenth century until recently it was customary to crown the pope with a three-tiered precious metal crown richly ornamented with costly jewels. This crowning signified both the sacred and secular power of the papacy. After the Second Vatican Council, Pope Paul VI sold a tiara and gave the proceeds to the poor. This action said that a pope ought not wear the crown of a national leader. Since then popes have been installed rather than crowned.[63]

After examining, considering, remembering, studying, exploring, sharing insights about, commenting on, praying with the symbols, symbolic actions, prayer texts, or readings in the life of the church, the catechetical community can understand more fully the meaning of the words and actions in the liturgical rite. In movement 2 of the catechesis, the community considers how the prayer texts or the scriptural readings or the symbolic actions of the rite relate to the concrete human experience. Ordinarily this meaning will be available through stories and images of Scripture or through the life of the church, its teaching and its history.

In movement 2 the community sometimes turns to biblical stories even though it is doing a liturgical catechesis. For example, if the catechesis is for baptism, the community could consider one or more of the following scriptural stories: the saving of the baby Moses in the water, the crossing of the Reed Sea to freedom, the baptism of Jesus, the words of Jesus about water or baptism, or the sending forth of the disciples to baptize.[64]

Catherine Dooley points out that "for the most part, the Christian community no longer has the biblical background to hear the word in depth."[65] This is particularly true within the Catholic Church. For this reason every liturgical catechesis is in a way also a biblical catechesis, and just as the catechist needs to understand the rite, so she needs to know how to interpret the appropriate biblical passages. We are asking a great deal from our catechists, but it is the work of the pastor and the director of catechetical ministry to see that catechists have both the education and the resources that they need for their ministry. In smaller parishes it may be best to let catechists specialize on a particular form of liturgical catechesis so that they can continue to probe the meaning and the significance of the symbols, symbolic actions, prayer texts, and readings of a rite. The one thing that is absolutely essential is that the catechist continue to prayerfully consider the symbols, prayer texts, and readings and not fall into a rut that limits the interpretation of the community and the creativity of the imagination to recognize the power of the symbols.

These are a few ways in which liturgical catechesis on baptism might develop. The catechesis does not examine only the symbol or the prayer texts or the Scriptures but how any one, two, or three of these are related in the rite. In liturgical catechesis the community looks beyond the visible and sees "the more," the invisible reality beyond the visible sign. Recognizing the unseen, the community interprets its life and its world in light of God's presence. A sacrament recognized as a "visible sign of an invisible reality" unveils the reality of God's constant loving presence always and everywhere available to the community and to the world. Liturgical catechesis brings the community face to face with the Divine Presence experienced in life and in the ritual, and in so doing it shapes the faith of the community.

Third, liturgical catechesis leads the catechetical community to do justice. Liturgical catechesis also considers how the liturgical event and human life merge and how the doing of justice is intimately related to every worship event. Justice, like worship, is at the core of Christian life. Like worship, justice is not something one *chooses* to do or not do. Christians, because they are Christians, worship and do justice. Worship and justice are at the heart of Christian faith, and catechesis leads the community to recognize their significance and their unity.

The church exists to do the work of Christ. Its mission is to proclaim the reign of God, which it does in its liturgy. Liturgy "effectively symbolizes in an incipient way the reign of God."[66] The church also proclaims God's reign in its works. Justice and liturgy are like two branches of the same palm. They share the same stem and bear the same life. Sometimes they diverge to carry out Christ's work in different ways. The artificial separation of works of justice and liturgy which the Catholic Church in the United States experienced in earlier decades was an aberration. Liturgy and justice both emerge from the same faith and both express the same commitment to God through Christ in the Spirit.

How can this be? How can we say that liturgy and justice are so closely related when they take place in different arenas with different symbols and words and call forth different responses from us? First, both justice and worship emerge from the heart of the Christian community. They express what it means to be a community of Christians. They are not optional for Christians. Both liturgy and justice are essential expressions of Christian faith. Both unite members of the community. Both promote the reign of God. They unify our lives and our time. We cannot differentiate what we do at the altar from what we do during the rest of our lives, nor what we do during the week from what we do at Sunday worship. Neither the individual nor the community can celebrate the reign of God in liturgy and not strive for it in daily life.

The Second Vatican Council enunciated the unity of the scriptural, sacramental and social justice dimensions of the church in three of its documents: the *Constitution on the Sacred Liturgy*, the

Dogmatic Constitution on the Church, and the *Pastoral Constitution on the Church in the Modern World*. The liturgy constitution sets forth the church's renewed understanding of sacrament. The *Constitution on the Church* examines and describes the inner life of the church using scriptural metaphors. The *Church in the Modern World* examines and describes the reach of the church outside itself to the world in which it lives. The three documents together give us a harmonious vision of the church as sacramental, scriptural, and socially responsible.[67]

The voices of the prophets and of Jesus speak to us from the scriptural readings of the liturgy, reminding us that "the quality of faith will always be tested by the way the women, the orphans, and the aliens are treated."[68] The voice of the church speaks to us in bishops' pastorals, papal encyclicals, and the witness of thousands of people working in hospitals, schools, shelters, kitchens, and organizations seeking justice. Justice and worship are at the heart of our faith.

The eucharistic vision of the world that the church proclaims to the wealthy and poor, to men and women, and to people of different races and ethnic groups is that the bread and wine of Christ is being offered as food and drink to the young and the elderly, to people of every educational level and to those of no education at all. This symbolizes the responsibility of the community and of each individual within it to do justice for all. The Eucharist tells us time and time again that the homeless and the hungry must be fed. The ignorant must be taught. Those who grieve must be comforted. The oppressed must be freed. The imprisoned must be visited. Worship and justice feed on and support each other. Without one, the other perishes.

Liturgical catechesis needs to uncover this truth in its catechesis of every sacrament. People too often separate the act of worship from the doing of justice. In liturgical catechesis the relationship needs to be rediscovered. The community can look back on what the church does in the world and reflect on the symbolism expressed in the liturgical event and recognize that every liturgy calls us to justice. The prayer texts, the scriptural readings, the symbols and symbolic actions of liturgy all remind us in different ways that Christian faith calls us to live and be in the world as Christ was, a healer, one who feeds, a liberator, a pray-er, a comforter, a friend, a teacher, a bearer of good news. Liturgical catechesis reminds the community that justice is at the heart of faith.

Fourth, liturgical catechesis climaxes with ritual prayer. The ritual prayer that is the climax of liturgical catechesis may not be sacramental, but this prayer is a perfect place for the community to pray with some of the symbolic actions, scriptural readings, and/or prayer texts of the liturgical event it considered. Few words and more use of the language of symbol and gesture might be called for at this time. In this prayer the human experience, the symbolic actions, the Scripture readings, the prayers, the focus on justice all come together in a single corporate event, the ritual prayer.

If the liturgical prayer is the intuitive and symbolic synthesis of all that has happened in the catechesis, then it is the climax of the session. It needs careful planning, an appropriate space and a variety of ministers all of whom need to be prepared for their ministry. When will the catechist do this? Careful planning of the prayer with attention to detail will take place long before the catechetical community meets. The immediate preparation for the prayer can take place within a few minutes before the ritual begins. Preparing for the ritual is important if the prayer is to be the climax of the catechesis, an experience of grace, of God's constant and loving presence.

Lectionary Catechesis

As noted earlier, the *Lectionary for Mass* is the book that contains the scriptural readings to be proclaimed in liturgical celebrations. It has, at the request of the Second Vatican Council, been revised so that "the treasures of the Bible" may be "opened up more lavishly so that a richer fare may be provided for the faithful at the table of God's word."[69] In the revised lectionary the readings are organized in a three-year cycle (A, B, and C), with each Sunday having one reading from the Old Testament, a second from a New Testament writing other than a Gospel, and the third from a Gospel. In the arranging of the lectionary the first and third readings were coordinated by theme; the second often shares images from the other readings.

As a form of symbolic catechesis, lectionary catechesis has as its core the mystery of Christ celebrated in the liturgical year. The human experience reflected on in catechesis may simply be the community's journey of faith as reflected in and interpreted by the Scriptures or the feasts and seasons of the liturgical year. Lectionary catechesis focuses on the scriptural readings that celebrate the seasons and feasts as the community lives through them. Or the catechist may choose a human experience related to the Scriptures as the focus of the initial reflection.

Lectionary-based catechesis is an excellent form of catechesis for adults. It is always paschal, a celebration of the life-death-resurrection of Jesus the Christ. It is a biblical and liturgical catechesis that relates adults' faith journey to their own lives and reinforces their identity as members of the faith community. It is based on previous catechesis either through a parish structure or through the family. It is trinitarian, christological, and ecclesial since it is based on the Scriptures. It is anthropological in that it relates the Scriptures to life, the life of the individual and his or her world, the life of the community and its world, and the tradition that forms the community. It is evangelical in that it calls the community to share its faith with others. It is ethical, as the Scriptures and liturgy both call the community to justice and because the voice of the prophets calling the community to care for widows, orphans, the poor, and the hungry often rings through the readings. It is a mystagogical catechesis, a reflection on Scriptures already celebrated.

Lectionary catechesis presumes that the catechist has a solid foundation in the Scriptures. This means that she is familiar with the Bible itself, both the Old and the New Testament, and that she knows, as *Sharing the Light of Faith* recommends, the major themes of the Old Testament, "creation and redemption, sin and grace, the covenant with Abraham and the chosen people, the exodus from Egypt and the Sinai covenant, the Babylonian captivity and the return, the Emmanuel and suffering servant passages in Isaiah."[70] Knowledge of Gospel parables and stories as well as of the teachings of Jesus is essential. Study, prayer to the Holy Spirit, and meditation on the Scriptures will help prepare catechists for this ministry.

I believe that lectionary catechesis, if it is the *only* catechesis offered to children, is inadequate for them. It is, however, an excellent form of supplemental catechesis for children. Children need to hear more of the Bible than is contained in the lectionary, and perhaps some stories that are not part of the Sunday readings. The lectionary's presentation of the Christian story or creed is subtle and sophisticated and not easily synthesized by children unless they have knowledge of the church's tradition also.

On the other hand, lectionary catechesis is certainly a satisfactory form of catechesis for adult catechumens. Catechumens are in the midst of a catechesis that envelops them cognitively, affectively, and ethically. With sponsors, catechists, and parish members, the catechumens experience a rich adult reflection on the Scriptures in the context of the liturgical rites they have experienced or are going to experience. The very fact that there are sponsors, members of the parish community, and catechists available to the catechumen means that the conversation on the Scriptures is ongoing throughout the week. The parish presents itself to the catechumens as a biblical community, an assembly formed by the Bible which prays through the Bible and lives out biblical values and biblical commitment. As a biblical community it recognizes the mystery of salvation, the mystery of God's love given to it always and everywhere.

The inquirers and catechumens are on a significant journey in their lives, and this journey involves reflection on the Scriptures. If the axiom *the law of prayer is the law of belief* is true, and for centuries the church has accepted it as true, then the doctrine the catechumens need will be prayed through as they listen to and reflect on the Scriptures, and celebrate their liturgical rituals. The catechumens will be enlightened and formed by the Scriptures into a biblical community through their lectionary-based catechesis.

In Summary

Liturgical catechesis is a catechesis on the symbols and language of a liturgical event, usually a sacramental celebration. But it may also be preparing people to be ministers at liturgical celebrations. Lectors, hospitality ministers, choir members, cantors, acolytes, eucharistic ministers, those who take communion to the sick can all be prepared for their ministry in a liturgical catechesis, a catechesis that reflects on a rite already celebrated or a rite to be celebrated in the future.

The law of prayer is the law of belief. As we pray, so we believe. In every liturgical experience the faith community joins itself to God through Christ, and the grace of the Holy Spirit pours out upon it. Hence all prayer begins in the name of the Father, and of the Son, and of the Holy Spirit. Liturgies are encounters with Christ. In our liturgies the great Holy Mystery who was, who is, who always will be reaches out and touches the worshipers. This touch has the power to transform the community, to turn it toward God's reign, where the lion lies down with the lamb, where the poor are fed and housed and reverenced, where all good things flourish. We worship with the people, with the "things" of creation—bread, wine, oil, and water—and with song and dance and every good human impulse. Everything is sacramental. All created reality symbolizes God. All creation is sacramental. We are sacramental.

Catechesis for liturgy simply unveils the grace that is already there in all that we do. The catechist leads the community to see "the more," and when we see "the more" we recognize the invisible reality beyond the visible signs in life. Such recognition leads us to turn to the Holy Mystery who is reaching out and enfolding the whole human race with love and with grace and simply say, *"Amen."*

FURTHER READINGS

Bernstein, Eleanor, ed. *Liturgy and Spirituality in Context: Perspectives on Prayer and Culture*. Collegeville, Minn.: Liturgical Press, 1990.

Bishops' Committee on the Liturgy. *Liturgical Music Today*. Washington, D.C.: United States Catholic Conference, 1982.

Collins, Mary. *Women at Prayer*. 1987 Madeleva Lecture in Spirituality. New York: Paulist Press, 1987.

Dooley, Kate. *To Listen and Tell: Introduction to the Lectionary for Masses with Children with Commentary*. Washington, D.C.: Pastoral Press, 1993.

Empereur, James L., and Christopher G. Kiesling, eds. *The Liturgy That Does Justice*. Theology and Life Series 33. Collegeville, Minn.: Liturgical Press, 1990.

Grosz, Edward M., ed. *Liturgy and Social Justice: Celebrating Rites—Proclaiming Rites*. Collegeville, Minn.: Liturgical Press, 1989.

Gusmer, Charles. *Wholesome Worship*. Washington, D.C.: Pastoral Press, 1989.

Hughes, Kathleen, and Mark R. Francis, eds. *Living No Longer for Ourselves: Liturgy and Justice in the Nineties*. Collegeville, Minn.: Liturgical Press, 1991.

Joncas, Jan Michael. *The Catechism of the Catholic Church on Liturgy & Sacraments*. San Jose, Calif.: Resource Publications, 1995.

Kavanagh, Aidan. *The Liturgy Documents: A Parish Resource*. Chicago: Liturgy Training Publications, 1991.

———. *On Liturgical Theology*. A Pueblo Book. Collegeville, Minn.: Liturgical Press, 1992.

The Milwaukee Symposia for Church Composers. Chicago: Liturgy Training Publications, 1992.

Rites of the Catholic Church. 2 volumes. New York: Pueblo Publishing Company, 1990.

Sacred Congregation for the Sacraments and Divine Worship. *The Lectionary for Mass*. Chicago: Liturgy Training Publications, 1999.

Afterword:
Catechesis as a Prophetic Ministry

Catechesis on the "signs of the times" is in many ways a prophetic ministry. In fact, there are remarkable similarities between catechesis and prophecy. Both are ministries of the word. Both are responses to God's call. Both address the significance of God's action in our daily lives. Both demand justice from individuals and communities. It is possible to find extraordinary resemblances between the two ministries, likenesses that permit or encourage us to say that catechesis is, itself, a prophetic ministry.

Prophets and Prophecy

"There are three ways," says Abraham Heschel, that we may respond to the world. "We may exploit it; we may enjoy it; we may accept it in awe."[1] Heschel notes that the prophets of the Old Testament enjoyed the world and accepted it in awe. They recognized that God communicated with humankind in and through the world and they embraced the mundane and ordinary as having a profound spiritual significance. For the prophets there was an intimate unity between the material and the spiritual world. For them God was present in this world and they experienced and recognized God in the simplicity and wonder of daily life.

The prophets were people who disturbed others by the power of their words and actions. They were people with insight, poets and preachers, oddly individualistic and fiercely communal. They

271

spoke with power. Their words were effective, not simply descriptive. Their words made a difference in their world because they were not their own words but God's word speaking through them. And the people recognized God's power in the words of the prophet. Heschel describes the power of words by telling us of his father's words:

> Words, he wrote, are themselves sacred, God's tools for creating the universe, and our tools for bringing holiness—or evil—into the world. He tried to remind us that the Holocaust did not begin with the building of crematoria, and Hitler did not come to power with tanks and guns; it all began with uttering evil words, with defamation, with language and propaganda. Words create worlds, he used to tell me when I was a child. They must be used very carefully. Some words, once having been uttered, gain eternity and can never be withdrawn. The book of Proverbs reminds us, he wrote, that death and life are in the power of the tongue.[2]

For the prophets, words were sacred. They exercised a "ministry of the word" and in this service they spoke verbally and through gesture the powerful word of God.

The prophets were not, however, simply dumb instruments through which God spoke. Again, Heschel wrote:

> The prophet is a person, not a microphone, He is endowed with a mission, with the power of a word not his own that accounts for his greatness—but also with temperament, concern, character, and individuality. As there was no resisting the impact of divine inspiration, so at times there was no resisting the voices of his own temperament. The word of God reverberated in the voice of man.[3]

The prophet was one who mediated and interpreted the divine mind and will.[4] Prophets were those who spoke in the name of God.[5]

We sometimes tend to consider the prophets as wholly other than ourselves. We think of them as famous people, leaders among the people or Israel. The biblical prophets Isaiah, Jeremiah, Ezekiel, Amos, Hosea, and the others are "extraordinary" prophets among many more prophets. Most of the prophets in the Hebrew Scriptures were men, though both Miriam and Deborah are called "prophets."[6] But not all prophets achieved the stature of these major figures. There were, besides the major and minor prophets of the Bible, schools of prophets, cult prophets, and court prophets. There were many prophets about whom we know nothing, who are for us anonymous.

One of the characteristics frequently attributed to prophets is that they were doomsayers, and sometimes they were. But most of the time they were people of hope. They saw and acknowledged the reality of evil. They confronted their people with the concreteness of sin in their world. But they never finished uttering their word without adding an offer and expectation of hope. God is still with us. God still upholds the covenant We are God's people. Righteousness will replace injustice.

Through their words the prophets tore down indifference and said no to complacency and sin. Heschel tells us, "Their words are onslaughts, scuttling illusions of false security, challenging evasions, calling faith to account, questioning prudence and impartiality."[7] They were social critics who illumined the consciousness of their time. Through their words and their actions the prophets led the community to recognize the injustice the people were hiding from themselves.

The prophets were reflective men and women who moved from reflection to action, who did not temper their condemnation of injustice, which was for them a catastrophe, "a threat to the world." According to Heschel, "Prophecy is the voice that God has lent to the silent agony, a voice to the plundered poor, to the profaned riches of the world."[8] The prophet made the rich and powerful see the misery in the lives of others, particularly in the lives of the poor, a misery too often caused by the actions of the wealthy.

The prophets did not volunteer to prophesy. They were called to a vocation most of them did not want. "Ah, Lord God! Truly I do not know how to speak, for I am only a boy," said Jeremiah (1:5). Amos described himself as a herdsman and tree farmer. "I am no prophet, nor a prophet's son; but I am a herdsman, and a dresser of sycamore trees, and the LORD took me from following the flock, and the LORD said to me, 'Go, prophesy to my people Israel'" (Am 7:14–15).

Why would anyone want to be a prophet? Prophecy included rejection by the people, suffering, and pain. In a classic moment of resistance to his vocation, Jeremiah, who was being rejected by the people, cried out:

> O LORD, you have enticed me
>   and I was enticed;
> you have overpowered me,
>   and you have prevailed.
> I have become a laughingstock, all day long
>   everyone mocks me.
> For whenever I speak, I must call out,
>   I must shout, "Violence and destruction!"
> For the word of the LORD has become for me
>   a reproach and derision all day long. (20:7–8)

The word of prophecy brought ridicule, reproach, rejection, and derision to Jeremiah. But Jeremiah is so taken up with God's word that he repents his lament and turns back to God proclaiming his commitment to prophecy and his love:

> If I say, "I will not mention him,
>   or speak any more in his name,"
> then within me there is something like a burning fire,
>   shut up in my bones;
> I am weary with holding it in,
>   and I cannot. (20:9)

Jeremiah and the other prophets were grasped and embraced by God, and they returned the embrace. They became God's spokespersons, ministers of God's word. They spoke words of condemnation and words of hope. They spoke not only of the future but primarily of the present. They spoke not their own word, but the word of God. For this reason the word they spoke seared and divided, healed and united. It condemned and it graced.

Jesus of Nazareth followed in the pattern of the prophets so that his friends and disciples said of him that he "was a prophet mighty in deed and in word before God and all the people" (Lk 24:19). When he healed the son of the widow in a town called Nain, the people were "seized with fear, and they glorified God, saying, 'A great prophet has risen among us!' and 'God has looked favorably on his people'" (Lk 7:16). He was the greatest of all prophets, and because of the word he preached in both action and language he was condemned to death as a common criminal. Yet it is for this same word that God raised him from the dead. He is the one of whom Luke writes: "He [Jesus] commanded us preach to the people and to testify that he is the one ordained by God as judge of the living and the dead. All the prophets testify about him that everyone who believes in him receives forgiveness of sins through his name" (Acts 10:42–43).

Catechesis as a Prophetic Ministry

Catechists are prophetic. They embody the prophetic spirit. Both prophets and catechists have been called to a ministry that no one particularly wants to do, and one that often comes at a very high cost. Being given to selfless service of God's word both prophets and catechists are generally anonymous people in their parishes. Their service is often hardly recognized by the community they serve.

The catechist, like the prophet, is a person endowed with the power of the word. For the catechist, words are sacred. As a minister of the word catechists echo or resound the word and the word catechists echo is not their own word but the word of God. Catechesis is a ministry of the word, a prophetic ministry in which the catechist through words of awe, of image, of story, of doctrine, of dogma, of ritual, of gesture calls the community to acknowledge and repudiate sin and to turn back to its covenant relationship with God through Christ and his church. The catechist like the prophet speaks the word that reminds the community that religion *is* justice and worship and that the Holy Mystery, who gives the whole universe life, deserves the praise and thanksgiving of the community.

The catechist emerges from the community of faith and speaks God's word within it.

Walter Brueggemann suggests that "the task of prophetic ministry is to nurture, nourish, and evoke a consciousness and perception alternative to the consciousness and perception of the dominant culture around us."[9] Catechists, like prophets, look at the signs of the times in daily life, personal and social, and they turn to the symbols of faith for interpretation. They lead their communities to look at the signs of the times in the light of their Christian faith. In so doing catechists evoke a consciousness that is an alternative to the dominant culture in which they live. Catechists lead the people to see that the values and meanings of the dominant culture are worthy of respect when they harmonize with the values and meanings of religious faith, and that they are a bondage wearing the people down when they conflict with that faith.

Directors of parish catechesis and catechists at the adult, youth, and elementary school levels are called from the faith community to bring Christ's liberating word of freedom and grace. Through the word of their lives and the word of their mouth catechists stir up the heart and stretch the minds of their listeners so they may lead them to an ever stronger faith. Because the prophets spoke from the heart as well as from the head they had power to move people to repentance. So the catechist whose voice emerges from a strong and compelling faith commitment has power, given by the Holy One through the Spirit, to move people to repentance and conversion.

In the days of the Old Testament most of the prophets were men. They were men because social norms and expectations made it almost impossible for women to be heard as speakers of God's word. Today most catechists are women, and in today's culture in the United States many people, though surely not all, recognize that women can and do speak God's word, often with a compelling voice. In this new millennium where women expect to be treated as equals, people can finally recognize that they can also expect to be given the gift of prophecy. They can speak as the prophets once did.

They can be and are a prophetic voice within the church. Their voices must be heard.

At the beginning of this new century it is the word of prophetic women and men that is going forth throughout the whole world, summoning other men, women, and children to awaken and recognize God in the wonders of ordinary daily life and relationships. Those who catechize with a prophetic spirit call the community to justice, not in generic terms but concretely as the prophets did: feed the hungry children, take care of abused women, educate the men and women who are immigrant strangers in our midst, provide care and health for those with AIDS, and protect the children. As the biblical prophets called for justice for widows and orphans, so now catechists call for justice and righteousness for those whom the dominant culture has marginalized. The prophetic spirit in catechists introduces the community not only to a fathering God but also to a mothering God, not a frail, helpless unknowing woman but a mother God who loves tenderly, fiercely, and well, a mothering God who protects and chastises and frees from bondage.

Marilyn Schaub has noted that prophets have had "the experience of being addressed by God."[10] Jeffrey Sobosan points out that among the prophets "the vocation to Christian living will endure as a vocation only as long as the initiating address by God and the enthusiasm and conviction it creates regarding what God has revealed is continually refreshed as an effective influence over our lives."[11] Today God addresses catechists and the enthusiasm *(en theos)* this address creates enables them to address the church. This second address often brings enthusiasm and conviction to the church, although it is sometimes resisted, ridiculed, and rejected. The word of the catechist, like the word of the prophet, is an utterance of hope and justice, of condemnation as well as of grace.

How can the catechist maintain both enthusiasm and conviction? Through looking at the world with awe, through study, and through prayer. Not through just one or the other of these three avenues but through all three together. First, the catechist needs to see, really see, the world in which she or he lives—not just look at it superficially, but look at it carefully, reflectively, prayerfully, with awe.[12] The catechist looks for the good in this world as well as all those factors that dehumanize humankind. She looks for signs of grace as well as signs of evil. He looks for signs of God's presence as well as for signs of God's absence. And as they look and see the unseen, the fire burns ever more brightly in their hearts.

The catechist needs to study daily. Why would anyone want to study? you might ask. I'm told that most people do not like to study. That seems a strange statement when the numbers of senior citizens taking adult education courses is increasing dramatically, and when most colleges and universities are making room and adjusting their curricula for "traditional" or "older" students. Every senior citizen I know is studying something: how to use the computer, oil painting, bird watching, Shakespeare's tragedies, the history of early California, a musical instrument, Italian opera, Mexican cooking. The variety of courses offered and the sheer number of adult education courses offered by neighborhood community centers and by colleges and universities are astounding. What this tells me is that when people have a little free time they have a variety of interests and they like to study. They particularly like to study together with other adults. They like participative study to which they can bring their experience and their insights. Why would catechists be any different from the senior citizens and those who study at community adult education programs? Most of them know that their vocation demands that they know more about God and the church, about Christian history and about the saints. Most catechists will study if there is opportunity for participative as well as private adult study.

We need to recognize that it can be through the word of study that God addresses the people and calls individuals within the community to prophesy. Often students have said to me, "I know this university study is not catechetical, but it inspires me. It calls me to conversion." Strange as it may seem, even the words of the brilliant theologian Karl Rahner can lift one into ecstasy. Good theology and good catechesis do not separate the heart from the intellect.

True study, whether it is study of biology or theology, engages the whole person and often spurs a change in the way one lives.

Where can the catechist receive guidance or assistance in preparing for the work of catechizing? The church in the United States has not even begun to recognize the hunger that people have for growth in faith through study, study for ministry and study for life.[13] It is true that some dioceses and a few parishes are leaders in providing ministry courses or parish courses such as the ones promoted through "occasional" catechesis. But we seem to have lost American ingenuity, imagination, and inventiveness when it comes to renewing parish opportunities for the people to reintroduce themselves to the beauty and grace of the gospel.

The third source of life for a catechist is prayer. A life without prayer is like a life without water. The person dries up spiritually, becomes arid, cannot grow, withers. Prayer takes many forms, but when we pray with others we have not only our own faith to support us but also the faith and hope and love of those with whom we pray. Ritual prayer with others enriches all of life. It is by nature physical, mental, relational, spiritual, imaginative. And when a community prays out of its heritage with symbols and symbolic actions that express the faith of past and present communities as well as the communities of the future, the prayer is full of power. Water and oil, bread and wine, word and action, names of our holy ones, dance and song, psalm and response, light and darkness, fire and air are dangerous symbols with which to interact. When they come together in prayer they lead the pray-ers to transformation and mission.

People can also pray alone and many people prefer that mode of prayer, but it is not easy for everyone to pray alone. Catechists need to pray. The parish director of catechesis can provide opportunities for catechists to pray together in ritual and scriptural prayer. This is one of her most significant works. Retreat weekends and/or common prayer a half hour before catechetical sessions for adults, children, or youth can be easily arranged. It is just a question of recognizing the value of ritual prayer in our lives.

Catechists resemble prophets in that they share in the prophetic character of ministry. Theirs is not the priestly ministry but the prophetic ministry. They resemble prophets not because they share the characteristics of individual prophets but because they share in the charism of prophecy, a gift given by God which enables the prophet to nurture, to nourish, to evoke a consciousness and perception alternative to the consciousness and perception of the dominant culture.

Catechesis is a prophetic ministry in that it resembles prophecy in four primary ways. First, prophets emerged from the community and called the community to conversion. So do catechists. Second, in searching for meaning prophets knew that genuine knowledge of God included both the knowledge of the religious tradition and personal insight and experience. They interpreted life out of their tradition and their insights, and they demanded that the people do the same. So do catechists. Third, for the prophets justice was not a duty imposed by religion; *it was religion*, and they challenged everyone to justice. This is an essential component of catechesis. And lastly, the prophets knew that Israel's service to God included prayer.[14] Both corporate and private prayer were integral dimensions of their lives. So it must be with catechesis.

The Prophet, the Catechist, and the Community

"The world is charged with the grandeur of God," wrote Gerard Manley Hopkins.[15] Sallie McFague describes "the world (or universe) as God's body."[16] Wilfrid Harrington wrote: "Because God is Creator, sustainer of all that is, there is no situation in which God is not present, no place in which [God] may not be found."[17] Karl Rahner points out that we do not have adequate language or insight to speak of God's presence. He wrote:

> Our basic starting point seems to say that God is everywhere insofar as he grounds everything, and he is nowhere insofar as everything that is grounded is created, and everything which appears in this way within the world of our experience is different from God, separated by an absolute chasm between God and what is not God.[18]

God is everywhere and the world is filled with God's glory. All of creation reflects God, symbolizes the Divine Mystery. The *Dogmatic Constitution on Divine Revelation* reminds us that "God who creates and conserves all things by [his] Word (see Jn 1:3) provides constant evidence of [himself] in created realities (see Rom 1:19–20).

Where is God? asked the *Baltimore Catechism*. And the children all responded, *God is everywhere.* Catechesis is a ministry in which the catechist leads the community to discover that profound reality: God is everywhere, active, dynamic, loving, as father, mother, sister, brother, spinner, weaver, potter, nurse. God is everywhere *for* us.

Thus says the catechist as did the prophet: there is no separation of spirit and body within human life, no separation of the physical from the material. Life is whole; we are one ourselves, and we are one with one another. God comes not just to me privately in a mystical revelation but to us, wholly, as a community, and we as a community are called to respond to God together. We are God's people and as God's people we are related and responsible for one another in our daily lives. Thus says the catechist, and as she or he builds and strengthens community bonds, the prophetic catechist builds relationships among the peoples and with people and the world, people and God. This is what catechists do daily. Unspectacularly they offer our people alternative perceptions of reality and so through their words and works show forth God's light of freedom and will for justice. This is no simple task. It is a vocation.

Catechists, like Jeremiah, are called to be prophetic, to speak in the name of the Lord. Like Jeremiah most of us protest and say, "I cannot. Not me, Lord. Send someone else." But then, like Isaiah, we say, "Here I am, Lord, send me." We are like Mary, the prophet, who said to the waiters at Cana, "Do whatever he tells you." And we know that if we do as God tells us and speak the word of the Lord, the word will be heard, justice will be done, worship will be given.

Prophecy is a gift, most of the time an unwanted one, for prophets are called to suffer and be rejected by the very ones they love, the ones with whom they share their fire. At this time in the United States we might say that a prophet is one who is called to be ridiculed. This is not because people in the United States are better or worse than people of other times and places, but it is because our culture often does not take religious faith seriously. Too often it does not take God seriously. Why would it take us seriously?

I am always conscious of the hundreds of women and men in Central America who within the past twenty-five years were martyred simply because they were catechists. I wonder why we do not hear more about them. Thousands and thousands of anonymous men and women in unspectacular ways brought the gift of God's word to their people, a word that empowered the people to search for freedom, and the anonymous ones were killed. Someone took them seriously.

Catechists are not irrelevant. We are a multitude of signposts that continually signal, whether or not we are seen or heard, that the Mystery is with us always and everywhere and that the Mystery loves us, each one of us, and all of us unconditionally. Every so often someone hears our word. The fire breaks in. The word is heard and people are graced and freed. The word we speak is an effective word. It changes lives. It is effective, like the two-edged sword of the Bible, when it is God's word and not our own.

Earlier I dedicated this book to all the catechists I have met in the past thirty years, each of whom has said to me in her or his own way, "There is a fire burning in my heart, imprisoned in my bones, the effort to restrain it wearies me, I cannot." I sometimes find this fire in diocesan offices. I find it very strong in the lives of authors of catechetical textbooks who work diligently for years with creativity and knowledge to share God's word. I find this fire in women and men catechists in parishes all over this country from east to west, from Washington, D.C., to Kauai, Hawaii. This Pentecost fire is what makes catechists. It warms us, enlightens us, burns us. It leads us to recognize the Mystery in our lives, at least glimpse it occasionally and share it. The only way we as catechists can continue to live and minister is to be on fire and share the fire that is in our hearts.

FURTHER READINGS

Brueggemann, Walter. *The Prophetic Imagination*. Philadelphia: Fortress Press, 1982.

Heschel, Abraham Joshua. *God in Search of Man: A Philosophy of Judaism*. New York: Farrar, Strauss, & Giroux, 1955. Reprint. New York: The Noonday Press, 1976.

————. *The Prophets*. 2 volumes. New York: Harper & Row, 1962.

Heschel, Susannah, ed. *Moral Grandeur and Spiritual Audacity: Essays of Abraham Joshua Heschel*. New York: Farrar, Strauss, & Giroux, 1966. Reprint. New York: The Noonday Press, 1997.

Nowell, Irene. *Women in the Old Testament*. Collegeville, Minn.: Liturgical Press, 1997.

Sobosan, Jeffrey G. *Christian Commitment: Prophetic Living*. Mystic, Conn.: Twenty-third Publications, 1986.

Notes

INTRODUCTION

1. The actual title of what we call the *Baltimore Catechism* is *A Catechism of Christian Doctrine Prepared and Enjoined by the Order of the Third Plenary Council of Baltimore* (New York: Catholic Publications Co., 1885).

2. Sacred Congregation for the Clergy, *General Catechetical Directory* (Washington, D.C.: United States Catholic Conference, 1971).

3. *Rite of Christian Initiation of Adults*, trans. International Committee on English in the Liturgy (Chicago: Liturgy Training Publications, 1988).

4. Pope Paul VI, apostolic exhortation *On Evangelization in the Modern World* (Washington, D.C.: United States Catholic Conference, 1975).

5. Pope John Paul II, *Catechesi Tradendae* (Washington, D.C.: United States Catholic Conference, 1979).

6. National Conference of Catholic Bishops, *Sharing the Light of Faith: National Catechetical Directory for Catholics of the United States* (Washington, D.C.: United States Catholic Conference, 1979).

7. *Catechism of the Catholic Church* (Washington, D.C.: United States Catholic Conference, 1994).

8. Congregation for the Clergy, *General Directory for Catechesis* (Washington, D.C.: United States Catholic Conference, 1997).

9. These four tasks are listed frequently in *Sharing the Light of Faith*. The *GDC* (1997) notes that there are not four but six "fundamental tasks of catechesis": (1) promoting knowledge of the faith, (2) liturgical education, (3) moral formation, (4) teaching to pray, (5) education for community life, and (6) missionary initiation (arts. 85–87). I believe these six tasks are included in the four tasks mentioned above, and since the four

are so well known in the United States I have continued to use them as the actions which when integrated make up the catechetical act itself. This will be more fully explained in part II, "The Process of Symbolic Catechesis."

10. George Elford, "Practical Answers from a National Study of Catechesis," *PACE* 24 (October 1994), issues 8–13.

11. Because most parish catechists and directors of catechetical ministry are women, I have often used the pronoun "she" when referring to catechists. When using quotations from documents or books with sexist language I have whenever possible changed the language to make it inclusive without changing the meaning of the statement.

12. Education Testing Service, *Toward Shaping the Agenda: A Study of Catholic Religious Education/Catechesis* (Washington, D.C.: Educational Testing Service, 1994), 9.

1. THE MYSTERY AS THE SOURCE OF MINISTRY

1. Karl Rahner writes, "In transcendence therefore is found, in the form of the aloof and distant which rules unruled, the nameless being which is infinitely holy. This we call mystery, or rather, the *holy mystery*." See Karl Rahner, "The Concept of Mystery in Catholic Theology," in *Theological Investigations*, vol. 4, trans. Kevin Smyth (New York: Seabury Press, 1974), 53.

2. Ibid., 60.

3. *On Divine Revelation*, art. 3.

4. Rahner, "Concept of Mystery," 60.

5. Elie Wiesel, *Legends of Our Time* (New York: Avon, 1968), 31.

6. Abraham Lincoln, "Emancipation Proclamation," in *Living American Documents*, ed. Isidors Starr, Lewis Paul Todd, Merle Curti (New York: Harcourt, Brace & World, 1961), 183–84.

7. Rom 2:17–21, Gal 6:6, 1 Cor 14:9, Lk 1:4, Acts 18:25 and 21:21, 24.

8. Hermann Wolfgang Beyer, *"katēchéo,"* in *Theological Dictionary of the New Testament*, vol. 3 (Grand Rapids, Mich.: Eerdmans, 1967), 638–40.

9. Walter J. Burghardt, "Catechetics in the Early Church: Program and Psychology," *The Living Light* 1 (Winter 1965): 100–118.

10. John L. McKenzie in an article about teaching in the "Primitive Church," noted: "Catechetical instruction, if it is true to its name and to its traditions, is not purely academic; it is intended to deepen the impression made by the proclamation, to make the commitment of faith more dynamic"

("'Proclamation' and 'Teaching' in the Primitive Church: Their Relevance to Catechetical Instruction Today," *The Living Light* 1 [Fall 1964]: 134).

11. *SLF,* art. 165.

12. *GDC,* art. 55.

13. *GCD,* art. 10.

14. Ibid., art. 20.

15. Ibid., art. 22.

16. National Conference of Catholic Bishops, *To Teach as Jesus Did: A Pastoral Message on Catholic Education* (Washington, D.C.: United States Catholic Conference, 1972), art. 43.

17. *CT,* art. 43.

18. *GDC,* art. 59,5.

19. David C. Leege and Joseph Gremillion, eds., *Notre Dame Study of Catholic Parish Life in the United States* (Notre Dame, Ind.: University of Notre Dame Press, 1984).

20. *SLF,* see arts. 32, 39, 70, 213, 215, 227, among others.

21. *To Teach as Jesus Did,* art. 14.

22. Anne M. Mongoven, "The Directory: A Word for the Present," *The Living Light* 16 (Summer 1979): 140.

23. *GDC,* art 85.

24. Catherine Dooley, "The *General Directory for Catechesis* and the Catechism: Focus on Evangelizing," *Origins* (4 June 1998): 36.

25. *GDC,* art. 86.

26. The revised *General Directory for Catechesis* notes that "the term catechesis has undergone a semantic evolution during the twenty centuries of the Church's history." In this Directory the concept of catechesis takes its inspiration from postconciliar magisterial documents, principally from *Evangelii Nuntiandi, Catechesis Tradendae,* and *Redemptoris Missio.*

"The concept of catechesis which one has, profoundly conditions the selection and organization of its contents *(cognitive, experiential, behavioral),* identifies those to whom it is addressed and defines the pedagogy to be employed in accomplishing its objectives" (art. 35).

27. *Notre Dame Study of Catholic Parish Life,* "Participation in Catholic Parish Life: Religious Rites and Parish Activities in the 1980's" (April 1985).

28. Philip J. Murnion, David DeLambo, Rosemary Dilli, S.S.N.D., and Harry A. Fagan, *New Parish Ministries: Laity and Religious on Parish Staffs* (New York: National Pastoral Life Center, 1992), 11.

29. Educational Testing Service, *Toward Shaping the Agenda: A Study of Catholic Religious Education/Catechesis* (Washington, D.C.: Educational Testing Service, 1994).

2. THE STORY OF RENEWAL

1. The ethnic origins were all of European descent, and there were a few Jewish families living among many Christian churches. This was a major change in my parents' lives.

2. *A Catechism of Christian Doctrine Prepared and Enjoined by Order of the Third Plenary Council of Baltimore* (New York: Catholic Publications Co., 1885).

3. St. Augustine, *The First Catechetical Instruction (De catechizandis rudibus)*, trans. Joseph P. Christopher (Westminster, Md.: Newman Press, 1962).

4. These included Erasmus's *Enchiridion militis christiani* (The Handbook of the Christian Soldier), ca. 1499, and a second catechism for adults published ca. 1533. Berard Marthaler, *The Catechism Yesterday and Today: The Evolution of a Genre* (Collegeville, Minn.: Liturgical Press, 1995), 16–17.

5. *Enchiridion: Der kleine Catechismus* (May 1529), in *Three Reformation Catechisms: Catholic, Anabaptist, Lutheran*, ed. Denis Janz, Texts and Studies in Religion, vol. 13 (Lewiston, N.Y.: Edwin Mellen Press, 1982), 179–217.

6. Marthaler, *Catechism Yesterday*, 24.

7. Ibid., 182.

8. St. Augustine, *Faith, Hope, and Charity*, trans. Wilfrid Parsons, Ancient Christian Writers, vol. 3 (New York: Newman Press, 1947).

9. Marthaler, *Catechism Yesterday*, 45–46.

10. Ibid., 42–47.

11. The *Catechism of the Council of Trent*, trans. J. Donovan (New York: Catholic School Book Co., 1829), 5.

12. Ibid., 6.

13. Ibid., 17.

14. Charles R. Morris, *American Catholic: The Saints and Sinners Who Built America's Most Powerful Church*, Times Book (New York: Random House, 1997), 53.

15. Mary Charles Bryce, *Pride of Place: The Role of the Bishops in the Development of Catechesis in the United States* (Washington, D.C.: The Catholic University of America Press, 1984), 88.

16. Ibid., 90.

17. The one question was no. 89: "On what day did Christ rise from the dead?" The response was, "Christ rose from the dead, glorious and immortal, on Easter Sunday, the third day after His death."

18. Bryce, *Pride of Place*, 90.

19. AAB, 94-B-1, Minutes of the Annual Meeting of the Most Rev. Archbishops, October 2, 1895.

20. In the encyclical *On the Teaching of Christian Doctrine (Acerbo nimis)*, April 15, 1905, Pius X ordered the reestablishment of the Confraternity of Christian Doctrine in all parishes. See *The Papal Encyclicals 1903–1939* (New York: McGraw-Hill, 1981), 29–35.

21. Ibid., art. 19.

22. See Berard L. Marthaler, "The Modern Catechetical Movement in Roman Catholicism: Issues and Personalities," in *Sourcebook for Modern Catechetics*, vol.1, ed. Michael Warren (Winona, Minn.: St. Mary's Press, 1983), 276.

23. Charles K. Riepe, "Josef A. Jungmann," in *The New Day: Catholic Theologians of the Renewal*, ed. Wm. Jerry Boney and Lawrence E. Molumby (Richmond: John Knox Press, 1968), 35.

24. Josef A. Jungmann, *The Good News Yesterday and Today*, Johannes Hofinger, S.J., gen. ed., trans. William A. Huesman, S.J. (New York: W. H. Sadlier, 1962).

25. Ibid., 4.

26. Ibid., 5–6.

27. Ibid., 4.

28. Ibid., 8.

29. Ibid., 9.

30. Ibid., 38.

31. Ibid., 33.

32. Ibid., 95.

33. Domenico Grasso described the publication of *Die Frohbotschaft* by stating that "few books in recent years have exercised more influence on the renewal of theology than Jungmann's *Die Frohbotschaft und unsere Glaubensverkündigung*....Even if not all could read the original text, many profited from the theological fruits that grew from a discussion of the book. The nature of theology has hardly ever been debated with such

lively enthusiasm as it has since Jungmann published this volume" *(Good News,* 201).

34. Ironically, it is through his work on the liturgy that Jungmann achieved recognition throughout the world as the preeminent scholar of the Latin liturgy.

35. G. Emmett Carter, *The Modern Challenge to Religious Education* (New York: William H. Sadlier, 1961), 89.

36. Françoise Derkenne, *La vie et la joie au catéchisme* (Paris: de Gigord, 1935; Marie Fargues, *Les methods actives dans l'enseignement religieux* (Paris: Editions du Cerf, 1934). Extracts from text are included in Marie Farques, *How to Teach Religion,* trans. Sister Gertrude (New York: Paulist Press, 1968), 99–101.

37. Georges Delcuve, "The Catechetical Movement in France," *Lumen Vitae* 12 (1957): 676.

38. Joseph Colomb, "The Inner Milieu of the Catechism Course," *Lumen Vitae* 5 (1950): 355.

39. Ibid.

40. Joseph Colomb, *Catéchisme progressif, Guide I.,* trans. Georges Delcuve (Lyon/Paris: Emmanuel Vitte, 1950), 5.

41. Joseph Colomb, *Doctrine,* 3:41, trans. Georges Delcuve and quoted in Delcuve, "The Catechetical Movement in France," 676.

42. Colomb, *Doctrine,* 1:115, trans. Delcuve as quoted in *The Catechetical Movement in France,* 677.

43. Ibid.

44. Ibid.

45. Sister Maria de la Cruz Aymes-Couche, S.H., "Johannes Hofinger, Remembered: 1905–1984," *The Living Light* 20 (June 1984): 345–46.

46. Published by Wm. H. Sadlier, Co., New York.

47. Georges Delcuve, "Nijmegen: Liturgy and the Missions," *Lumen Vitae* 15 (1960): 153–58.

48. *Teaching All Nations: A Symposium on Modern Catechetics,* ed. Johannes Hofinger, trans. Clifford Howell (New York: Herder & Herder, 1961), xiii.

49. Marthaler, "Modern Catechetical Movement," 280.

50. Luis Erdozain, "The Evolution of Catechetics: A Survey of Six International Study Weeks on Catechetics," in Warren, *Sourcebook for Modern Catechetics,* vol. I, 87.

51. Alfonso Nebreda, "Some Reflections on Father Gleeson's Paper on History and Present Scene in Religious Education," in *Teaching All Nations* 11 (1974): 85.

52. Johannes Hofinger, ed., "General Conclusions," in *Teaching All Nations*, 398.

53. In the "official record" of this East Asian Study Week, Alfonso Nebreda presented a brief survey of the discussions which took place in "East Asian Study Week on Mission Catechetics," *Lumen Vitae* 17 (1962): 717–30.

54. Pierre-André Liégé introduced the word *preevangelization* into catechetical vocabulary in the article "Evangelization" in *Catholicisme*, vol. 4 (Paris, 1951), col. 761. Liégé stated: "It is the work of preevangelization—not necessarily chronologically distinct from evangelization—to work at men's own milieu in order to make them accessible to the evangelical message" (trans. Erdozain, p. 17).

55. Theodore Stone, "The Bangkok Study Week," *Worship* 37 (1963): 186–87.

56. Robert J. Ledogar, ed., *Katigondo: Presenting the Christian Message to Africa* (London: Geoffrey Chapman, 1965), 126.

57. Austin Flannery, O.P., ed., *Vatican Council II: Constitutions, Decrees, Declarations* (Northport, N.Y.: Costello Publishing, 1966), 163–282, 443–497.

58. Luis Erdozain, 7–13.

59. Terence J. Sheridan, "The Occasion," in *The Medellín Papers*, ed. Johannes Hofinger and Terence Sheridan (Manila: East Asian Pastoral Institute, 1969), 11–12.

60. Ibid., 11.

61. François Houtard, "The International Catechetical Week, Medellín, Colombia, August 11–17, 1966," *The Living Light* 5 (Winter 1968–69): 123–24.

62. "General Conclusions of the International Study Week," in *The Medellín Papers*, 213.

63. Ibid., 215.

64. Ibid., 217.

65. Ibid., 218.

66. Gerard S. Sloyan, *Shaping the Christian Message: Essays in Religious Education* (New York: Macmillan, 1958).

67. Gerard S. Sloyan, *Modern Catechetics: Method and Message in Reli-*

gious Formations (New York: Macmillan, 1963); *Speaking of Religious Education* (New York: Herder & Herder, 1968).

68. Marthaler also followed Sloyan as chair of the Department of Religion and Religious Education in the Religious Studies School of the Catholic University of America. Marthaler's writings have had a major influence on catechetical renewal in the United States. See Catherine Dooley and Mary Collins, eds., *The Echo Within: Emerging Issues in Religious Education* (Allen, Tex.: Thomas More, 1997). This book is a collection of essays in "tribute to Berard L. Marthaler."

69. Gabriel Moran, *Theology of Revelation* (New York: Herder & Herder. 1966); *Catechesis of Revelation* (New York: Herder & Herder, 1966).

70. Gabriel Moran, *Design for Religion* (New York: Herder & Herder, 1970). He wrote: "I am trying to move forward into the birth of a new field rather than to revivify an old one. The term, 'ecumenical education,' is an attempt to coin a name for that field" (Preface, p. 9).

3. THE STORY OF AFFIRMATION

1. "Decree on the Pastoral Office of Bishops in the Church," in Austin Flannery, gen. ed., *Vatican Council II* (Northport, N.Y.: Costello Publishing, 1966), 283–315.

2. Ibid., art. 44.

3. See *Catéchèse* 14 (January 1964). This issue of *Catéchèse* included the French directory and commentary on each of its principal parts.

4. Italian Episcopal Conference (Roma: Edizioni Pastorale Italiane, 1970). The Italian directory was translated into English as *The Renewal of the Education of Faith*. It was adopted by the Australian bishops, who added a supplement that focused on Australian Catholic schools. The Italian directory was published with an authoritative but unofficial commentary produced by the Salesian Catechetical Center in Turin, *Documento di base: Il rinnovamento della catechesi, Commento a cura del centro catechistico*.

5. *International Catechetical Congress: September 20–25, 1971, Selected Documentation*, ed. William J. Tobin (Washington, D.C.: United States Catholic Conference, 1972).

6. The eight persons included Bishop Anthyme Bayala of Upper Volta (Africa); Bishop Benitez of Vilarrica, Paraguay; Canon Joseph Bournique from Paris, France; Monsignor Aldo Del Monte from Italy;

Reverend Robert Gaudet from Canada; Monsignor Russell Neighbor from the United States; Reverends Klemens Tilmann and A. Zenner from Germany. At least four of the eight members of the commission—Benitez, Bournique, Neighbor, and Tilmann—as well as Villot had participated in the Medellín Study Week.

7. Mary Perkins Ryan and William J. Tobin, eds., "Foreword," *The Living Light* 9 (Fall 1972): 4.

8. *GCD*, p. 1.

9. Only the *Decree on the Up-to-Date Renewal of Religious Life and the Decree on the Ministry and Life of Priests* are not included as references.

10. *GCD*, art. 74.

11. Ibid., art. 20.

12. Ibid.

13. *CSL*, art. 64.

14. Ibid.

15. *SLF*, arts. 115, 227; *GDC*, art. 59.

16. *GDC*, art. 59, quoting 1977 Synod, "Message to the People of God," no. 8.

17. *SLF*, art. 35.

18. *EMW*, art. 1.

19. Ibid., art. 4.

20. Ibid., art. 2.

21. Ibid., art. 8.

22. Ibid., art. 14.

23. Ibid., art. 18 (Rv 21:5; cf. 2 Cor 5:17; Gal 6:15).

24. *EMW*, art. 20.

25. *Synod of Bishops—1977* (Washington, D.C.: United States Catholic Conference, 1978), "Message to the People of God" (pp. 5–16).

26. *CT*, art. 4.

27. Ibid., art. 3.

28. Ibid.

29. Ibid., art. 5.

30. Ibid., art. 6.

31. Ibid., art. 7.

32. Ibid., art. 18.

33. Ibid., art. 10.

34. For a study of "systematic catechesis" in *On Catechesis in Our Time*, see Anna S. Campbell, "Toward a Systematic Catechesis: An Inter-

pretation of *Catechesis Tradendae,*" *The Living Light* 17 (Winter 1980): 311–20.

35. *CT,* art. 26.

36. Ibid., art. 43.

37. Bishops on the committee were Archbishop John F. Whealon (chairman), Archbishop John R. Quinn, Archbishop William W. Baum, Bishop Clarence E. Elwell, Bishop John J. Ward, Bishop William E. McManus, Bishop Raymond A. Lucker. After the death of Bishop Elwell, the bishops' conference appointed Bishop Rene H. Gracida to the committee.

38. *SLF,* art. 6.

39. Ibid., art. 11.

40. Ibid., art. 32.

41. Ibid., art. 42.

42. Jean Jadot, "Dimensions of Catechesis," *Origins* 8 (15 March 1979): 612.

43. Catherine Dooley writes: "The invention of the printing press affected the history of catechetics in a radical way. Until the end of the 15th century catechesis, despite its weaknesses, was oral and experiential. Its success or failure clearly depended upon those who shared their faith. The printing press brought standardization and uniformity" ("Commentary on Catechesis in Our Time," in Louvain Studies [Spring 1979], 195–211).

44. Michael Donnellan, "Bishops and Uniformity in Religious Education: Vatican I to Vatican II," in *Sourcebook for Modern Catechetics,* ed. Michael Warren (Winona, Minn.: St. Marys's Press, 1983) 1:235.

45. *CT,* art. 50.

46. *CCC, Fidei depositum,* p. 3.

47. Ibid., art. 3 (emphasis added).

48. *Fidei depositum,* art. 3.

49. *CCC,* art. 24.

50. Ibid., art. 136.

51. *GDC,* art. 2.

52. Ibid.

53. Ibid., art. 7.

54. Ibid., art. 11.

55. Ibid.

56. Ibid., art. 9.

57. Ibid., art. 11.

58. Ibid., art. 47. See also Catherine Dooley, O.P., "The *General Directory for Catechesis* and the Catechism: Focus on Evangelizing," in *Origins* (4 June, 1998): 34–39.

59. Ibid., art. 59, citing *GCD*, art. 20; *CT*, art. 43.

60. Ibid., art. 78.

61. Ibid., art. 30.

62. Ibid., art. 87.

63. J. Stephen O'Brien, *An Urgent Task: What Bishops and Priests Say About Religious Education Programs* (Washington, D.C.: National Catholic Education Association, 1988), 10.

4. A THEOLOGY OF CATECHESIS

1. Avery Dulles, *Revelation Theology* (New York: Seabury Press, 1969), 75.

2. Namely, fideism, rationalism, and semi-rationalism. See Dulles, *Revelation Theology*, 69–76; René Latourelle, *Theology of Revelation* (New York: Alba House, 1966), 255–59.

3. *GDC*, art. 8.

4. In contrast, the *Dogmatic Constitution on the Church* has sixty-nine articles, and the *Pastoral Constitution on the Church in the Modern World* has ninety-three articles.

5. Joseph Ratzinger, "Dogmatic Constitution on Divine Revelation: Origins and Background," in *Commentary on the Documents of Vatican II*, vol. 3, ed. Herbert Vorgrimler (Montreal: Palm Publishers, 1968), 155–198. Cardinal Ratzinger points out that Text E, the fifth schema or draft prepared by the Theological Commission, is the first to include a chapter on the nature of revelation itself.

6. Ibid., 167.

7. Ibid., 168.

8. *Constitution on the Church*, art. 48.

9. Avery Dulles, "The Meaning of Revelation," in *The Dynamics of Christian Thought*, ed. Joseph Papin (Philadelphia: Villanova University Press, 1970), 52–80.

10. First Vatican Council, *Constitution on the Catholic Faith*, chap. 3 "On Faith" (DS 1789 [3008]).

11. Second Council of Orange, Canon 7 (DS 180 [377]); First Vatican Council, *Constitution on the Catholic Faith* (DS 1791 [3010]).

12. Karl Rahner distinguishes between what he calls "transcendental revelation," the unreflective consciousness of God's presence, and "categorical revelation," the objectification of God's self-communication in love and wisdom (*Foundations of Christian Faith: An Introduction to the Idea of Christianity*, trans. William V. Dych [New York: Seabury Press, 1978], 171–74).

13. Avery Dulles, *Models of Revelation* (Garden City, N.Y.: Doubleday, 1983), 259.

14. The word *Tradition* (singular) with a capital "T" refers to the whole life of the church. The church's "doctrine, life, and worship" are the symbols of the church's faith, *that through which* it expresses and constitutes itself. The word *tradition* with a lower case "t" refers to customs or traditions of the community (plural).

15. Ratzinger, 185.

16. Ibid.

17. Dulles, *Models of Revelation*, 131.

18. Karl Rahner, "The Theology of the Symbol," in *Theological Investigations*, vol. 4, trans. Kevin Smyth (New York: Seabury Press, 1974), 221–52.

19. *CCC*, art. 1146.

20. *CCC*, art. 42.

21. Ratzinger, "Dogmatic Constitution on Divine Revelation," 184–85.

22. Albert Gregory Cardinal Meyer, cited in Ratzinger, "Dogmatic Constitution on Divine Revelation," 185.

23. *Sharing the Light of Faith* lists some of the created realities and signs of the times as "creation, the events of daily life, the triumphs and tragedies of history" (art. 35). In other articles it refers to "human beings," "human cultures," "the religions of humanity," "the arts and the sciences, " as symbols of God's self-revelation.

24. *GDC*, art. 108; *GCD* (1971) 72; see also *CCC*, arts. 39–43.

25. Mt 16:3: "You know how to interpret the appearance of the sky, but you cannot interpret the signs of the times."

5. SYMBOLIC CATECHESIS

1. The subtitle of Stephen L. Carter's book, *The Culture of Disbelief: How American Law and Politics Trivialize Religious Devotion* (New York: Basic Books, 1993).

2. T.S. Eliot, "The Dry Salvages," in *Four Quartets* (New York: Harcourt, Brace & World, 1971), 39.

3. *Self-Esteem Survey* (Princeton: The Gallup Organization, 1982). Cited in Robert Wuthnow, *Rediscovering the Sacred: Perspectives on Religion in Contemporary Society* (Grand Rapids: William B. Eerdmans, 1992), 22.

4. "God Decentralized," *New York Times Magazine*, 7 December 1997. This issue included articles about faith and loneliness, culture, intermarriage, materialism, ethics, experimentation, and other concerns of people who consider themselves "religious" but find little help in developing their faith from the religious institutions to which they belong, whether Christian, Jewish, or Muslim institutions. The articles point out that believers say that the religious institutions are not speaking either to or about their questions.

5. A theological method of "correlation" emerged in the nineteenth century, particularly among Protestant theologians. While the correlation method in theology is more complex than the correlation method in catechesis, the theological practice has led me to see correlation as related to catechesis. Most Catholic theologians in the United States who use a correlation method draw on the insights of Paul Tillich as presented in *Systematic Theology* (Chicago: University of Chicago Press, 1951–65). Anne E. Carr describes a "feminist" methodology that might be called "critical correlation," in "The New Vision of Feminist Theology: Method," in *Freeing Theology: The Essentials of Theology in Feminist Perspective*, ed. Catherine Mowry LaCugna (San Francisco: Harper, 1993), 5–29. Some Catholic theologians who have described their theological method as one of correlation are Edward Schillebeeckx in *Interim Report on the Books "Jesus" and "Christ"* (New York: Crossroad, 1981), 50; David Tracy, *Blessed Rage for Order* (New York: Crossroad, 1975); Hans Küng as described in *Consensus in Theology? A Dialogue with Hans Küng and Edward Schillebeeckx*, ed. Leonard Swidler (Philadelphia: Westminster, 1980); and Rosemary Ruether, "Feminist Interpretation of the Method of Correlation," in *Feminist Interpretation of the Bible*, ed. Letty Russell (Philadelphia: Westminster, 1983).

6. *Catholic Rites Today* (Collegeville, Minn.: Liturgical Press, 1992), 489–521.

7. Second General Assembly of the Synod of Bishops, *Justice in the World* (Washington, D.C.: United States Catholic Conference, 1972), 34.

8. *SLF,* 170,11.

9. Ibid., 170.

10. C. S. Lewis, *Letters to Malcolm: Chiefly on Prayer* (New York: Harcourt, Brace, Jovanovich, 1964), 4.

11. The four characteristics or "marks" of the church are the same as the four "tasks" of catechesis as presented in *Sharing the Light of Faith*. These "marks" correlate with the four tasks in *SLF.* See arts. 32; 181,5; 181,12; 212; 213; 215; 224; 226; 227; 228a; 229; 232; 243.

12. In an article in *America*, Michael McGarry notes that his parish has an agenda of topics for preaching. He states: "Those [concerns] pressed on me are the effects of child sexual abuse, alcoholism, the rights of gays and lesbians in the church, the importance of Catholic schools, racism, nuclear weapons, breast cancer and Mother's Day." People want to know, sometimes desperately want to know, what the church has to say about their lives, whether in preaching or in catechizing ("For Less Appealing Preaching," *America* 179 [3 October 1998]: 20–22).

13. See James W. Fowler, *Stages of Faith: The Psychology of Human Development and the Quest for Meaning* (San Francisco: Harper & Row, 1981). There are multiple texts describing, delineating, and defining different "stages" of faith development. It is my understanding that the "faith of the community" sustains and supports the faith of individuals as they participate in symbolic catechesis.

14. Programs for children usually meet weekly for twenty to thirty weeks, and youth programs meet on a regular weekly basis also, but for about twelve to fifteen weeks a year. These programs are ordinarily more "comprehensive. They are surely not "occasional." Ordinarily they initiate the children and youth into the faith community. The structure of symbolic catechesis works very well with children and youth because it begins by addressing their life experiences or concerns. Its success depends on the catechist.

15. *GDC*, art. 71.

16. Linda J. Vogel presents "the household of the faith" as one of four metaphors that describe particular forms of religious education in *Teaching and Learning in Communities of Faith: Empowering Adults Through Religious Education* (San Francisco: Jossey-Bass Publishers, 1991), 84–88. David N. Power uses *households of faith* to mean "small, informal, and often spontaneous groups, associations and communities," which may or may not be related to official church structures (see Power, "Households of Faith in the Coming Church," *Worship* 57, no. 3 [May 1983]: 237–54. When I use this term I am referring to small groups that are related to the parish or church structure, though perhaps loosely.

6. CATECHESIS AS A CRITIQUE OF LIFE AND CULTURE

1. Benedict Viviano, O.P., "The Gospel According to Matthew," in *The New Jerome Biblical Commentary*, ed. Raymond E. Brown, Joseph A. Fitzmyer, and Roland E. Murphy (Englewood Cliffs, N.J.: Prentice-Hall, 1990).

2. Pope John XXIII, *Humanae salutis* (symbolically dated December 25, 1961; AAS. 54 [1962]: 5–13).

3. Pope John XXIII, Address at the Solemn Opening of the Second Vatican Council ("Council Daybook," in *Destination Vatican II: An Interactive Exploration of the Second Vatican Council* [Allen, Tex.: RCL Enterprises, 1997]).

4. Rino Fisichella, "Signs of the Times," in *Dictionary of Fundamental Theology*, ed. René Latourelle and Rino Fisichella (New York: Crossroad, 1994): 995–1001.

5. Pope John XXIII, *Peace on Earth*, Encyclical Letter (Washington, D.C.: National Catholic Welfare Conference, 1963).

6. *Peace on Earth*, art. 126.

7. Ibid., arts. 40–42.

8. Pope Paul VI, *Ecclesiam Suam* (Glen Rock, N.J.: Paulist Press, 1964), art. 65.

9. Ibid., art. 15.

10. *CMW*, art. 4.

11. Ibid., art. 11.

12. *MLP*, art. 9.

13. *RL*, art. 15.

14. United States Bishops, "Sharing Catholic Social Teaching: Challenges and Directions," *Origins* 28 (2 July 1998): 102–106.

15. See John T. Noonan, Jr., "On the Development of Doctrine," *America* (3 April, 1999): 6–8, vol. 180.

16. Edward Schillebeeckx, *Christ: The Experience of Jesus as Lord*, trans. John Bowden; A Crossroad Book (New York: Seabury Press, 1980): 29.

17. Dermot Lane, *The Experience of God: An Invitation to Do Theology* (New York: Paulist Press, 1981), 1.

18. Donald Gelphi, *The Turn to Experience in Contemporary Theology* (New York: Paulist Press, 1994): 1.

19. T.S. Eliot, "The Dry Salvages," in *Four Quartets* (New York: Harcourt, Brace & World, 1971), 39.

20. The following description of experience is based primarily but not solely on Dermot Lane's description of experience in *Experience of God*,

1–31. See also Gerald O'Collins, *Contemporary Theology* (New York: Paulist Press, 1981), 32–52; idem, *Retrieving Fundamental Theology: The Three Styles of Contemporary Theology* (New York: Paulist Press, 1993), 98–119. See also Edward Schillebeeckx, *Christ: The Experience of Jesus as Lord*, 30–64, especially chapter 1, "The Authority of New Experiences," which demonstrates the relationship of revelation and human experience(s).

21. Lane, p. 6.

22. Schillebeeckx, *Christ: The Experience of Jesus as Lord*, 32.

23. *GDC*, art. 31.

24. Ibid., art. 32.

25. For examples of how different parishes approach ministry, see Karen Sue Smith, "Following Up on Parish Renewal," *Church* (Fall 1998, vol. 14): 24–28.

26. T. Howland Sanks, S.J., "Postmodernism and the Church," *New Theology Review* 11, no. 3 (August 1998): 51–59.

27. Aylward Shorter, *Toward a Theology of Inculturation* (Maryknoll, N.Y.: Orbis Books, 1988), 5.

28. Raymond Williams, *The Sociology of Culture* (New York: Schocken, 1982), 13, in Michael Warren, *Communications and Cultural Analysis: A Religious View* (Westport, Conn.: Bergin & Garvey, 1992), 30–31. Warren's excellent text is the academic foundation of my premises about the relationship of religion and culture.

29. Thomas H. Groome, *Sharing Faith: A Comprehensive Approach to Religious Education & Pastoral Ministry* (San Francisco: Harper, 1991), 98.

30. Joseph P. Fitzpatrick, *One Church Many Cultures: The Challenge of Diversity* (Kansas City, Mo.: Sheed & Ward, 1987), 28.

31. Ibid.

32. Maria Elena Gonzales, "Diverse Races and Cultures: Implications for Catholic Education in the United States," in *Catholic Education: Toward the Third Millennium*, The Catholic Education Futures Project (Washington, D.C.: The Catholic Education Futures Project, 1996), 74.

33. For an excellent book of essays on the "United States Hispanic Reality," see *Dialogue Rejoined: Theology and Ministry in the United States Hispanic Reality*, ed. Ana Maria Pineda and Robert Schreiter, with a foreword by Donald Senior (Collegeville, Minn.: Liturgical Press, 1995).

34. Shorter points out that at the Second Vatican Council, "unlike its predecessor of 1869, the non-Western cultures were not exclusively represented by missionary bishops. Of the 2,540 Council Fathers a high proportion were natives of Latin America, Africa, Asia and Oceania.

There were also the representatives of the Eastern rites who celebrated their liturgies in the Vatican Basilica during the Council sessions. The cultural diversity of the Church was distinctly visible at Vatican Two" (*Toward a Theology of Inculturation*, 189).

35. *CMW*, art. 58.

36. Ibid., art. 62.

37. Ibid.

38. *CT*, art. 53.

39. *GCD*, art. 2.

40. Extraordinary Synod of Bishops, Rome 1985, *A Message to the People of God and the Final Report* (Washington, D.C.: United States Catholic Conference, 1986), *Final Report*, II, D, 4.

41. Ibid.

42. Eugene Hillman, "Inculturation," in *The New Dictionary of Theology*.

43. Pope John Paul II, speaking at the National Congress of Catholic Cultural Organizations, *Insegnamenti*, V/1 (1982): 131. See also John Paul II, *Epistula Qua Pontificium Consilium pro hominum Cultura instituitur* (AAS 74 [1982]: 685).

44. AG, 10; cf. AG, 22n.

45. *GDC*, art. 109. The quotation in art. 109 refers to a footnote which states that "the term 'inculturation' is taken from diverse documents of the Magisterium." See *CT*, art. 53; *RM*, 52–54. The concept of culture, either in a general or in an ethnological sense is clarified in *CMW*, art. 53.

46. *GDC*, art. 110.

47. An excellent resource for assistance in planning is Richard Reichert, *Developing a Parish Program*, The Effective DRE: A Skills Development Series, National Conference of Catechetical Leadership, ed. Richard Reichert (Chicago: Loyola Press, 1998). See also Robert G. Howes, *Parish Planning: A Practical Guide to Shared Responsibility* (Collegeville, Minn.: Liturgical Press, 1994). An older but still helpful text is Kennon L. Callahan, *Twelve Keys to an Effective Church: The Planning Workbook* (San Francisco: Harper & Row, 1987).

48. *CMW*, art. 4.

7. THE BIBLE AS A SYMBOL OF FAITH

1. Karl Rahner, *Foundations of Christian Faith: An Introduction to the Idea of Christianity*, trans. William V. Dych (New York: Seabury Press, 1978), 371.

2. Gerard S. Sloyan, "The Bible as the Book of the Church," *Worship* 60 (January 1986): 9–21.

3. *Dogmatic Constitution on Divine Revelation*, art. 21.

4. Ibid., art. 24.

5. The *Dogmatic Constitution on Divine Revelation* states: "The Church has always venerated the divine Scriptures just as she venerates the body of the Lord, since, especially in the sacred liturgy, she unceasingly receives and offers to the faithful the bread of life from the table both of God's Word and of Christ's Body" (art. 21).

6. David C. Leege and Thomas A. Trozzolo, "Participation in Catholic Parish Life: Religious Rites and Parish Activities in the 1980's," in *Notre Dame Study of Catholic Parish Life*, Report No. 3, April 1985, p. 7.

7. George Gallup, Jr., and Jim Castelli, *The American Catholic People: Their Beliefs, Practices, and Values* (Garden City, N.Y.: Doubleday, 1987), 30–32.

8. Commission on Certification and Accreditation United States Catholic Conference, *Certification Manual* (St. Louis, Mo.: United States Catholic Conference, 1990), 6.

9. Committee on Certification and Accreditation, National Federation of Catholic Youth Ministry, Inc. *NFCYM Competency-Based Standards for the Coordinator of Youth Ministry* (Washington, D.C.: National Federation for Catholic Youth Ministry, 1990), 2.

10. "The Word of God is the full manifestation of the Father; thus He may be called a symbol, an icon, an image of the Father. Created through the Word, the world is in its very reality a symbol of its creator" (*SLF*, art. 114).

11. Rahner, *Foundations*, 371.

12. Joseph Cardinal Ratzinger, "Preface," in Pontifical Biblical Commission, *The Interpretation of the Bible in the Church* (Washington, D.C.: United States Catholic Conference, 1993), 1.

13. Joseph Grassi, *Rediscovering the Jesus Story: A Participatory Guide* (New York: Paulist Press, 1995), vi.

14. Ratzinger, "Preface," in *Commentary on the Documents of Vatican III*, vol. II, p. 167.

15. *CCC*, art. 101ff.

16. *CCC*, art. 105.

17. Gerald O'Collins, *Fundamental Theology* (New York: Paulist Press, 1981), 243.

18. Gerald O'Collins points out that a strict version of apostolic origin would not always work today, as some of the New Testament books (Hebrews and 2 Peter) are of uncertain authorship. O'Collins, p. 244.

19. O'Collins, Ibid., 242–49.

20. Pontifical Biblical Commission, *The Interpretation of the Bible in the Church* (Vatican City: Libreria Editrice Vaticana, 1993).

21. This section depends on chapter 4, revising it and sometimes expanding it through examples, but remaining faithful to the principles it suggests.

22. *IBC*, 34.

23. Ibid.

24. Ibid.

25. Different publications of the Bible offer study guides and notes. The *New American Bible*, the *New Revised Standard Version*, and the *New Jerusalem Bible* are excellent translations.

26. One of the finest recent introductions is Raymond E. Brown, *An Introduction to the New Testament*, Anchor Bible Reference Library (New York: Doubleday, 1997). For a fine introduction to the entire Bible, see David Noel Freedman, *The Anchor Bible Dictionary*, 6 volumes (New York: Doubleday, 1992).

27. Different publishers offer different study guides with the approved translations. *The New Jerome Biblical Commentary* (Englewood Cliffs, N.J.: Prentice-Hall, 1990), the *Sacra Pagina* series and/or the *Zacchaeus Studies* (Collegeville, Minn.: Liturgical Press) are all excellent study guides. One of the best study Bibles is, in my opinion, the New American translation in *The Catholic Bible: Personal Study Edition* (New York: Oxford University Press, 1995). These represent what Gerald O'Collins refers to as "the consensus of centrist exegetes." Other works are listed in "Further Readings" at the end of this chapter.

28. *IBC*, 36.

29. *IBC*, 18.

30. Ibid., 19.

31. Sandra Schneiders, *Beyond Patching: Faith and Feminism in the Catholic Church* (New York: Paulist Press, 1991), 40–42.

32. For development of these insights, see ibid., 15–25.

33. Elisabeth Schüssler Fiorenza, *Bread Not Stone: The Challenge of Feminist Biblical Interpretation* (Boston: Beacon Press, 1984), xii. Schüssler Fiorenza writes, "Feminist interpretation therefore begins with a hermeneutics of suspicion that applies to both contemporary androcentric interpretations of the Bible and the biblical texts themselves."

34. Elisabeth Schüssler Fiorenza, "The Will to Choose or Reject: Continuing Our Critical Work," in *Feminist Interpretation of the Bible*, ed. Letty Russell (Philadelphia: Westminster Press, 1985), 130.

35. Ibid.

36. Ibid.

37. Phyllis Trible, *Texts of Terror* (Philadelphia: Fortress Press, 1984), xiii.

38. Schneiders, *Beyond Patching*, 39.

39. Sandra M. Schneiders, *The Revelatory Text: Interpreting the New Testament as Sacred Scripture* (San Francisco: Harper, 1991); idem, *Beyond Patching*.

40. Schneiders, *Beyond Patching*, 57.

41. Schneiders gives the example of the text "all men are created equal," which in its original sense meant all adult, white, free, property owning males. Today the American experience enables us to interpret that phrase to include all people, men, women, and children of different races and classes, with or without property (*Beyond Patching*, 61).

42. Ibid., 63.

43. Gerald O'Collins points out that the church's Tradition has been shaped by and evaluated by the church's interpretation of the biblical texts. This is a living Tradition in which Scripture and Tradition dialogue with and shape each other (Gerald O'Collins and Daniel Kendall, *The Bible for Theology: Ten Principles for the Theological Use of Scripture* [New York: Paulist Press, 1997], 15).

44. *IBC*, 18.

45. *Constitution on the Sacred Liturgy*, art. 51.

46. Gerard Sloyan, "Richer Fare for God's People?" in *Liturgy* 90 (July 1990): 8–10.

47. National Conference of Catholic Bishops, *Lectionary for Mass* (Chicago: LTP, 1999).

48. Gerard S. Sloyan, "Overview of the *Lectionary for Mass: Introduction*," in *The Liturgy Documents*, 3rd edition (Chicago: Liturgy Training Publications, 1991), 119.

49. Ibid.

50. "Introduction," art. 4, in *Lectionary for Mass*.

51. Gerard S. Sloyan, "The Hebrew Scriptures Apart from Their Fulfillment in Christ," in *Liturgy* 90 (October 1990): 10.

52. See Joseph Grassi, *The Hidden Heroes of the Gospels: Female Counterparts of Jesus* (Manila: St. Paul Publications, 1991); Ruth Fox, "Women in the Bible and the Lectionary," *Liturgy* 90 (May/June 1996): 4–9, 15; Marjorie Procter-Smith, "Images of Women in the Lectionary," in *Women: Invisible in Church and Theology*, Concilium 182 (Edinburgh: T. & T. Clark, 1985), 51–62.

53. Joseph A. Grassi, *Rediscovering the Jesus Story: A Participatory Guide* (New York: Paulist Press, 1995), v.

54. Ibid., 2.

55. Michael E. Moynahan, a former colleague of mine, has written four books that present creative and imaginative dramas on the miracles and parables of Jesus or relate biblical narratives to modern-day life. See *Once Upon a Mystery: What Happens Next* (New York: Paulist Press, 1998); *Once Upon a Parable: Dramas for Worship and Religious Education* (New York: Paulist Press, 1984); *Once Upon a Miracle: Dramas for Worship and Religious Education* (New York: Paulist Press, 1993); *How the Word Became Flesh: Story Dramas for Worship and Religious Education* (New York: Paulist Press, 1981).

56. Ibid., 2.

57. See nn. 26 and 27 above; Walter Brueggemann, *The Bible Makes Sense*, rev. ed. (Winona, Minn.: St. Mary's Press, 1997).

58. For an excellent introductory form of biblical basics, including principles of interpretation, see Maureen Gallagher, *The Art of Catechesis: What You Need to Be, Know, and Do* (New York: Paulist Press, 1998), principally chapters 2 and 3, pp. 31–73.

59. For an excellent participatory introduction to the four Gospels, see Grassi, *Rediscovering the Jesus Story*.

60. *IBC*, 39.

61. Ibid.

62. Ibid.

63. This commentary is taken from the *Christian Community Bible* (Manila: Claritian Publications, 1988). It was "translated, presented and commented for the Christian Communities of the Philippines and the Third World; and for those who seek God."

8. THE CHURCH SYMBOLS: DOCTRINE AND SAINTS

1. *GDC*, art. 51e.

2. Gerald O'Collins, "Theology," in *The Harper Collins Encyclopedia of Catholicism.*

3. Elizabeth A. Johnson, *She Who Is: The Mystery of God in Feminist Theological Discourse* (New York: Crossroad, 1992), 17; Dermot Lane, *The Experience of God: An Invitation to Do Theology* (New York: Paulist Press, 1981), 3; Gregory Baum, *Man Becoming: God in Secular Experience* (New York: Seabury Press, 1970), xii; Anne E. Carr, *Transforming Grace: Christian Tradition and Women's Experience* (San Francisco: Harper & Row, 1988), 56.

4. Francis A. Sullivan, *Magisterium: Teaching Authority in the Church* (Mahwah, N.J.: Paulist Press, 1983), 24–34; see also idem., *Creative Fidelity: Weighing and Interpreting Documents of the Magisterium* (New York: Paulist Press, 1996).

5. *CCC*, art. 892.

6. *SLF*, art. 37.

7. David Tracy, James Fowler, Edward Farley, and others address this question in *Practical Theology*, ed. Don S. Browning (San Francisco: Harper & Row, 1983).

8. Two of Shea's books on story are *Stories of God* (Chicago: Thomas More Press, 1978), and *Stories of Faith* (Chicago: Thomas More Press, 1980).

9. John Shea, "Introduction: Experience and Symbol, An Approach to Theologizing," *Chicago Studies* 19 (Spring 1970): 5–20.

10. Abraham Joshua Heschel, *God in Search of Man: A Philosophy of Judaism* (New York: Farrar, Straus & Giroux), 74.

11. *CCC*, art. 234.

12. Gregory Baum, "Dogma as Symbolic Truth," *The Ecumenist* (March–April 1971, vol. 9), 41–46.

13. Ibid.

14. *Summa Theologiae* 1a. 13.1–6, in *Thomas Aquinas: Selected Philosophical Writings*, ed. and trans. Timothy McDermott, World Classics (Oxford: Oxford University Press, 1993), 214–30.

15. *CCC*, art. 90: "In Catholic doctrine there exists an order or 'hierarchy' of truths since they vary in relation to the foundation of the Christian faith."

16. Ibid., art. 234.

17. *On Divine Revelation*, 8, 2.

18. Ibid., 23, 24.

305

19. Ibid., 8, 2.

20. St. Gregory the Great, *Hom. in Ez.* 1, 7, 8; *PL* 76:843 D.

21. For example, "Guidelines for Equal Treatment of the Sexes in McGraw Hill Book Company Publications."

22. *Bishops' Committee on the Liturgy Newsletter, National Conference of Catholic Bishops,* October–November, 1990, p. 38.

23. As quoted in Peter Hebblethwaite, "Rome manhandled catechism's language," *National Catholic Reporter,* July 1, 1994, p. 16. Hebblethwaite quotes from an article written by Law and published in *The Pilot,* February 12, 1994. Fr. Clark describes his work of translating the catechism from French to English in "On 'Englishing' the Catechism," *The Living Light* (Summer 1993) 13–28.

24. Pope John Paul II, Apostolic Constitution *Fidei Depositum* in *Catechism of the Catholic Church* (Washington, D.C.: United States Catholic Conference, 1994), 1–2.

25. Cardinal Joseph Ratzinger, "The *Catechism of the Catholic Church* and the Optimism of the Redeemed," trans. Cyprian Blamires, in *Sourcebook for Modern Catechetics,* ed. Michael Warren (Winona, Minn.: St. Mary's Press, 1997), 2:262.

26. Raymond A. Lucker, Patrick J. Brennan, and Michael Leach, eds., *The Peoples' Catechism: Catholic Faith for Adults* (New York: Crossroad, 1995). The editors note: *"The Peoples' Catechism* attempts to bring life and a fresh understanding of the truths contained in the *Catechism of the Catholic Church,* 1.

27. Johann Baptist Metz, *Faith in History and Society: Toward A Practical Fundamental Theology,* trans. David Smith (New York: Seabury Press, 1980), 88–99.

28. See Elizabeth A. Johnson, *Friends of God and Prophets: A Feminist Theological Reading of the Communion of Saints* (New York: Continuum, 1998). This treatise is an extraordinary *tour de force* of scholarship and spirit, and the brief excursus here on the communion of saints will, one hopes, lead you to read Johnson.

29. Gordon Bowen's article "No Roadblocks to Death," *Commonweal* (15 June 1984): 362–64, gives a horrifying account of the killing of lay leaders, priests, and religious in Guatemala in the first four years of the 1980s. He points out that catechists in particular were the target of government soldiers and hundreds of catechists were killed simply because they were catechists. Bowen wrote: "One hundred and fifty catechists (lay preachers) were killed in El Quiche during 1976, but only one priest, Father Bill

Woods (an American) died that year in a suspicious plane crash" (p. 362). And, "to discourage any other religious presence, catechists were killed by the hundreds" (p. 364). "In November 1983, Monsignor Pellecer stated that over five hundred catechists remained missing" (p. 364).

30. In writing about the murder of the six Jesuits, their housekeeper and her daughter in El Salvador, Jon Sobrino, S.J., a companion and brother of the Jesuits at the University of Central America wrote the following about Christians in El Salvador: "Another thing that cannot be ignored is that this church has been ferociously persecuted; it has generously shed its blood and produced innumerable martyrs, who are the proof of the greatest love. And if the end of life is what expresses the deepest truth about life itself, it cannot be denied that in this way of being a church there has been much that is Christian. If so many have died like Jesus, it is because so many lived like Jesus. This is what is illustrated in the life and death of Archbishop Romero, the murdered priests and nuns, so many ordinary Christians, *catechists*, preachers of the word, members of base communities, and now these six Jesuits" (*Companions of Jesus: The Jesuit Martyrs of El Salvador* [Maryknoll, N.Y.: Orbis Books, 1990], 45).

31. Johnson, *Friends of God*, 118.

32. Ibid., 16.

33. Lawrence Cunningham, *The Meaning of Saints* (New York: Harper & Row, 1980), 3.

34. For example, the communion of saints is not mentioned in *Effective and Faithful: Catechetical Ministry to the United States, A Study of the Studies*, or in George Gallup, Jr., and Jim Castelli, *The American Catholic People: Their Beliefs, Practices, and Values* (Garden City, N.Y.: Doubleday, 1987).

35. National Conference of Catechetical Leadership, *National Certification Standards for Professional Parish Directors of Religious Education* (Washington, D.C.: NCCL, 1996), 4.

36. Johnson, *Friends of God*, 102.

37. Ibid., 102–3.

38. *CCC*, art. 948.

39. Berard Marthaler, *The Creed: The Apostolic Faith in Contemporary Theology*, rev. ed. (Mystic, Conn.: Twenty-third Publications, 1993), 329.

40. *DCC*, art. 3.

41. Johnson, *Friends of God*, 8.

42. Sallie McFague, *The Body of God: An Ecological Theology* (Minneapolis: Fortress Press, 1993).

43. Ibid., xi.

44. *CMW*, art. 22.

45. Abraham Joshua Heschel wrote: "God's unconditional concern for justice is not an anthropomorphism. Rather, man's concern for justice is a theomorphism." *The Prophets*, vol. 2 (New York: Harper & Row, 1962), 51–52.

> Justice is not an ancient custom, a human convention, a value, but a transcendent demand, freighted with divine concern. It is not only a relationship between man and man, it is an act involving God, a divine need. Justice is His line, righteousness His plummet (Isa 28:17). It is not one of His ways, but in all His ways. Its validity is not only universal, but also eternal, independent of will and experience.
>
> People think that to be just is a virtue, deserving honor and rewards, that in doing righteousness one confers a favor on society. No one expects to receive a reward for the habit of breathing. Justice is as much a necessity as breathing is, and a constant occupation." (The Prophets: An Introduction [New York: Harper & Row, 1962], 198–99) (Written long before our recognition of the need for inclusive language.)

46. Gabriel Moran, *Showing How: The Act of Teaching* (Valley Forge, Pa.: Trinity Press International, 1997), 15.

47. *DCC*, art. 1.

9. LITURGICAL SYMBOLS OF FAITH

1. It is interesting to note that a recent survey regarding Mass attendance conducted by CARA indicated that 73 percent of Catholics in Northern Ireland attended Mass weekly and 68 percent of Catholics in the Republic of Ireland attended Mass weekly. The next highest percentage was from Poland, where 39 percent attended. The United States was fourth with 36 percent of Catholics attending weekly Mass ("Mass Attendance Declining," *The CARA Report: Research on Catholics and the Catholic Church in the United States* 4 [Summer 1998]: 3).

2. A recent study pointed out that "the number of the nation's parishes without a full-time, resident priest grew from 549 in 1965 to 2161 in 1995." The number of priests declined from 58,132 diocesan and religious-order priests to 48,097 in 1998. During that same period the number of Catholics increased from 46.6 million in 1965 to 61.2 million in

1998 (Jack Gischer, "Aging Gracefully," *San Jose Mercury News*, August 23, 1998, sec. B, p. 1).

3. *Constitution on the Sacred Liturgy*, art. 10; *Dogmatic Constitution on the Church*, art. 11.

4. *CSL*, art. 1.

5. Ibid.

6. Mary Collins, *Worship: Renewal to Practice* (Washington, D.C.: Pastoral Press, 1987), 3.

7. Regis A. Duffy, "The Sacramental Economy," in *Commentary on the Catechism of the Catholic Church*, ed. Michael J. Walsh (Collegeville, Minn.: Liturgical Press, 1994), 227.

8. Ibid.

9. The *CCC* notes that when applied to humankind "the word 'blessing' means adoration and surrender" to the Creator in thanksgiving (art. 1078). Regis Duffy calls attention to the appropriateness of *berakah* when he reminds us that "the importance of this form of prayer,…is the profound experience of salvation that it presupposes" ("The Sacramental Economy," in *Commentary on the Catechism of the Catholic Church*, ed. Michael J. Walsh [Collegeville, Minn.: Liturgical Press, 1994], 229).

10. Jan Michael Joncas, *The Catechism of the Catholic Church on Liturgy & Sacraments* (San Jose, Calif.: Resource Publications, 1995), 5.

11. Peter Fink, "The Liturgy and Eucharist in the Catechism," in *The Universal Catechism Reader: Reflections & Responses*, ed. Thomas J. Reese (San Francisco: Harper, 1990), 98.

12. *CCC*, art. 1068.

13. *CSL*, art. 7.

14. Though this may seem obvious to most Christians, I mention it because I have been present at Christian celebration of liturgies in which neither the Paschal Mystery nor Christ was referred to or mentioned. The prayer form had an introspective and individualistic character.

15. *CCC*, art. 1099. The catechism uses this image to describe the Holy Spirit, relying on Jn 14:26, which describes Jesus as saying that the Holy Spirit "will remind you of all that I have said to you."

16. *CCC*, art. 1112.

17. The word *credo* comes from the Latin *cŏr dŏ*, which means "to give one's heart."

18. *DCC*, art. 1.

19. *CSL*, art. 2.

20. James Dallen, *Gathering for Eucharist: A Theology of Sunday*

Assembly (Daytona Beach, Fla.: Pastoral Arts Associates of North America, 1982), 44–45.

21. Robert Hovda, "Celebrating Sacraments 'For the Life of the World,'" in *Robert Hovda: The Amen Corner*, ed. John Baldovin (Collegeville, Minn.: Liturgical Press, 1994).

22. John Baldovin, *Worship: City, Church and Renewal* (Washington, D.C.: Pastoral Press, 1991), 120–21.

23. Gerard Austen, "In *Persona Christi* at the Eucharist," in *Eucharist Toward the Third Millennium*, ed. Martin F. Connell (Chicago: Liturgy Training Publications, 1997), 81–86.

24. *CSL*, art. 8.

25. Annie Dillard, "Expedition to the Pole," in *Teaching a Stone to Talk* (New York: Harper & Row, 1982), 40–41.

26. *CSL*, art. 14.

27. Ibid., 343.

28. Aidan Kavanagh, "How Rite Develops: Some Laws Intrinsic to Liturgical Evolution," *Worship* 41 (1967): 343. Kavanagh describes ritual as "the hinge on which personal interiorization of the religious tradition swings" (p. 342).

29. Kavanagh, "How Rite Develops," 335.

30. *CSL*, art. 62.

31. Aidan Kavanagh, *On Liturgical Theology: The Hale Memorial Lectures of Seabury-Western Theological Seminary, 1981* (Collegeville, Minn.: Liturgical Press, 1992), 113.

32. See Catherine Dooley, "Liturgical Catechesis: Mystagogy, Marriage or Misnomer? *Worship* 65 (September 1992), 396–97.

33. *CSL*, art. 7.

34. *The Liturgy Documents*, "General Instruction of the Roman Missal," art. 9.

35. Ibid., art. 33.

36. Ibid., "Afterword."

37. *The Milwaukee Symposia for Church Composers* (Chicago: Liturgy Training Publications, 1992), art. 1.

38. "General Instruction of the Roman Missal," art. 19.

39. See Bishops' Committee on the Liturgy, *Liturgical Music Today* (Washington, D.C.: United States Catholic Conference, 1982), 9–11.

40. Kavanagh, *On Liturgical Theology*, 86–87 (emphasis added).

41. *Bishops' Committee on the Liturgy Newsletter: National Conference of Catholic Bishops*, October–November 1990, pp. 37–41.

42. Ibid., 38.

43. Donald Trautman, "Inclusive Language and Revised Liturgical Books," *Origins* (10 April 1997): 690.

44. Dooley, "Liturgical Catechesis," 390.

45. *CT*, art. 23.

46. Ibid.

47. *SLF*, art. 113.

48. Charles Gusmer, *Wholesome Worship* (Washington, D.C.: Pastoral Press, 1989), 31.

49. See Anne Marie Mongoven, "Catechists and Liturgists: Can We Bring Them Together?" in *PACE* 15 (February 1985): G 1–5; idem, "Forum: Catechesis and Liturgy," *Worship* 61 (May 1987): 249–57; Mary Charles Bryce, "The Interrelationship of Liturgy and Catechesis," *American Benedictine Review* 28 (March 1997): 1–40.

50. John Westerhoff, "Liturgics and Catechetics," *Worship* 61 (November 1987), 510–11; idem, "Catechetics and Liturgics," *PACE* 19 (1989): 140–43.

51. Westerhoff, "Catechetics and Liturgics," 142.

52. Dooley, "Liturgical Catechesis," 386–87.

53. See Congregation for Divine Worship, "Directory for Masses with Children," in *The Liturgy Documents* (Chicago: Liturgy Training Publication, 1990), 235–47, art. 24. Also Catherine Dooley, "Overview of the Directory for Masses with Children," in *The Liturgy Documents*, 230–233.

54. See "Part Two: Rites for Particular Circumstances, Christian Initiation of Children Who Have Reached Catechetical Age," in *RCIA Study Edition* (Chicago: Liturgy Training Publications, 1988), 155–203.

55. Anne Marie Mongoven, "Overview of the Rite of Christian Initiation of Adults," in *The Catechetical Documents: A Parish Resource*, Martin Connell, ed. (Chicago: Liturgy Training Publications, 1966), 418–21.

56. 1977 Synod, *Message to the People of God*, art. 8; *GDC*, art. 59.

57. *GDC*, art. 71.

58. Aidan Kavanagh, "Theological Principles for Sacramental Catechesis," *The Living Light* 23 (June 1987): 322.

59. Ibid. Kavanagh also says: "None of these things are done only once by normal people. They do them over and over again; and the acts are usually joined together like words in a sentence, the repeated utterance of which makes us who we are."

60. Hovda, "The Vesting of Liturgical Ministers," in *Robert Hovda*, ed. Baldovin, 220.

61. Ibid.

62. *The Rites of the Catholic Church (Study Edition)*, 2 vols. (New York: Pueblo Publishing Company, 1990). For the Eucharist, see *Sacramentary*, now being revised and soon to be published, and *The Lectionary for Mass*, Sacred Congregation for the Sacraments and Divine Worship (Chicago: Liturgy Training Publications, 1999).

63. See "Coronation, papal," and "Tiara," in *The Harper Collins Encyclopedia of Catholicism*, gen. ed. Richard McBrien (San Francisco: HarperSanFrancisco, 1995).

64. This listing in no way includes all of the possible scriptural references.

65. Dooley, "Liturgical Catechesis," 393.

66. Duffy, "Sacramental Economy," 236.

67. J. Brian Hehir, "Liturgy and Social Justice: Past Relationships and Future Possibilities," in *Liturgy and Social Justice*, ed. Edward M. Grosz (Collegeville, Minn.: Liturgical Press, 1989), 40–61.

68. Ibid., 56.

69. *CSL*, art. 51.

70. *SLF*, art. 60, i.

AFTERWORD: CATECHESIS AS A PROPHETIC MINISTRY

1. Abraham Joshua Heschel, *God in Search of Man: A Philosophy of Judaism* (New York: Farrar, Strauss, & Giroux, 1955), 33–34.

2. Susannah Heschel, ed., *Moral Grandeur and Spiritual Audacity: Essays of Abraham Heschel* (New York: Farrar, Strauss, & Giroux, 1996), viii–ix.

3. Abraham Joshua Heschel, *The Prophets: An Introduction* (New York: Harper & Row, 1962), x.

4. Bruce Vawter, "Introduction to Prophetic Literature," in *The New Jerome Biblical Commentary*, ed. Raymond E. Brown, Joseph A. Fitzmyer, and Roland E. Murphy (Englewood Cliffs, N.J.: Prentice-Hall, 1990), 187.

5. John J. Schmitt, "Prophecy: Pre-exilic Hebrew Prophecy," in *The Anchor Bible Dictionary*.

6. Deborah was unique in that she was both prophet and judge; see Ex 15:20 (Miriam) and Jgs 4:4 (Deborah).

7. Heschel, *Prophets*, xiii.

8. Ibid., 5.

9. Walter Brueggemann, *The Prophetic Imagination* (Philadelphia: Fortress Press, 1978), 13.

10. Marilyn Schaub, "The Chaplain as Prophet" (unpublished paper).

11. Jeffrey G. Sobosan, as cited in Shaub, *Christian Commitment, Prophetic Living* (Mystic, Conn.: Twenty-third Publications, 1985), 31.

12. At one time a former student met me and said, "I will never forget what you told us was the most important thing for catechists to do." I hesitated, but finally and fearfully asked, "What was that?" "Read the daily newspaper," she replied. Not too bad an answer.

13. We need to learn from our friends in community education. The courses adults want are four to six weeks in length; they are at a convenient time for the people; they are not modeled on schooling through lecture processes; and they are totally at the service of those who participate in courses. We need to provide resources such as books and videos and opportunities for conversation and dialogue about our readings and the videos we see. Study is the opening of the mind to new insights. It is a seeking and searching for meaning. It is a uniquely human process, and it develops and restores our humanity.

14. These characteristics of prophecy and others were presented by Marilyn Schaub of Duquesne University in a lecture given at Santa Clara University on July 1, 1998. Dr. Schaub, friend and colleague, has generously enabled me to use her insights in this chapter as a basis for my understanding of the ministry of the catechist as a prophetic ministry.

15. Gerard Manley Hopkins, "God's Grandeur," in *Poems and Prose of Gerard Manley Hopkins* (Baltimore: Penguin Books, 1954), 27.

16. Sallie McFague, *The Body of God: An Ecological Theology* (Minneapolis, Minn.: Fortress Press, 1993), xi.

17. Wilfrid Harrington, *God Does Care: The Presence of God in Our World* (Westminster, Md.: Christian Classics, 1994), 4.

18. Karl Rahner, *Foundations of Christian Faith: An Introduction to the Idea of Christianity*, trans. William V. Dych (New York: Seabury Press, 1978), p. 92.

Index